W9-DEB-863

CHINESE MUSIC

GARLAND REFERENCE LIBRARY
OF THE HUMANITIES
(VOL. 75)

14/077

ML
120
. C5
L5
1979

CHINESE MUSIC
An Annotated Bibliography

Second Edition;
Revised and Enlarged

Fredric Lieberman

GARLAND PUBLISHING, INC. • NEW YORK & LONDON
1979

GOSHEN COLLEGE LIBRARY
GOSHEN, INDIANA

©1979 by Fredric Lieberman
All rights reserved

Library of Congress Cataloging in Publication Data

Lieberman, Fredric.
  Chinese music.

  (Garland reference library of the humanities; v. 75)
  Includes indexes.
  1. Music, Chinese—Bibliography.   I. Title.
ML120.C5L5   1979   016.7817'51   76-24755
ISBN 0-8240-9922-2

Printed on acid-free, 250-year-life paper
Manufactured in the United States of America

To Liang Tsai-ping

CONTENTS

PREFACE

This bibliography attempts exhaustive coverage of publications in Western languages as well as critical annotation. Materials are included on Chinese music, dance, and drama as these are essentially interdependent. Oriental languages have not been included. In annotating I have adopted two conventions: the abbreviation "NE" follows entries that I have not personally examined; if neither an annotation nor "NE" follows an entry, then the annotation "contains no unique or important information" is implied. The abbreviation "RR" identifies annotations contributed by Ronald Riddle.

In matters of format, I try for clarity and consistency; when, however, problems arise which set these ideals at odds, the choice is clarity. I have included incomplete or questionable entries culled from various sources; my own work is certainly not free from errors of commission and omission; and by the time this volume appears in print, it will no longer be up to date. Since the first edition of this bibliography appeared, many readers have kindly sent corrections and additions, and reviewers have sympathetically identified weaknesses and omissions. This new edition does not eliminate all shortcomings of the previous one, but sufficient new material has accumulated to warrant its publication. Corrections and additions from users of this volume will be greatly appreciated.

Special thanks to Bruce Brooks, Kuo-huang Han, Kai Jacobs, Fritz A. Kuttner, Colin Mackerras, Rulan Chao Pian, Laurence Picken, Barbara Rehm, Ronald Riddle, Stanley Sadie, A.C. Scott, Barbara B. Smith, Bang-song Song, Gloria Strauss, F. John Thompson, Martin Tracy, and Graeme Vanderstoel for contributions of information and advice. Michael Feldman, Faye Dion, and Lee Nackman prepared several computerized interim editions; Barb Shurin typed the copy for this edition.

The dedication of this book reflects both a public and a private debt to a scholar who has, through his activities on behalf of Chinese music, been a leader in encouraging the study of its history and literature and in preserving and enriching its living tradition.

ABBREVIATIONS

The following abbreviations are used freely in titles of periodicals:

Amer = America, American

Bull = Bulletin

Jl = Journal, Journale

Mus = Music, Musical, Musik

Soc = Society, Société, Società

BIBLIOGRAPHY AND DISCOGRAPHY

1. Anonymous. *Bibliography of Dr. R.H. Van Gulik.* Boston:
   Boston University Libraries, [n.d.], 82p. A thorough chronological bibliography of this prolific
   and fascinating sinologist. Compiled from his own
   notes, with biographical information, and annotations of some items. Compiled for the Robert Van
   Gulik Collection at the Mugar Memorial Library,
   Boston University.

2. _____. "Notes Bibliographiques sur la Musique Chinoise" *Bulletin de l'Association Amicale Franco-
   Chinoise* (Paris) 2(3):276-278, July 1910.

3. Chan Wing-tsit. *An Outline and an Annotated Bibliography of Chinese Philosophy.* New Haven: Far Eastern Publications, Yale University, 1961. vi+127p.
   Excellent guide to topics and literature of Chinese
   philosophy and aesthetics.

4. *CHINOPERL News.* A yearly publication of the Conference
   on Chinese Oral and Performing Literature, with
   headquarters at the China-Japan Program, Cornell
   University. Frequently includes special bibliographies, discographies and lists of field collections.
   Also features articles and edited proceedings of the
   yearly meeting.

5. Cordier, Henri. *Bibliotheca Sinica.* 2nd ed. Paris:
   Guilmoto, Guenther, 1904-1924. 4 vols. plus supplement.

6. Craig, Dale A., ed. *Holdings of the Chinese Music Archives.* Hong Kong: Music Department, Chung Chi College, The Chinese University of Hong Kong, 1974.
   24, 502, 42p. il., index. Reproduction of card catalog including books, scores, records, tapes and
   instruments. Cards are both in Chinese characters
   and Romanization. An impressive and useful collection.

7. Crossley-Holland, Peter. "International Catalog of
   Records of the Folk and Classical Music of the Orient" *Recorded Sound* 2(10-11):78-80, 1963.

8. _____. "Oriental Music on the Gramophone" *Music and Letters* 40(1):56-71, Jan 1959. A review-essay; sections on each country, including China, stressing European discs.

9. Endo, Hirosi. *Bibliography of Oriental and Primitive Music*. Tokyo: Nanki Music Library, 1929. [viii]+ 62p. 625 entries giving worldwide coverage, no annotation. Indexed by countries.

10. *Ethnomusicology*. "Current Bibliography" sections in most issues provide good general coverage of contemporary materials.

11. Ferenczyné-Wendelin, Lidia. *Chinese-Hungarian Bibliography.* Budapest: National Széchényi Library, 1959. 334p. Arranged by topic, p. 99-109 on Music, Dance, and Theater.

12. Gerboth, Walter. *Music of East and Southeast Asia: A Selected Bibliography of Books, Pamphlets, Articles and Recordings*. New York: State Department of Education, 1963. 23p. Keyed to library holdings in New York City area.

13. Gillis, Frank and Alan P. Merriam. *Ethnomusicology and Folk Music: An International Bibliography of Dissertations and Theses*. Middletown, Conn.: Wesleyan University Press, 1966. 160p. An expanded version of material presented in two earlier articles in *Ethnomusicology*. 873 entries, well indexed, with numerous annotations.

14. Goodrich, L. Carrington and Chaoying Fang, eds. *Dictionary of Ming Biography, 1368-1644*. New York: Columbia University Press, 1976. 2 vols. NE.

15. Hornbostel, Erich Maria von. "Musik des Orients auf der Schallplatte" *Kultur und Schallplatte* 2(10-11): 161-162, Apr-May 1931. Also in *Musik* 23:829-830, 1931.

16. Hu, William C.C. "A Bibliography for Yüan Opera" *Occasional Papers, University of Michigan Center for Chinese Studies* 1:1-37, 1962.

17. Hucker, Charles O. *China: A Critical Bibliography*. Tucson: University of Arizona Press, 1962. x+126p. An excellent general bibliography. 2285 entries with brief annotations and author index.

18. International Institute for Comparative Music Stud-
    ies and Documentation—Berlin, compilers. *Oriental
    Music: A Selected Discography*. New York: Uni-
    versity of the State of New York and National
    Council of Associations for International Stud-
    ies, 1971. (Foreign Area Materials Center, Occa-
    sional Publication No. 16) iv+100p. China, p. 66-
    71, lists 10 discs, 5 of which are of Chinese
    origin. A very meager selection.

19. Jacobs, Kai. *Deutschsprachige Schriften zur Revolu-
    tionären Musik der Volksrepublik China: Eine Bib-
    liographie*. [n.p.]: Archiv für Populäre Musik,
    1976. (Schriften, Band 6). 538 entries, indexes.
    64p. Arranged by topics. This is a thorough and
    useful compilation. Though entries are not anno-
    tated, topic headings are introduced by brief es-
    says. Includes material from German magazines and
    newspapers difficult to locate in other countries.
    Numerous items not included in my list.

20. *Journal of Asian Studies*. Every September issue of
    this scholarly journal is devoted to a comprehen-
    sive listing of new books and periodical litera-
    ture, arranged by country and topic.

21. Knosp, Gaston. "Bibliographia Musicae Exotica" *Revue
    Musicale de la Société Internationale de la Mu-
    sique*, Supplement, Nov 1910. [8]p. 123 entries on
    Chinese music.

22. Kunst, Jaap. *Ethnomusicology*. 3 ed. The Hague: Nij-
    hoff, 1959. x+303p. Includes a bibliography on
    ethnomusicological subjects of over 4500 entries;
    well indexed.

23. _____. *Supplement to the Third Edition of Ethnomusi-
    cology*. The Hague: Nijhoff, 1960. vii+45p. Adds
    over 500 titles.

24. Laade, Wolfgang. *Gegenwartsfragen der Musik in
    Afrika und Asien: Eine Grundlegende Bibliographie*.
    Baden-Baden: Verlag Valentin Koerner, 1971. (Col-
    lection d'Études Musicologiques, Band 51) 110p.
    See p. 62-66, 91 for entries on China.

25. _____. *Neue Musik in Afrika, Asien und Ozeanien: Dis-
    kographie und Historisch-Stilistischer Ueberblick*.
    Heidelberg: Privately printed, 1971. 463p. China,
    passim.

26. Lachmann, Robert. "Orientalische Musik auf Schall-
    platten" *Musik* 24(4):254f., Jan 1932. NE.

27. Leslie, Donald and Jeremy Davidson. *Author Catalogues of Western Sinologists*. Canberra: Australian National University, 1966. A guide to bibliographies of individual scholars, including many who have written on music.

28. Liang Tsai-ping, ed. *Bibliography on Chinese Music*. Taipei: Chinese National Music Association, 1956. 50p. English, 25p. Chinese. Includes selected chronological listing of works arranged by language, and reprint of China section from Waterman (44, below). Chinese language section adapted from Yuan T'ung-li in *Yin-Yüeh Tsa-chih* [Journal of Music] (Peking, 1928).

29. Lieberman, Fredric. *An Annotated Bibliography of Materials Related to the Notation of Chinese Music*. Unpub. ms., 1963. 11p. 54 entries on notation in general, Chinese notation, and other Sinic-area notations. Copy deposited in Institute of Ethnomusicology Archives, UCLA, Catalog No. KA293.

30. _____. *Chinese Music: An Annotated Bibliography*. New York: Society for Asian Music, 1970. xii+157p. The first edition of the present work, containing 1483 entries. Reviewed by Rulan Chao Pian in *Notes* 28 (2):227-229, Dec 1971; Laurence Picken in *Ethnomusicology* 18(1):157-158, Jan 1974.

31. _____. "Chinese Music: An Annotated Bibliography, First Supplement" *Asian Music* 5(1):56-85, 1973. 224 entries, supplementing this book's first edition; all have been included in this edition.

32. _____. *Contemporary Ch'in Repertoire: Preliminary Discography*. Providence: the author, 1975. Edition 3, Feb 1975, 24p, computer printout. Compilation of information on all known discs of ch'in performances, and attempt to include private tape recordings whenever possible. Arranged by composition, indexed to performer. The discography must remain preliminary until major collections in Taiwan, Hong Kong, and Peking become accessible for study.

33. _____. "Robert Hans van Gulik: A Bibliography" *Asian Music* 1(1):23-30, Winter 1968-1969. Published as a memorial tribute to this great sinologist. List of 68 items compiled without access to Item 1 above, which should be consulted first, if available.

34. Liu Chun-Jo, with Liao Ling-te and Michael Welch. *The Serendipity Chants: A Descriptive Catalog of the Recordings of the Buddhist Rite for the Dead*, "Yü-chia yen-k'ou shih-shih yao chi." Ithaca: China-Japan Program, Cornell University, 1973 (*CHINOPERL News*, No. 3, Jan 1973). xv+110p. Recordings were made in Shan-tao Szu, Taipei, in 1969. Catalog is thorough and useful for students of liturgy. Includes data on duration, titles, textual forms, musical styles, metric configurations, text incipits and sources.

35. Lust, John and Werner Eichhorn. *Index Sinicus: A Catalog of Articles Relating to China in Periodicals and Other Collective Publications, 1920-1955*. Cambridge: Heffer, 1964. xxx+663p. About 20,000 entries arranged by topic, with author and topic indices.

36. MacGillivray, D. "A List of Hymn Books" *China Mission Yearbook*, p.253-259, 1912. NE.

37. Malm, William P. "Notes on Bibliographies of Japanese Materials Dealing with Ethnomusicology" *Ethnomusicology* 7(1):39-40, Jan 1963.

38. *Music Index*. Monthly publication with annual cumulations. Indexes selected music periodicals. Relevant subheads "China" and "Far East."

39. Pian Rulan Chao. "Primary Sources of Materials from the Chinese Oral Tradition" *CHINOPERL News* 4:78-84, Jan 1974. An annotated survey of source materials including collections of recordings, varied genres of folk music, narrative, and drama, many of which are unobtainable thus far on Western commercial discs.

40. Purcell, William L. "A Discography of the Music of Asia. Part One: China, Korea and Japan" *American Record Guide* 26(1):8-11, 56-60, Sept 1959. Review essay and list of 16 discs of Chinese music.

41. *Revue Bibliographique de Sinologie*. Covers publications in both Western and Oriental languages. Numerous musical entries by Laurence Picken.

42. Schmieder, Wolfgang, ed. *Bibliographie des Musikschrifttums*. Leipzig, Frankfurt A.M.: Hofmeister, 1950--. A continuing series of annual volumes; extensive listings arranged topically and fully indexed.

43. Stevens, Catherine. "Chinese Folk Entertainment: A Collection of Tapes with Matching Texts" *CHINOPERL News* 4:85-109, 1974. Catalog of an extraordinarily rich collection of music, musical drama, narrative song, storytelling, and other genres of Chinese oral tradition; altogether 145 reels recorded in Taiwan in 1960.

44. Waterman, Richard A., William Lichtenwanger, Virginia H. Herrman, Horace I. Poleman, and Cecil Hobbs. "Bibliography of Asiatic Musics" *Notes* 2s 5-8, 1947-1951. A rich source; 377 entries on Chinese music; more on related areas.

45. _____, et al. "Survey of Recordings of Asiatic Music in the United States, 1950-1951" *Notes* 2s 8(4): 683-691, Sept 1951. 15th installment of the "Bibliography of Asiatic Musics"; lists 72 private, public, and university collections and indexes their holdings by area.

46. Wu, K.T. "Books on East Asiatic Music in the Library of Congress (Printed Before 1800). 1. Works in Chinese" in *The Library of Congress Catalogue of Early Books on Music ... Supplement*, by Hazel Bartlett (Washington: Library of Congress, 1944), p. 121-131. 47 works listed, with full descriptive annotations.

47. Yang, Daniel Shih-p'êng. *An Annotated Bibliography of Materials for the Study of the Peking Theatre.* Madison: University of Wisconsin, 1967. x+98p. (Wisconsin China Series, No. 2); 160 entries on all phases of Peking theater; items 62-78 on music. Most entries are of Chinese materials, but some are English.

48. Yuan Tung-li. *Russian Works on China 1918-1960 in American Libraries.* New Haven: Yale University, 1961. Arranged by topic, author index; about 1350 entries.

49. _____. *China in Western Literature.* New Haven: Yale University Far Eastern Publications, 1958.

BOOKS AND ARTICLES ON CHINESE MUSIC

50. Aalst, J.A. van. *Chinese Music*. Shanghai: Statistical Department, Inspectorate General, 1884. London: King, 1884. Reprinted--- Peiping: French Book Store, 1933, 1939. Taipei: Chinese Classical Music Society, 1955, 1965 (in Liang Tsai-ping, *Chinese Music*). New York: Paragon, 1964. iv+84p., il., mus. An early and much-quoted survey with sections on the *lü*, scales, *kung-chih* notation, ritual music, popular music, and instruments, repeating Chinese authority without investigation, the whole being based on the assumption that "it is incontestable that Chinese music compares unfavorably with European music" (p.84).

51. _____. "Exposé de la Musique des Chinois" *L'Echo Musicale* 20:246-249, 257-259, 271-274, 282-285, 295-297, 309-311, 1890. mus. NE.

52. Aarflot, Olav. *Kinesisk Musikk*. Oslo: Brøgger, 1948. 127p., il., mus., index. [Håndbøker utgitt av Etnografisk Museum, 2.] Survey of genres and theory, more detailed coverage of instruments. Numerous short musical examples.

53. Abraham, Otto and E.M. von Hornbostel. "Studien über das Tonsystem und die Musik der Japaner" *Sammelbände der Internationalen Musikgesellschaft* 4:302-360, 1902-1903. Reprinted in *Sammelbände für Vergleichende Musikwissenschaft* I:197-231, 1922. Reprinted with parallel English translation by Gertrud Kurath in *Hornbostel Opera Omnia* (The Hague: Nijhoff, 1975) I, 1-84. Because Japanese music historically is related to Chinese, this study is expanded to include data on Chinese scales and instruments when available; charts summarize measurements on several museum instruments.

54. Achilles [pseud.]. "Mei Lan Fang: China's Foremost Actor" *The Living Age* 321:1053-1055, 1924. NE.

55. Ackerman, Phyllis. *Ritual Bronzes of Ancient China*. New York: Dryden Press, 1945. vi+114p., il. See p. 74-75, 106-107, and *passim*.

56. Adams, Mrs. Crosby. "Chinese Fragments" *Music* 6:491-495, Sept 1894. Brief note on folk tunes picked up or composed by missionaries.

57. Adams, George. "The Chinese Drama" *Nineteenth Century* 37:497-515, March 1895. NE.

58. Addison, Don. "Elements of Style in Performing the Chinese P'i-P'a" *Selected Reports* (U.C.L.A.)2(1): 119-139, 1974. mus. "This study treats the realization of the Chinese notation for the p'i-p'a (lute) and its more common characteristic ornamental techniques. The notation of a short composition, Chao Chun Yuen, is reviewed, and the recorded performance of the same piece by six different p'i-p'a artists is transcribed into Western staff notation and melographed. The melograph helps to point out ... the exact manner in which the music is realized by these six performers; it tends to clarify the approaches to the study of different ornamental techniques and it helps to indicate which items are shared by all performers and which are particular to a given performance" (from author's abstract).

59. Adler, Johannes. "Musikinstrumente in der Volksrepublik China" *Musik und Gesellschaft* 9(12):715-717, Dec 1959. On the manufacture of various Western instruments in Communist China.

60. Agnew, R. Gordon. "The Music of the Ch'uan Miao" *Journal of the West China Border Research Society* 11:9-22, 1939. il., mus. An excellent survey of this important tribal group's music. Transcriptions numerous but not reliable, as they were done by the singer repeating phrases while Agnew fit the tunes to his piano. Inexplicable translation of *lu-sheng* (six-tube mouth organ) as "lute."

61. _____. "Revived Interest in Music" *China at War* 11:95-100, 1943.

62. Ah Wen. "Face Designs in Chinese Opera" *Chinese Literature* 7:95-99, 1963. il. NE.

63. _____. "New Attractions in Peking Theatres" *Chinese Literature* 2:89-94, 1965. il. A song-and-dance show presented by the Army, proving that "The People's Soldiers can do anything."

64. _____. "Three Young Artists in the Revolution in Peking Opera" *Chinese Literature* 9:95-103, 1974. il. Bio-ideological sketches of Li Kuang, Li Pingshu, and Yang Chun-hsia, who play leading roles in model revolutionary operas.

*   Ahrweiler, Alice. See Association des Amitiés Franco-
    Chinoises, ed.

65. Ai K'o-en.   "The Furnace of Labor Molds New People:
    Talk on the Honan Opera Chao-Yang Kou" *Selections
    from China Mainland Magazines* 414:26-29, April 27,
    1964. From *Hung-Ch'i* 6, 1964. NE.

66. Albini, Eugenio.   "La Musica in China (Un Libro di
    Mr. Mei Lan-fang)" *Revista Mus Italiana* 42:34-45,
    1938. mus.   Review essay based on Liu T'ien-hua's
    Selections from the Repertoire of Mei Lan-fang.

67. Aleksandrov, B.   "Moskva—Pekin (Putevye Zametki)"
    [Moscow—Peking (Traveling Observations)] *Sovets-
    kaya Muzyka* 4:92f., 1953. NE.

68. Alender, Izrail Z., ed.   *Muzykalniye Instrumenti
    Kitaya* [Chinese Musical Instruments]. Moscow: Gosu-
    darstvennoe Muzikal'noe Izdatel'stvo, 1958.   50p.
    text, 64 plates.   A useful, illustrated introduc-
    tion to Chinese musical instruments.   Good photos
    are explained by short notes, and pitch ranges are
    given.   Pictorial material supplied from China by
    Professor Yang Yin-Liu, Peking.

69. Alexiev, B.A.   "Der Schauspieler als Held in der
    Geschichte Chinas" *Asia Major* 10:33-58. NE.

70. Allen, B.S.   *Chinese Theatres Handbook.*   Tientsin: La
    Librairie Française [ca. 1922].   56p.   NE.

71. Alley, Rewi and Eva Siao. *Peking Opera.* Peking: New
    World Press, 1957.   German translation by Ruth
    Weiss: *Die Peking-Oper.*   Peking: Verlag Neue Welt,
    1957.   An introductory picture book; stress on mod-
    ern practice; Alley's journalistic prose enlivened
    by many photos in color and black and white by Eva
    Siao. Illustrations and back cover by Kuan Liang.

72. Ames, J.W.   "Day in Chinatown" *Lippincott's Magazine*
    16:498-501, Oct 1875. Description of Chinese music
    in a San Francisco cafe. [RR]

73. Amiot, Jean Joseph. *Divertissements chinois: ou Con-
    certs de Musique Chinoise, les Notes Chinoises
    mise sur les Lignes à Notre Manière.* Manuscript,
    1779. 105 leaves. Paris: Bib. Nat. Dept. de Mss.
    Fonds chinois Bréquigny 14. Music with annotations.

74. _____. "De la Musique des Chinois, tant Anciens que
Modernes" in *Mémoires Concernant l'Histoire, les
Sciences, les Arts, les Moeurs, les Usages, etc.
des Chinois, par les Missionnaires de Pe-kin*
(Paris: Nyon l'Ainé, 1776-1814), VI, 1-254. 30
plates, mus. German abstract published by J.N.
Forkel in the *Almanach Musical* p. 223-275, 1784.
The first major study of Chinese music, devoted
largely to theory, based on Chinese sources, with
excellently engraved plates. Used as the authority
for many later studies.

75. _____. "Extrait d'une Lettre Inédite du Père Amiot,
Jésuite Missionnaire à Péking, Adressée a M. Bertin, Ministre Secrétaire d'Etat, le 2 Octobre 1784,
sur le tam-tam et sur la musique chinois" *Revue
Musicale* 1:365-369, 1827. Knosp lists this entry
under Henri Cordier, who possibly wrote notes or
introduction. NE.

76. _____. *Memoria Sobre la Musica de los Chineses.*
Madrid: Imprenta di Bablo y Texero, 1780. Spanish
translation of Amiot's French translation of Li
Kuang-ti's work on Chinese music. Cordier (*Bibliotheca Sinica*, Column 1572) questions the existence
of this book. NE.

77. Anastas'ev, A.V. *V Kitaiskom Teatre: Putevye Zametki*
[In the Chinese Theater: Travel Notes]. Moscow:
Sovetskii Pisatel', 1957. 69p., il. NE.

78. Anderson, Aeneas. *A Narrative of the British Embassy
to China, in the Years 1792, 1793, and 1794 ...*
London: 1795. 2nd ed. Passages on music excerpted
in Frank Harrison, *Time, Place and Music* (q.v.).

79. Anderson, E.N., Jr. "The Folksongs of the Hong Kong
Boat People" *Journal of American Folklore* 80(317):
285-296, July-Sept 1967. Text and context; report
of field study. No music.

80. _____. "Songs of the Hong Kong Boat People" *CHINOPERL News* 5:8-114, 1975. Translations,
with Chinese texts, of a series of songs and excerpts recorded in 1965 and 1966; context, language, and themes are discussed in a general introduction, and the texts are annotated as needed.
No music.

81. Anderson, Eleanor MacNeill. "Chinese Melodies and
Christian Worship" *Chinese Recorder* p. 107-110,
Feb 1934. NE.

82. Anderson, John. *Mandalay to Momien: A Narrative of the Two Expeditions to Western China of 1868 and 1875.* London: Macmillan, 1876. xvi+479p. il., maps. See p. 134 and 142 for brief discussion and illustration of Kachin (primarily Burmese) instruments.

83. Anderson, Lily Strickland. "On Chinese Music" *Musical Courier* 96(2):6,7,10, Jan 12, 1928. il. Brief, non-technical notice.

84. Anisimov, A. "Poezdka v Kitaiskuyu Narodnuyu Respubliku" [A Trip to the Chinese People's Republic] *Sovetskaya Muzyka* 8:91-97, Sept 1950. il., mus. NE.

85. Ankerson, W.A. "The Chinese Shadow Play" *Journal of the Royal Asiatic Society, North China Branch* 72: 46-54, 1946. NE.

* * * * * * * * * *

86. Anonymous. "The Academy of Chinese Music" *Chinese Literature* 12:113-114, 1964. Report of opening.

87. _____. "Albanian Song and Dance Ensemble Visits China" *China Reconstructs* 23(9):38-39, Sept 1974. il.

88. _____. "Allegorical Lama Dance" *China Reconstructs* 7(2):17-19, Feb 1958. il. Description, with good color photos, of annual spring festival dance at the Yung Ho Kung Lamaist Temple in Peking.

89. _____. "Americans in China" *High Fidelity and Musical America* 23:MA 30-31, June 1973. NE.

90. _____. "Ancient Musical Instruments" *People's China* (16):39, Aug 16, 1957. il. Reports discovery of complete set of 13 *pien chung* and 3 *seh* in Sinyang, Honan, Warring States tomb.

91. _____. "Ancient Uighur Music Restored" *Chinese Literature* 11:147-148, 1959. Report on research and pending publication of "Mukam," the major collection of ancient Uighur music.

92. _____. "Another Form of Local Opera Revived" *Chinese Literature* 9:119, 1965. On the *Hai-ch'ü* from Anhwei.

93. _____. "An Appreciation of the Ballet 'The White-Haired Girl'" *Chinese Literature* 4:75-86, 1969.

94. _____. "Arab Folk Dancers in China" *China Reconstructs* 14(3):27, March 1955. il. Peking performance by Reda Folklore Dance Co. of the U.A.R.

95. _____. "Army Takes Over Opera" *New York Times* 6:1, Dec 6, 1966. NE.

96. _____. *The Art of Peking Opera in China.* Peking: Peking Lantern Slide Film Studio, [n.d.]. 14p., 48 slides. Filmstrip with explanatory booklet.

97. _____. "The Art of the Chinese Theater" *Literary Digest* 38:970-971, 1909. [RR]

98. _____. "Art Troupe of Peking Garrison Forces: Brilliant Example of the Revolution in Peking Opera Music" *Chinese Literature* 2:92, 1970. NE.

99. _____. "The Ballad Goes Contemporary—and Collective" *China Reconstructs* 23(10):22, Oct 1974. il. Ballads on contemporary themes are sung to the accompaniment of a chamber group of traditional instruments by a troupe of girls with the Shanghai Philharmonic Society.

100. _____. "Ballet: First Success in Revolutionization" *Peking Review* 8(6):30-31, Feb 5, 1965. NE.

101. _____. "Battle of Chihpi" *Chinese Literature* 3:167-168, 1959. Note on a newly revised version of the Peking Opera, "The Meeting of Gallant Men."

102. _____. "Big Traitor Ma Sitson's Letter Made Public" *Selections from China Mainland Magazines* 616:10-15, March 25, 1968. Ma's letter, originally published in the Russian journal *Literature* (July 19, 1967), is reprinted in China by the editors of *Shuang-ch'en-yüeh* with an angry prefatory note. From *Shuang-ch'en-yüeh* 1:Jan 10, 1968.

103. _____. "The Bolshoi Ballet in China" *China Reconstructs* 8(12):23, Dec 1959. il.

104. _____. "'Brother Dragon,' US Deejay in Far East, Ribs 'n Rocks Reds" *Variety* 209:217, Jan 8, 1958. NE.

105. _____. "Camel with Four Musicians and a Dancer" *China Reconstructs* 7(7):12-13, July 1958. il. Brief description and a full-page photo of T'ang terra cotta figurine.

106. _____. "Canton Music Festival" *China Reconstructs* 11 (6):38, June 1962. Traditional and modern music performed in 16-day gala.

107. _____. "Canton Music Festival" *Chinese Literature* 7:
     111, 1962.

108. _____. "Celebrations of the 25th Anniversary of the
     'Talks'" *Chinese Literature* 8:194-202, 1967. il.,
     mus. On the fruition and influence of Mao's doc-
     trine on art: *Talks at the Yenan Forum on Litera-
     ture and Art*. With two quotations set to music.

109. _____. "A Chekiang Opera Company in Peking" *Chinese
     Literature* 2:120-121, 1963.

110. _____. "Chiang Ching" *New York Times* 1:7, June 2,
     1967.

111. _____. "Chicago Musician Brings Culture of Ancient
     China to Western Audiences" *Musical America* 44(4):
     30, May 15, 1926. il. Report of recital series
     given by Bernice Austin, who studied for four
     years in China.

112. _____. "Children's Ballads and Dramas Published"
     Chinese Literature 9:100-101, 1973.

113. _____. "The Ch'in" *Canon* 11:396-397, July 1958. il.
     Prompted by rediscovery of "Kuanglingsan"—a short
     introduction to the *ch'in* based on secondary
     sources.

114. _____. "China Assails Beethoven and Schubert" *New
     York Times*, p. 8:3, Jan 15, 1974. il. Report on
     the campaign against music without titles.

115. _____. *China Handbook*. Taipei: China Publishing Co.,
     1951—. After 1956 *China Yearbook*. Includes re-
     ports on musical activities, organizations and
     education.

116. _____. "China Remolding Writers, Artists" *New York
     Times* 9:1, May 28, 1972. NE.

117. _____. "'China Town' in San Francisco" *Cornhill* 54:
     50-59, July 1886. Several paragraphs on Chinese
     theatre, audiences, lives of actors. [RR]

118. _____. "China's Music Comes Back to Life" *Chinese
     Literature* 2:180-181, 1955. il. Accomplishments of
     the People's Government in encouraging traditional
     music.

119. _____. "Chinese-Albanian Friendship on the Revolu-
     tionary Stage" *China Reconstructs* 17(1):40-42,
     Jan 1968. il.

120. _____. "Chinese and Japanese Music Compared" *China Review* 5(2):142-143, 1877. NE.

121. _____. "Chinese Ballet Goes Abroad" *Peking Review* Jan 26, 1962. NE.

122. _____. "Chinese Dancer Reviving Lost Art" *China Institute Bulletin* 38:5, Dec 1946. il. On Tai Ai-lien, ballet dancer visiting America.

123. _____. "Chinese Drama—Lord Amherst's Embassy" *Quarterly Review* 16:396-416, 1917. NE.

124. _____. "Chinese Folk Songs" *Chinese Literature* 4:141-142, 1960. Reports new publications.

125. _____. "The Chinese in California" *Lippincott's Magazine* 2:36-41, July 1868. Passing mention of Chinese theatre in San Francisco. [RR]

126. _____. "Chinese in San Francisco" *Leisure Hour*, p. 383-384, June 1, 1870. Brief description of theatrical performance. [RR]

127. _____. "Chinese Like Scotch Bagpipes" *California Outlook* 10(7):341-342. Facetious note on tastes in Tientsin. [RR]

128. _____. "Chinese Mainland Delegation Now Visiting Music Industry" *Music Trades* 124:52f., March 1976. NE.

129. _____. "Chinese Music" *Metronome* 19:11-12, Feb 1933. NE.

130. _____. "Chinese Music" in *Newport Folk Festival 1967*, edited by Henry Glassie and Ralph Rinzler ([n.p.]: Gilbert Kravette, 1967), p. 16. il. On Chang Ming Quang and the Chinese Music Ensemble of New York. NE.

131. _____. "Chinese Music: Invention and Character Thereof, Musical Instruments, Etc." *Music News* 1(11):15-16, 1909. NE.

132. _____. "Chinese Music and Musical Instruments" *Musical Herald* 7:33-34,38,65,97-99,129-131,161-162, 193-195,225-226,257-259,321-322,353-354, 1886. il. NE.

133. _____. *Chinese Music in l'Exposition Universelle de Londres en 1884*. London: Clowes, 1884. NE.

14

134. _____. "Chinese Music: The Flying Dragon Music Club" *Life* p. 81-84, Nov 15, 1943. il. NE.

135. _____. "Chinese Musical Instruments" *Boston Musical Gazette* 1(8):57-58, May 11, 1846. NE.

136. _____. "Chinese Musical Instruments" *Eastern Horizon* 5(10):43-46, Oct 1966. il. Eight photos of traditional instruments.

137. _____. *Chinese Musical Instruments*. A set of 12 watercolor paintings on rice paper, probably from mid-19th century, of women musicians. In Daane Collection, New York Public Library, Oriental Library. NE.

138. _____. *Chinese Musical Instruments Used in the Confucian Temple Worship*. Lawrence: University of Kansas, 1941. 21 plates. Pictures purchased in China by University of Kansas Chancellor, minimal description.

139. _____. "Chinese Musicians Give Recital" *China Institute Bulletin* 33:9, April 1946. Liang Tsai-ping (*cheng* and *ch'in*) and Yi-an Chang (piano) perform at China House.

140. _____. "Chinese Now Praise Classical Composers" *Detroit Free Press*, March 19, 1977, p. 14c. NE.

141. _____. "A Chinese Orchestra" *Musician* 19:869, 1914. NE.

142. _____. "The Chinese Opera, 1948-1953" *China News Analysis* 16:1-5, Dec 11, 1953. An excellent account of attempts at reform, popular resentment, and compromise in the Chinese Opera during the formative years of the Communist government. Based on Communist magazines and newspapers, written from anti-Communist point of view.

143. _____. "Chinese Operas on the Screen" *Chinese Literature* 1:188-190, 1956. il.

144. _____. "Chinese Plan Increase in Musical Exports to U.S." *Music Trades* 124:44f., Feb 1976. NE.

145. _____. "Chinese Plays, Real and False" *Literary Digest* 64: -- , March 13, 1920. Notes on Mei Lanfang. [RR]

146. _____. "Chinese Shadow Theatre, First Visit to Europe" *The Times* (London), June 17, 1957. NE.

147. _____. "Chinese Stringed Instruments: Ch'in" *Musical Standard* 29:243, 1908. NE.

148. _____. "Chinese Theatres in San Francisco" *Harper's Weekly* 27:295-296, May 12, 1883. il. Brief, straightforward descriptions of performances.[RR]

149. _____. "The Chinese Theatres of Shanghai" *Living Age* 325:208-212, 1925. NE.

150. _____. "A Chinese Theatrical Triumph" *Studio* 101:31-35, 1931. NE.

151. _____. "Chinese Violins, Guitars Penetrating Canadian Market" *Music Trades* 120:33, July 1972. NE.

152. _____. "City Performers Tour the Countryside" *China Reconstructs* 13(1):27, Jan 1964. il. Report of four touring Peking groups.

153. _____. "Classical Theatre of China" *Musical Opinion* 76:139, Dec 1955. On tour of Peking Opera troupe.

154. _____. "Chinesische Musikinstrumente" *Über Land und Meer* 43(50):—. NE.

155. _____. "'Cogs and Screws' The Performing Arts in New China" *Current Scene* 3(9):1-15, Dec 15, 1964. A well-documented survey.

156. _____. "A Collection of Local Operas" *Chinese Literature* 5:178-179, 1959. Reports planned publication of anthology.

157. _____. "Collections of Folk Songs Published" *Chinese Literature* 2:133, 1960.

158. _____. "Collective Concerto" *Newsweek* 82:57, Sept 10, 1973. il. On the "Yellow River Piano Concerto" and its performance by the Philadelphia Orchestra.

159. _____. "Coming From Life, But Higher Than Life—Some Thoughts on the Choreographic Molding of Proletarian Heroic Images" *Selections From China Mainland Magazines* 670:11-17, Dec 31, 1969. From *Hung-ch'i* 12, Nov 29, 1969.

160. _____. "Commemorating the People's Musicians Nieh Erh and Hsien Hsing-hai" *Chinese Literature* 1:182-183, 1961. Report of commemoration meeting and concert.

161. _____. "Commemoration Cheng Yen-chiu" *Chinese Literature* 6:154, 1959. Report of performances in memory of this famous opera star.

162. _____. "Commentaries on the October 1969 Version of the Peking Opera *Taking the Bandit's Stronghold*" *Current Background* 898:1-41, Dec 22, 1969.

163. _____. "Comments on the Ballet 'The White-Haired Girl'" *Chinese Literature* 8:133-146, 1966. NE.

164. _____. "Commune Life on the Stage" *China Reconstructs* 8(1):25, Jan 1959. Descriptive review of "Hundred Flowers Farmers' Song and Dance Ensemble."

165. _____. "The Compass for the Great Proletarian Cultural Revolution" *China Reconstructs* 15(9):8-9, Sept 1966. On Mao's *Talks at the Yenan Forum*.

166. _____. "Concert of Folk Songs" *Chinese Literature* 3:119-120, 1964.

167. _____. "A Concert on the Grassland" *Chinese Literature* 2:120, 1974. Chronicle note on Kazakh folk singers.

168. _____. "A Concerto Praising People's War" *China Reconstructs* 19(11):42-45, Nov 1970. il. "The Yellow River Piano Concerto," a creative adaptation of Hsien Hsing-hai's "Yellow River Cantata."

169. _____. "The Connection Between Chinese Music, Weights, and Measures" *Nature* 30:565-566, 1884. NE.

170. _____. "Contests for Young Instrumentalists" *China Reconstructs* 12(8):20, Aug 1963. il. *Erh-hu* and violin competitions in 4th Shanghai Spring Music Festival.

171. _____. "Cultural Activities of National Minorities in Yunnan" *Chinese Literature* 3:127-128, 1974.

172. _____. "Cultural Front: Ballad Singers of Kwangsi" *People's China* (14):37, July 16, 1962.

173. _____. "Cultural Front: A Ballet for Peace" *People's China* 2(7):30, Oct 1, 1950. Report of the ballet "Doves For Peace," presented by the Central Dramatic Academy Ballet Corps.

174. _____. "Cultural Front: Blind Minstrels of the People" *People's China* 3(8):27, April 16, 1951. Ballad singers trained at new Blind Artists Training School.

175. _____. "Cultural Front: Chairman Mao's Talks on Art Commemorated" *People's China* (13):33, July 1, 1952.

176. _____. "Cultural Front: Choi Sung Hi, a Korean Dancer in China" *People's China* 4(8):16, Oct 16, 1951.

177. _____. "Cultural Front: Dances of the People" *People's China* (1):22-23, Jan 1, 1952. il.

178. _____. "Cultural Front: 'Little Son-in-Law'" *People's China* (5):30, March 1, 1952. Modern *ping-chu* opera.

179. _____. "Cultural Front: The People Dance" *People's China* 2(12):23, Dec 16, 1950. Folk dances of national minorities in National Day Festivities.

180. _____. "Cultural Front: The People's Records" *People's China* 3(11):30, June 1, 1951. Surveys many new releases.

181. _____. "Cultural Front: The PLA's Cultural Troupes" *People's China* 4(3):30, Aug 1, 1951.

182. _____. "Cultural Front: The Rhythm of the Waist Drum" *People's China* 3(10):28, May 16, 1951. mus. The flower drum in New China.

183. _____. "Cultural Front: Why They Love 'The White-Haired Girl'" *People's China* 4(11):18-21, Dec 1, 1951. il.

184. _____. "Cultural Life: Ancient Music Played by Peasants" *People's China* (7):38, April 1, 1957. Nahsi performers from Yunnan.

185. _____. "Cultural Life: Concert of Foreign Folk Songs" *People's China* (14):38, 1957.

186. _____. "Cultural Life: Fifteen Strings of Cash" *People's China* (11):37-38, June 1, 1956. Report of *k'un-ch'ü* revival in Peking.

187. _____. "Cultural Life: Films of Chinese Opera" *People's China* (24):38-39, Dec 16, 1956.

188. _____. "Cultural Life: Kwangtung Opera in Peking" *People's China* (12):41, June 16, 1956. il.

189. _____. "Cultural Life: Music Festival Opens" *People's China* (16):37, Aug 16, 1956. First national music festival in Peking.

190. _____. "Cultural Life: National Song and Dance Festival" *People's China* (4):37-38, Feb 16, 1957. il.

191. _____. "Cultural Life: A New Kunshan Opera Theatre" *People's China* (15):43, Aug 1, 1957. On the success of *k'un-ch'ü* in Peking.

192. _____. "Cultural Life: Old Operas Come into Their Own" *People's China* (1):40-41, Jan 1, 1957. il. Revivals of some neglected Peking operas.

193. _____.   "Cultural Life: Pioneers of Modern Chinese Music" *People's China* (2):33-34, Jan 16, 1956. Concert review; music by Nieh Erh and Hsien Hsing-hai.

194. _____.   "Cultural Life: Sunday Concerts" *People's China* (10):39, May 16, 1956.   Report of Peking series.

195. _____. "Cultural Life: Theatres to the Villages!" *People's China* (3):37, Feb 1, 1956.

196. _____. "Cultural Life: Tien Ma Studio's Dance Performance" *People's China* (24):42-43, Dec 16, 1957. il.

197. _____. "Cultural Life: La Traviata in Peking" *People's China* (3):38, Feb 1, 1957. il. Report of first all-Chinese production by the Central Experimental Opera Theatre.

198. _____. "Cultural Life: Uday Shankar Dance Company at Peking" *People's China* (18):38, Sept 16, 1957. il.

199. _____. "Cultural Life: Yunnan and Hunan Operas" *People's China* (14):37-38, July 16, 1956. Revivals in Peking.

200. _____. "Cultural Revulsion, Or the Case of the Viennese Revisionists" *High Fidelity and Musical America* 24:27, May 1974. NE.

201. _____. "Cultural Workers in Shanghai Criticize Confucius and Mencius" *Chinese Literature* 5:131, 1974. Joining the critical movement, "Shanghai's Peking Opera Troupe, Dancing Academy, People's Art Theatre and Philharmonic Society have composed a number of militant songs, skits, and other stage items."

202. _____. "Cultural World: Dr. Mei Lan-fang" *People's China* 1(2):23, Jan 16, 1950. Mei optimistic on drama reform.

203. _____. "Cultural World: 2000-year-old Bell" *People's China* 1(11):23, June 1, 1950. A Chou bell presented to Academia Sinica.

204. _____. "The Current Scene in Peking" *New York Times* 6:1,7, June 1, 1969. NE.

205. _____. "Dances of the People" *China Reconstructs* 4 (10):15-17, Oct 1955. il.

206. _____. "Dancing Display" *China Reconstructs* 5(10): 31, Oct 1956. On program given by the Peking School of Dance, "including excerpts from classical ballet, Chinese and international folk dances and Chinese classical items ..."

207. _____. "Dockers Hail the Performance of 'On the Docks'" *Chinese Literature* 1:73-80, 1969.

208. _____. "The Drama in Peking" *Saturday Review* 72:104-105, July 25, 1891. NE.

209. _____. "Dramatic Festival Victoriously Concluded in Peking" *Chinese Literature* 11:103-104, 1974. Brief report of Aug-Sept 1974 festival of local adaptations of model revolutionary Peking operas.

210. _____. "Dramatizing Today's Reality" *China Reconstructs* 7(9):23, Sept 1958. il. Developments in modern opera.

211. _____. "Etwas über die Neuere Chinesische Musik" *Berlinische Musikalische Zeitung,* p. 105f., 1793. NE.

212. _____. "Festival Discussions" *Peking Review* 7(32): 30-31, Aug 7, 1964. NE.

213. _____. "Festival of Films of Model Revolutionary Theatrical Works" *Chinese Literature* 7:97-98, 1974.

214. ____. "Festival of Peking Opera on Contemporary Themes" *Chinese Literature* 9:125-129, 1964. il.

215. ____. "Festival of Local Operas on Modern Themes" *Chinese Literature* 8:159, 1960.

216. ____. "Festivals of Local Operas on Contemporary Themes" *Chinese Literature* 4:104-105, 1965.

217. ____. "Festivals Reveal New Burst of Creativity" *China Reconstructs* 14(2):34, Dec 1965. il. Modern opera.

218. ____. "Fifth Shanghai Spring Music Festival" *Chinese Literature* 9:131-132, 1964.

219. ____. "'Fighting on the Plains,' a Modern Revolutionary Peking Opera" *China Reconstructs* 23(8): 26-30, Aug 1974. il. Plot summary, with color and black-and-white photos.

220. ____. "Fighting Spirit in Songs" *China Reconstructs* 15(2):21-31, Feb 1966. mus. On Nieh Erh and Hsien-hai, with a song by Hsien, "In the Taihang Mountains." [Hsien-hai = Hsien Hsing-hai.]

221. ____. "The First National Music Festival" *Chinese Literature* 1:194-195, 1957.

222. ____. "Five Hundredth Performance" *China Reconstructs* 11(6):38, June 1962. il. On the folk opera, *Third Sister Liu*, based on Chuang songs.

223. ____. "A Flowering Spring in the Great Proletarian Cultural Revolution" *China Reconstructs* 15(9):26-33, Sept 1966. il. On the 7th "Shanghai Spring" Music Festival. Color photos.

224. ____. "Folk Music Concerts" *Chinese Literature* 2: 123, 1964.

225. ____. "Folk Music of the National Minorities" *Chinese Literature* 9:121, 1962. Report of research collecting field trip by team from Chinese Musical Research Institute to Fukien, Yunnan, and Hainan.

226. ____. "Folksongs from China" *China Reconstructs* 4: Supplement, 1955. 12p. Seven songs, English text only; piano arrangement of varying quality.

227. ____. "Folk Songs in Manchuria" *Contemporary Manchuria* 4(2):71-87, April 1940. Collection of texts, in characters and translation, arranged topically. No music or musical information.

228. _____.   "Friends of Five Continents Highly Praise Revolutionary Performances" *China Reconstructs* 18: 20-21, April 1969.

229. _____.   "Gentle Drums" *Mitteilungen des Seminars für Orientalische Sprachen zu Berlin* 14:339-348, 1911. NE.

230. _____. "George Kin Leung" *China Journal* 34:48, 1941. NE.

231. _____.   "Ghosts and Spirits on the Stage" *China News Analysis* 502:1-7, Jan 31, 1964. NE.

232. _____.   "Government Supports Western Music in Chungking" *China At War* 7:71-72, July 1941.

233. _____.   "Grosser Erfolg des Farbfilms 'Tigerberg'—Oper in Hong Kong" *China-Analysen* 10:8, May 1971. NE.

234. _____.   "Les Guitares en Chine" *Études Japonaises* 4: 159, 1885. NE.

235. _____.   "Hail the Great Victory of the Revolution in Peking Opera" *Chinese Literature* 8:125-128, 1967. Editorial from *Hung-ch'i* 6, 1967.   Reprinted in Chiang Ching, *On the Revolution in the Peking Opera*, p. 8-12.

236. _____.   "Honouring Two Great Artists" *China Reconstructs* 4(8):29, Aug 1955. il. On Mei Lan-fang and Chou Hsin-fang celebrating their 50th year of acting. Color cover of Mei Lan-fang.

237. _____.   "Hsiao Chung-hua's Seventy Years in Peking Opera" *Chinese Literature* 2:143-145, 1958. il.

238. _____.   "Important Play Revived" *China Reconstructs* 5(8):30, Aug 1956. il. On the performance of the *k'un-ch'ü* opera "Fifteen Strings of Cash."

239. _____.   "In Commemoration of Mei Lan-fang" *Chinese Literature* 11:110-112, 1962.

240. _____. "In Commemoration of Nieh Erh and Hsien Hsing-hai" *Chinese Literature* 1:190-192, 1956. il., mus.

241. _____.   "In Tune with Chairman Mao: Revolutionary Music in People's China" *Current Scene* 3(29):1-12, Oct 15, 1965. Survey based on mainland sources.

242. _____.   "Information: Peking Opera, Kunchu Opera" *Chinese Literature* 11:101-103, 1961.

243. _____. "Inner Mongolian Folksong Exhibition" *Chinese Literature* 3:167, 1959.

244. _____. "Inno Republicano Cinese" *Musica* 6:3, 1912. NE.

245. _____. "Innovations in Traditional Musical Instruments" *Chinese Literature* 5:178, 1959. Exhibition of "improved" instruments by the Chinese Musician's Union.

246. _____. "Insipid Water Torture; Peking Opera 'The Red Lantern'" *Time* 92(18):58, Nov 1, 1968. il.

247. _____. "Japanese Kabuki in China" *China Reconstructs* 5(1):31, Jan 1956. il. Review of touring troupe.

248. _____. "Japan's Progressive Art" *China Reconstructs* 9(5):30, May 1960. il. Tour by Zenshinza Kabuki company.

249. _____. "Kai Chiao-tien: Peking Opera Star" *Chinese Literature* 2:220-221, 1957. il.

250. _____. "Kompository Narodnogo Kitaja" [Composers of People's China] *Sovetskaya Muzyka* 10:106-114, Oct 1952. NE.

251. _____. "Letter From Paris" *New Yorker* 31:66, June 25, 1955. On the Peking Opera performances in Paris. NE.

252. _____. "Liberated Serfs Sing and Dance" *Chinese Literature* 3:126-127, 1974. New Tibetan folk songs.

253. _____. "Long Ago" *China Pictorial* 2:41, 1966. il. Three *hsün* discovered in Shang tombs at Liulike, Honan, 1951, are pictured here.

254. _____. "Lu," "Pian" in W. Gurlitt, ed. *Riemann Musik Lexicon* 12th ed. (Mainz: B. Schott's Söhne, 1967), Sachteil, 535, 734. Brief, unsigned entries, possibly by Fritz Bose.

255. _____. "Lyrichord's Superb Chinese Series—No. 8" *American Record Guide* 32:432, Jan 1966.

256. _____. "Ma Sitson and His Tone Poeme Tibertia" *China Digest* 1(8):18, April 10, 1947. mus. Brief review.

257. _____. "Madame Butterfly in Peking" *China Reconstructs* 11(3):40, March 1962. il. First produced in 1958; now done successfully with an all-Chinese cast featuring soprano Li Chin-wei. *Madame Butterfly* "... represents the racism with which United States imperialism justifies its trampling on the Asian peoples and committing of every kind of vile crime against them."

258. _____. "Mao Tze Tung Knows Quality—Red China Buys a Steinway" *Music Trades* 121:65, Nov 1973. NE.

259. _____. "Mao Tsetung Thought Forever Sheds its Radiance" *Chinese Literature* 6:94-101, 1969. On "Taking the Bandit's Stronghold."

260. _____. "Mao's Wife Keeps Control of the Arts" *New York Times* 12:1, Sept 22, 1968. NE.

261. _____. "Maramures Folk Song and Dance Ensemble in China" *Chinese Literature* 11:105-106, 1974. il. Visit of Romanian troupe.

262. _____. "Mathew Ricci and Chinese Music" *Catholic Choirmaster* 43:63, Summer 1957. NE.

263. _____. "Dr. Mei Lan-fang" *China Journal* 31:303, 1939. NE.

264. _____. "Mei Lan-fang in Various Roles" *Chinese Literature* 11:[n.p.], 1961. il. A collection of 7 fine plates, 1 in color. No text.

265. _____. "Millions of Voices Sing" *China Reconstructs* 7(11):25, Nov 1958. Song festival in Shanghai.

266. _____. "A Ming Dynasty Painting" *New China Review* 1 (2):164, May 1919. Color plate. Note accompanying reproduction of a scroll by Ch'iu Ying depicting Yang Kuei-fei and T'ang Ming-huang listening to music. See comments by C.M. below, and related articles by Kishibe and Rowley.

267. _____. "Miss Tai Speaks of her Search for Native Chinese Dances" *China Institute Bulletin* 41:11, Mar 1947. il. Report of Tai Ai-lien's lecture-recital at China Institute.

268. _____. "Mr. T.P. Liang Revives Lost Musical Art" *China Institute Bulletin* (30):8, Jan 1946. Notice on Liang Tsai-ping, *cheng* virtuoso and scholar, then at Yale.

269. _____. "Mix With the Masses" *New York Times* 3:3, Dec 11, 1966. NE.

270. _____. "A Model for Revolutionary Peking Opera" *China Reconstructs* 16(9):12-16, Sept 1967. il. On "Taking the Bandit's Stronghold."

271. _____. "Model Revolutionary Theatrical Works Further Popularized and Developed" *Chinese Literature* 8: 99-101, 1974.   The list of model works expands. Some made into films, some adapted into local opera genres, and performed all over the country.

272. _____.   "Modern Minstrels of Inner Mongolia" *Peking Review* 8(7):30-31, Feb 12, 1965. NE.

273. _____.   "Modern Revolutionary Peking Opera: Taking Tiger Mountain by Strategy: Selected Songs (musical score and words)" *China Pictorial* 4:Supplement, 1971. 25p. Arranged and presented by a group of the Shanghai Peking Opera Troupe working on "Taking Tiger Mountain by Strategy." NE.

274. _____. "Mosaic of Major Events: Western Music" *China News Analysis* 948:2, Feb 1, 1974. Brief report on the opening shots in the campaign against untitled music.

275. _____. "Music and Dance from Three Countries" *China Reconstructs* 15(1):17-18, Jan 1966. il. Song and dance troupes from Albania, Cambodia, and Nepal.

276. _____.   "The Music Capabilities of the Chinese" *Dwight's Journal of Music* 27(3):20, April 27, 1867. Communication from a Hong Kong missionary on difficulties of forming a Chinese choir and teaching them to sing. See defense by E. Syle "Music Among the Chinese."

277. _____.   "Music from Argentina" *China Reconstructs* 9 (4):37, April 1960. il. Tour by Osualdo Pugliese Orchestra.

278. _____.   "Music, 1949-1961" *China News Analysis* 381: 1-7, July 21, 1961; 386:1-7, Aug 25, 1961. Reliable, concise survey of musical activities, both Western and traditional, in Communist China, based on Communist newspapers and magazines.

279. _____.   "Music in the Model Settlement" *China Today* 7:254-257, 1936. NE.

280. _____.   "Musician Escapes from China, Ma-szu-tsung" *New York Times* 1:7, April 13, 1967. NE.

281. _____.   "Die Musik der Chinesen" *Signale für die musikalische Welt* 59(20):--. NE.

282. _____. "La Musique Chinoise" *Revue des Revues* 24:442-447, Feb 15, 1898. mus. NE.

283. _____. "Nasi Umelci Boli v Cine" *Slovenska Hudba* 2:119-120, March 1958. NE.

284. _____. "National Music Ensemble" *Chinese Literature* 7:152-153, 1960.

285. _____. "National Music and Dance Festival" *Chinese Literature* 2:226-228, 1957. il.

286. _____. "New Appointment for Mao's Wife Adds to Her Responsibilities" *New York Times* 6:1, Dec 6, 1966. NE.

287. _____. "A New Blossoming of Revolutionary Peking Opera" *China Reconstructs* 16(3):8-11, March 1967. il. On "Taking the Bandit's Stronghold."

288. _____. "New Chinese Stage Technique Due?" *Chinese Digest*, p.10,13, Jan 31, 1936. NE.

289. _____. "New Colour Films of Model Revolutionary Theatrical Works" *Peking Review* 7:20, Feb 12, 1971. il. Announcing films of "The Red Lantern" and "The Red Detachment of Women."

290. _____. "A New Development in Traditional Chinese Opera" *Chinese Literature* 6:164-165, 1958.

291. _____. "New Envoys of Art From an Old Neighbor" *China Reconstructs* 14(6):18, June 1965. NE.

292. _____. "New Film on Nieh Erh, the People's Composer" *China Reconstructs* 9(10):36-37, Oct 1960. il. On the first Chinese musical cinema hagiography.

293. _____. "A New Form of Proletarian Art" *China Reconstructs* 17(10):19-22,43, Oct 1968. il. On the piano music "The Red Lantern," with Peking Opera singing.

294. _____. "A New Generation of Peking Opera Artists" *Chinese Literature* 7:170, 1954. Report of first performance by the youth company of the National Peking Opera Theatre.

295. _____. "A New Look at China's Operas" *Chinese Literature* 2:221-224, 1957. il.

296. _____. "New Masters of the Stage" *Chinese Literature* 12:91-99, 1966. il. NE.

297. _____. "New Music for an Ancient Instrument" *China Reconstructs* 23(11):14-15, Nov 1974. il. On the composition of the new work "Fighting the Typhoon" for remodeled *cheng*. The composition is recorded on Chung-Kuo Ch'ang-pien M-1019, "The Red Flower of Tachai Blossoms Everywhere," Side B, Band 1.

298. _____. "A New Opera" *China Reconstructs* 5(4):29, April 1956. il. On "Song of the Grassland" by Lo Tsung-hsien, a new-style opera using folk tunes.

299. _____. "The New Opera 'Hsiangyang Store'" *China Reconstructs* 23(6):42-43, June 1974. Background of genesis of this new *ping-chu* opera, with plot summary.

300. _____. "The New Political Campaign, Part III" *China News Analysis* 954:1-7, March 22, 1974. Reports and analysis from the cultural revolution, focusing on Chiang Ching and the odd incident of the supposedly critical opera "Three Visits to Peach Peak."

301. _____. "New Programme by Shanghai Philharmonic Orchestra" *Chinese Literature* 2:119-120, 1974. Includes new *cheng* solo "Fighting the Typhoon."

302. _____. "New Programme of the Tienma Dancing Academy" *Chinese Literature* 4:142, 1960.

303. _____. "New Recordings" *China Reconstructs* 12(3):24, March 1963.

304. _____. "New Repertoire of the Hainan Song and Dance Troupe" *Chinese Literature* 9:114, 1974. Brief note.

305. _____. "New Stage Entertainments" *Chinese Literature* 7:104-105, 1973. Local amateur variety shows.

306. _____. "New Style Puppet Plays" *Chinese Literature* 8:144-146, 1966. On a glove-puppet theater from Lunghsi Fukien.

307. _____. "New Tunes for the Old Folk Music of Fukien" *Chinese Literature* 5:122, 1965.

308. _____. "Nieh Erh and Hsien Hsing-hai" *Peking Review* 45:33-34, Nov 8, 1960. NE.

309. _____. "North China Theatrical Festival" *China Reconstructs* 23(5):27-28,48, May 1974. il.

310. _____. "North-China Theatrical Festival in Peking" *Chinese Literature* 4:102, 1974.

311. _____. "Notes on Chinese Musicians and Writers" *Asia* 46(3):144, March 1946. Hsien Hsing-hai, Ma Ssu-tsung.

312. _____. "O Činském Lidovém Tanci" [On Chinese Folk Dance] *Hudebni Rozhledy* 5(8):11, 1952. NE.

313. _____. "Ode to the Dragon River" in *Selections from China Mainland Magazines* 725-726:37-92, April 3-10, 1972. Script of new model opera; Jan 1972 revision by the Shanghai Operatic Group. From *Hung-ch'i* 3, March 1, 1972.

314. _____. "Of Devils and Demons" *Time* 89(16):40, April 21, 1967. Portrait. On Ma Ssu-tsung's defection.

315. _____. "Old Mongolian Musical Instrument Found in Yunnan" *Chinese Literature* 5:124, 1964. Rediscovery of *sugoto* among Nahsi people.

316. _____. "Old Songs for Young Singers" *China At War* 2:27-28, June-July 1939. NE.

317. _____. "Oldest Operas Come to Life" *China Reconstructs* 6(9):31, Sept 1957. il. On a *k'un-ch'ü* troupe established in Peking.

318. _____. *On the Docks—A Modern Revolutionary Peking Opera*. Revised by the "On the Docks" group of the Peking Opera Troupe of Shanghai (January 1972 script). Peking: Foreign Languages Press, 1973. 41p. il. Script, color plates.

319. _____. "An Opera for Millions" *China Reconstructs* 10(9):33-35, Sept 1961. il., mus. On "The Red Guards of Lake Hunghu," with musical excerpt.

320. _____. "The Opera Form in China Today" *Chinese Literature* 4:178-179, 1957.

321. _____. "Opera With a Difference" *China Today* 8(5):33-35, May 1965. il.

322. _____. "Os Chinêses e Música" *E. Musical* 6(241):27-28, 1916. NE.

323. _____. "P.L.A. Festival" *Chinese Literature* 10:156-157, 1959. Reports Second Music and Drama Festival of the People's Liberation Army.

324. _____. "Paeans to People's War—The South Vietnam Liberation Army Song and Dance Ensemble" *China Reconstructs* 17(6):40-41, June 1968. il.

325.   . "Peasant Cultural Festival in Shanghai" *China Reconstructs* 13(7):11, July 1964. il. Report.

326.   . "Peking Literary and Art Workers Discuss Yenan 'Talks'" *Chinese Literature* 8:103-104, 1974.

327.   . "Peking Opera" *Chinese Literature* 1:205- 08, 1957. il.

328.   . "Peking Opera Portrays Today's People" *China Reconstructs* 13(10):26-27, Oct 1964. il. Color photos of modern opera scenes.

329.   . "Peking to Paris" *Time* 65:40, June 20, 1955. il. On Peking Opera Troupe tour.

330.   . "Peking Theatrical Troupes Tour the Country" *China Reconstructs* 24(7):44-46, July 1975. illus. Report of March tours by opera and music groups, "their second large-scale tour since 1972."

331.   . "Peking's Revolutionary Opera Gives Ideology a Leading Role" *New York Times* 20:1, Nov 20, 1966. NE.

332.   . "People's Commune Cantata" *Peking Review* 35: 22-23, Aug 30, 1960. NE.

333.   . "A Performance of Story-Telling and Ballads" *Chinese Literature* 7:131-134, 1961. il. About the *ping-tan* genre of storytelling with accompaniment of *p'i-p'a* and/or *sanhsien*.

334.   . "Probleme der Musikkultur in der Volksrepublik China" *Musik und Gesellschaft* 10:602-607, 1960. NE.

335.   . "Professional Artists Learn from Amateurs" *Chinese Literature* 4:107-108, 1965.

336.   . "Psychologie de la Musique Chinoise" *Revue de Psychologie et de Psychologie Appliquée* 33(4):--, 1924. NE.

337.   . "Raid on the Tiger Regiment" *Peking Review* 8(3):30-31, Jan 15, 1965. NE.

338.   . *Raid on the White Tiger Regiment. Model Peking Opera on Contemporary Revolutionary Theme*. Colombo: Afro-Asian Writer's Bureau, 1967. 69p., il. Script, black-and-white photos.

339.   . "Random Talk on Drama, Hua Chü" *China News Analysis* 481:1-7, Aug 16, 1963. This is about Western-style spoken drama, not traditional opera.

340. _____. "Rapid Development of Tibetan Cultural and Art Workers" *Chinese Literature* 9:113-114, 1974. Brief note.

341. _____. "Une Réalisation Exceptionelle: l'Opéra Chinois" *Disques* 72:507, May-June 1955. Review of the recording made by the traveling troupe.

342. _____. "Recital of Ancient Songs" *Peking Review* 4 (18):21, May 5, 1961. NE.

343. _____. "The Red Detachment of Women" *New York Times* 85:2, Nov 23, 1969. NE.

344. _____. "Red Detachment of Women" in *Selections from China Mainland Magazines* 727-728:52-104, May 1-8, 1972. January 1972 script of Peking opera "transplanted collectively by the China Peking Opera Troupe from the ballet of the same name." From *Hung-ch'i* 4, April 1, 1972.

345. _____. *Red Detachment of Women—A Modern Revolutionary Ballet*. Revised collectively by the China Ballet Troupe (May 1970 script). Peking: Foreign Languages Press, 1972. 169., il., mus. Illustrated synopsis of the story, color plates, 86 pages of selected orchestral scores.

346. _____. "'Red Detachment of Women': A New Road for Chinese Ballet" *Chinese Literature* 1:262-267, 1970. NE.

347. _____. "The Red Lantern" *China Reconstructs* 19(9): 1-17, Sept 1970. il. (cover). Synopsis, discussion, many photos of the stage version.

348. _____. *The Red Lantern—A Modern Revolutionary Peking Opera*. Revised collectively by the China Peking Opera Troupe (May 1970 script). Peking: Foreign Languages Press, 1972. 98p., il., mus. Script, with color plates and music for 11 songs; song texts in both Chinese and English.

349. _____. *The Red Lantern. Model Peking Opera on Contemporary Revolutionary Theme*. Colombo: Afro-Asian Writer's Bureau, 1967. 59p., il. Script, with photos of scenes from the production.

350. _____. "'The Red Signal Lantern'—A Peking Opera" *China Pictorial* 9:18-19, 1965. il. NE.

351. _____. "Reminiscences of a Chinese Official. IX. The Making of a Singing Girl" *Oriental Affairs* 11:291-296, May 1939. NE.

352. _____. "Research on National Minorities Music" *Chinese Literature* 2:128-129, 1960. Report on field collections by a team from the Central Conservatory of Music.

353. _____. "Revisionist Music; Discrediting the Chinese Opera 'Three Ascents up Peach Mountain'" *Time* 103: 45, March 18, 1974. il. NE.

354. _____. "Revolution in Peking Opera" *Selections from China Mainland Magazines* 656:18-31, May 26, 1969. Translations of three articles from *Pei-ching Jih-pao*: 1) "P'eng Chen the Butcher Strangling the Revolution in Peking Opera" by Liu Tse-t'ien and Kuo Ch'uan-lin (Sept 20, 1968); 2) "Build a Revolutionary Force of Literary and Art Workers for the Proletariat" by Revolutionary Committee of the Peking Opera Troupe of China (July 4, 1968); 3) "Comrade Chiang Ch'ing Leads Us to March Bravely Along Chairman Mao's Revolutionary Line on Literature and Art" by Wei Ch'ing-tien (July 15, 1968).

355. _____. "A Revolutionary Ballet" *China Pictorial* 5: 22-23, 1965. il. On "The Red Detachment of Women." NE.

356. _____. "A Revolutionary Creation in the Art of Peking Opera" *Selections from China Mainland Magazines* 427:1-5, July 23, 1964. NE.

357. _____. "Revolutionary Model Operas Performed in the Mountains" *Chinese Literature* 11:106-107, 1974.

358. _____. "Revolutionary Songs and Dances" *China Pictorial* 1:52-53, 1967. NE.

359. _____. "Revolutionary Theme for Ballet" *China Reconstructs* 14(2):20-23, Feb 1965. il. On the new production "The Red Detachment of Women."

360. _____. "Rich Cultural Season" *China Reconstructs* 7 (1):28, Jan 1958. il. Survey of musical events, mostly international.

361. _____. "Scène Chinoise et Théâtre Européen" *Orient et Occident* 1(12):--, July 1935. NE.

362. _____. "Search for Old Szechuan Operas" *Chinese Literature* 9:119, 1962. Reports new publication.

363. _____. "Serve the Broadest Masses of the People" *Peking Review* 22:6-9, June 1, 1962. NE.

364. _____. "Seeking Themes from Life" *China Reconstructs* 8(4):36, April 1959. il. New compositions infused with the spirit of the people.

365. _____. "Selected Songs of Li Chieh-fu" *Chinese Literature* 6:128, 1964. Reports new publication.

366. _____. "The Seventh 'Shanghai Spring' Music Festival" *Chinese Literature* 8:141-142, 1966. Brief report of musical events.

367. _____. "Shachiapang, A Modern Revolutionary Peking Opera" *China Reconstructs* 20(2):14-16,18-24, Feb 1971. NE.

368. _____. *Shachiapang. A Modern Revolutionary Peking Opera.* Revised collectively by the Peking Opera Troupe of Peking (May 1970 script). Peking: Foreign Languages Press, 1972. 101p., il., mus. Script, with color plates, and music for 7 songs.

369. _____. "'Shachiapang': Strive to Portray Proletarian Heroes of People's War" *Chinese Literature* 11, 1970. Reprinted in *Drama Review* 15(2):270-273, Spring 1970. NE.

370. _____. "Shanghai Dockers Perform New Work Chants" *Chinese Literature* 12:109, 1973.

371. _____. "Shanghai Spring Music Festival" *Chinese Literature* 9:115, 1963.

372. _____. "Shanghai Workers', Peasants' and Soldiers' Festival of the Performing Arts" *China Reconstructs* 16(9):24-28, Sept 1967. il.

373. _____. "Shantung Liutzu Opera Is Performed in Peking" *Chinese Literature* 2:131-132, 1960. Reports revival of this obsolescent form.

374. _____. "The Sheng" *New Music Review* 23:267, Feb 1924. NE.

375. _____. *The Shiao Chiao Chinese Music Research Institute in a Commemoration of its Tenth Anniversary Presents its Orchestra in a Concert of Classical Chinese Music—Lyceum Theatre, Shanghai, November 1, 1935.* Shanghai: Mercury Press, 1935. 16[20]p. il. NE.

376. _____. "A Shining Example from the Great Proletarian Cultural Revolution" *China Reconstructs* 15(8):28-36, Aug 1966. il. On the ballet "The White-Haired Girl." Color photos.

377. _____ . "Silly Symphony; Chinese Opinion of the Philadelphia Orchestra Tour" *Newsweek* 83:81, Jan 28,
1974. NE.

378. _____ . "Singer of the Steppes" *Chinese Literature* 2:
174-176, 1956. il. About Tuokhin, a famous ballad
singer from Inner Mongolia.

379. _____ . "Singing in the Peking of Chairman Mao" *Chinese Literature* 1:120-126, 1967. il. On the amateur theatrical troupe of Hopei peasants. NE.

380. _____ .   "Singing Quotations from Chairman Mao Tse-
tung" *China Reconstructs* 16(4):25-27, April 1967.
il., mus. On the spread of this craze of the "Cultural Revolution."

381. _____ . "Singing Today's Songs" *China Reconstructs* 15
(6):7, June 1966.   Contemporary opera in Yunnan
Province. NE.

382. _____ .   "Sinkiang Song and Dance Troupe in Shanghai"
Chinese Literature 3:126, 1974.   Song and dance
drama "The People's Commune is Fine" in *mukkam*
style.

383. _____ . "A Sino-Soviet Swan Lake" *Peking Review*, Dec
1, 1961.

384. _____ . "Soldiers Act Soldiers" *China Reconstructs* 14
(5):16-18, May 1965. il. Amateur music, dance, and
theater groups of the People's Liberation Army.

385. _____ .   "Some National Minority Musical Instruments"
Chinese Literature 3:89-92, 1965. il. Photos and
descriptions of five unusual instruments. Useful.

386. _____ . "Some New Recordings" *China Reconstructs* 8(6):
16, June 1959. Description of recent releases.

387. _____ .   "Some Popular Chinese Records" *China Reconstructs* 4(6):29, June 1955.   Group of short reviews.

388. _____ .   "Song and Dance: 'Flames Over the Cocoanut
Groves'" *China Pictorial* 7:36-37, 1965.   il. Photographs by Ho Shih-yao and Ao En-hung. NE.

389. _____ . *Song of the Dragon River—A Modern Revolutionary Peking Opera*.   Revised by the "Song of the
Dragon River" Group of Shanghai (January 1972
Script).   Peking: Foreign Languages Press, 1973.
43p. il. Script, color plates.

390. _____. "Songs and Dances from Inner Mongolia" *China Reconstructs* 12(1):38-39, Jan 1963. il. Review of Peking performance by the Song and Dance Ensemble of the Inner Mongolian Art Theatre.

391. _____. "Songs and Dances from South Sinkiang" *China Pictorial* 4:18-19, 1966. il. Photos and descriptions of Khotan song-and-dance troupe visiting Peking.

392. _____. "Songs in Praise of Chairman Mao" *Chinese Literature* 10:67-74, 1966. NE.

393. _____. "Songs of Shanghai Dockers" *Chinese Literature* 5:131-132, 1974. Report of a concert by docker choruses, in which "... the worker audience joined in the choruses, making the concert hall a scene of heart-stirring solidarity."

394. _____. "Songs of the Revolution" *China Reconstructs* 10(5):27, May 1961. Review of 5 new song books.

395. _____. "Spare-Time Singers from Hsishuangpanna" *Chinese Literature* 8:105, 1974.

396. _____. "Spare-Time Songsters of Luta" *Chinese Literature* 10:121, 1974. Brief note on mass composition.

397. _____. "Splendid Stage Art: Selected Scenes from Model Revolutionary Theatrical Works" *China Pictorial* 7-8:22-23, 1971. NE.

398. _____. "Staging Yüan Drama: A Colloquium" *Literature East and West* 14(4):547-567, 1970. Report of session at CHINOPERL Traditional Theater Conference, 1970. NE.

399. _____. "Stamps of New China: Chinese Folk-Dance Specials" *China Reconstructs* 12(1):44, Jan 1963. il. A series of six stamps, Special 49, Nos. 246-251, depicting local folk dances.

400. _____. "Stamps of New China: Chinese Folk-Dance Specials" *China Reconstructs* 12(9):43, Sept 1963. il. A second set of six stamps, Special 53, Nos. 261-266.

401. _____. "Stamps of New China: Chinese Folk-Dance Specials" *China Reconstructs* 12(10):44, Oct 1963. il. Third and last set of six stamps, Special 55, Nos. 279-284, 246-251, depicting local folk dances.

402. _____. "Stamps of New China: Mei Lan-fang Miniature Sheet" *China Reconstructs* 11(12):42, Dec 1962. il. An addition to the previously issued set, depicting Mei as Yang Kuei-fei.

403. _____. "Stamps of New China: Opera Artist Mei Lanfang" *China Reconstructs* 11(11):44, Nov 1962. il. Description and photo of a set of 8 commemorative stamps issued on the first anniversay of Mei Lanfang's death, depicting Mei in his most famous roles.

404. _____. "Stamps of New China: The Revolutionary Modern Dance Drama, 'The White-Haired Girl'" *China Reconstructs* 23(2):48, Feb 1974. il.

405. _____. "Stamps of New China: Three More Stamps on Model Revolutionary Theatrical Productions" *China Reconstructs* 17(7):33, July 1968. il. Scenes from the ballets "Red Detachment of Women," "The White-Haired Girl," and from the symphony "Shachiapang."

406. _____. "Stamps of New China: Victory of Chairman Mao's Revolutionary Line on Literature and Art" *China Reconstructs* 17(6):35, June 1968. il. Scenes from five new operas.

407. _____. "State Theatre for Northern Kunchu Opera Set Up" *Chinese Literature* 4:180-181, 1957.

408. _____. "Street Songs of China" *Musician* Oct 1930. NE.

409. _____. "Strive to Create the Brilliant Images of Proletarian Heroes—Impressions on Creating the Heroic Images of Yang Tzu-jung and Others" *Selections from China Mainland Magazines* 667:11-19, Nov 24, 1969. From *Hung-ch'i*, 11, Oct 29, 1969. Also in *Peking Review* 12(51-52):34-39, Dec 26, 1969.

410. _____. "Studying China's Folk Music" *Chinese Literature* 5:113, 1963. Report on activities of Chinese Music Research Institute.

411. _____. "Studying 'Talks at the Yenan Forum on Literature and Art'" *China Reconstructs* 15(9):10-19, Sept 1966. il. Article translated from the *Jiefangjun Bao* [Liberation Army Daily] May 23, 1966.

412. _____. "Success of a New 'Kunchu' Opera" *Chinese Literature* 5:118-119, 1965. On "Ching-hua," a new *k'un-ch'ü* opera with a revolutionary theme.

413. _____. "A Successful Example of Opera Reform" *Chinese Literature* 4:230-234, 1956. il. On the revision of Chu Su-chen's "Fifteen Strings of Cash."

414. _____. "The Sun Shines on the Ballet Stage" *Selections from China Mainland Magazines* 629:33-36, Sept 30, 1968. "In praise of the ballet 'White-Haired Girl.'" From *Shou-tu Hung-wei-ping* [Capital's Red Guards] May 27, 1967.

415. _____. "Sunday Concerts" *China Reconstructs* 5(7):31. July 1956. Describes a series of concerts held by the Central Ensemble of Song and Dance, including new pieces on folk themes.

416. _____. "Symfonimusik I Kina" *Musikern* 1:8, Jan 1963. NE.

417. _____. "A Szechuan Comedy" *China Reconstructs* 12(7): 20, July 1963. il. "The Young Scholar," produced in Peking.

418. _____. "Szechuan Opera Festival" *Chinese Literature* 4:166-168, 1955. il.

419. _____. "Take That, Ludwig; Denouncing Western Classical Composers" *Time* 103:51, Jan 28, 1974. il. NE.

420. _____. "Taking the Bandits' Stronghold" *Chinese Literature* 8:129-181, 1967. 12p. color plates. Complete text of new opera.

421. _____. *Taking the Bandits' Stronghold. Model Peking Opera on Contemporary Revolutionary Theme*. Colombo: Afro-Asian Writer's Bureau, 1967. 68p., il. Script, black-and-white photos.

422. _____. "Taking the Bandits' Stronghold—Revised Collectively by the 'Taking the Bandits' Stronghold' Theatrical Unit of the Peking Opera Theatre of Shanghai" *Selections from China Mainland Magazines* 668:1-46, Dec 1, 1969. From *Hung-ch'i* 11, Oct 29, 1969.

423. _____. "Taking Tiger Mountain by Strategy (Oct 1969 script) Revised Collectively by the 'Taking Tiger Mountain by Strategy' Group of the Peking Opera Troupe of Shanghai" *Peking Review* 12(51-52):12-33, Dec 26, 1969. il.

424. _____. *Taking Tiger Mountain by Strategy—A Modern Revolutionary Peking Opera*. Revised collectively by the "Taking Tiger Mountain by Strategy" group of the Peking Opera Troupe of Shanghai (July 1970 script). Peking: Foreign Languages Press, 1971. 113p. il., mus. Script, color photos, music for nine songs.

425. _____. "Tenth Anniversary Celebrations" *Chinese Literature* 12:158-166, 1959. il. Reports events—operas, dance, theatre, etc.—held to celebrate the 10th anniversary of the People's Republic.

426. _____. "Das Theater der Chinesen. Über ein Gastspiel der Peking-Oper und ein Buch von Obraszow" *Theater Heute* 5:30-31, June 1964. il. NE.

427. _____. "The Theatre in China" *Cornhill* 9:297-303, March 1864. NE.

428. _____. "Theatre" *Chinese Literature* 3:159-163, 1955. Introduction to the Chinese periodical *Theatre*, with discussion of main topics of the Chinese operatic and theatrical world.

429. _____. "Theatre Festival in Peking" *Chinese Literature* 8:152-153, 1959.

430. _____. "Le Théâtre National contre le Théâtre Impérial" *Est-Orient* 1(4):26-37, 1967. NE.

431. _____. "Theatrical Festival Held by Heilungkiang Young People" *Chinese Literature* 10:121-122, 1974.

432. _____. "Theatrical Festival Opens in Peking" *Chinese Literature* 10:119-120, 1974.

433. _____. "Theatrical Performances During Spring Festival" *Chinese Literature* 4:104-105, 1974.

434. _____. "Third Sister Liu, a Kwangsi Opera Performed in Peking" *Chinese Literature* 11:154-155, 1960.

435. _____. "A Thirteenth Century Relief of a Chinese Stage" *Chinese Literature* 5:176, 1958. Reports discovery of "earliest tangible replica of ancient Chinese theatre."

436. _____. "Three Chinese Work Songs" *China Reconstructs* 6(1):37, Jan 1957. mus. Transcriptions.

437. _____. "Three Dramatic Revivals" *China Reconstructs* 11(10):30-31, Oct 1962. il. "White-Haired Girl" (Yangko), "The Pressgang" (topical play), "Three Attacks on Chu Family Village" (new Peking opera), presented in Peking for 20th anniversary of Mao's *Talks at the Yenan Forum.*

438. _____. "Town Hall (Shantung Traditional Music)" *Music Journal* 30:61, Sept 1972. NE.

439. _____. "Traditional Music, Contemporary Themes" *China Reconstructs* 13(5):19, May 1964. il. Report of highlights of Peking music season.

440. _____. "Traditional Orchestra" *China Reconstructs* 11 (11):34, Nov 1962. il. Review of a tour by the Shanghai Traditional Music Orchestra, led by Ho Wu-chi.

441. _____. "Triumphs of Mao Tse-tung's Thought in Literature and Art" *China Reconstructs* 16(9):8-11, Sept 1967. il. On the numerous modern operas and what they owe to Mao and Chiang Ching.

442. _____. "Turkish Musicians Give Première in Peking" *Chinese Literature* 3:129, 1974. Violin concert.

443. _____. "Two Stirring Operas" *Chinese Literature* 1: 112-113, 1965. New operas presented at a festival.

444. _____. "Über das chinesische Theater. Eine Betrachtung anlässlich des Klabundschen Kreiderkreises" *Chinesische Blätter* 1(1):79-90, 1925. NE.

445. _____. "Über die Musik der chinesen" *Allgemeine Musikalische Zietung* 17-18:--, 1817. NE.

446. _____. "Ueber die Musik der chinesen" *Ebendaselbst* 11:43-44, 1824. NE.

447. _____. "Ulan Muchir Troupes—In the Vanguard of Culture for the People" *China Reconstructs* 23(8):34-37, Aug 1974. il. On local revolutionary cultural troupes of musicians and dancers in Inner Mongolia.

448. _____. "Unrest in East China, Troubles in Peking" *China News Analysis* 643:1-7, Jan 13, 1967. On the political infighting surrounding the reform of performing arts; 3 sections: 1) Chiang Ching (a biopolitical sketch); 2) Lin Piao and the theater; 3) Mao on Lin Piao's stage.

449. _____. "Upsurge in the Arts: A 'China Reconstructs' Symposium" *China Reconstructs* 8(12):8-17, Dec 1959. Reports on progress in music, dance, opera. Includes the following: Tuan Cheng-pin "We Learn From the People"; Yu Chen-fei "An Old Style Through Today's Eyes"; Yang Yu-ho "Teaching Drama in a New Way"; Tsaidan "From Serf to Artist"; Tu Chin-fang "Rising Generation in Opera"; Yen Liang-kun "Symphony: Richer and Better"; Hou Pao-lin "A Lively Art Wins Respect"; Kuan Wei-chi "We Serve the Children"; Ah Chia "Never Before So Fast, So Well, So Cooperatively."

450. _____. "A Very Old Opera" *China Reconstructs* 4(11): 31, Nov 1955. il. On a production of "Chen San and Wu-niang," a Fukien opera of the *Li Yüan* style.

451. _____. "Victorious Close of the Festival of Peking Opera on Contemporary Themes" *Chinese Literature* 10:105-110, 1964.

452. _____. "Vigorous Spare-Time Literary and Art Activities in Peking, Shanghai and Tientsin" *Chinese Literature* 8:102-103, 1974. Amateur groups perform model revolutionary operas.

453. _____. "Volume Three of 'New Songs from the Battlefield' Published" *Chinese Literature* 7:98, 1974.

454. _____. "We Sing of Chairman Mao with Infinite Love" *China Reconstructs* 16(11):19-21, Nov 1967.

455. _____. "A Well-Loved Story in New Guise" *China Reconstructs* 7(7):33, July 1958. il. "The White-Haired Girl" staged as ballet and a Peking opera.

456. _____. "What 'The White-Haired Girl' Teaches Us" *China Reconstructs* 15(8):47-50, Aug 1966. il. A symposium with members of the ballet cast.

457. _____. "The 'White-Haired Girl'—A New Revolutionary Ballet" *Peking Review* 9(21):25-27, May 20, 1966. il. NE.

458. _____. "Wood-Block Prints of Early Peking Opera" *Chinese Literature* 9:140, 1959. Reports new publication.

459. _____. "A Worker's and PLA Men's Propaganda Team Mobilize the Masses to Use Mao Tsetung Thought to Transform the Literary and Art Front" *Peking Review* 12(31):13-15, Aug 1, 1969. NE.

460. _____. "Workers, Peasants and Soldiers on 'Shachia-pang'" *Chinese Literature* 3:85-91, 1969.

461. _____. "World Renowned Harmonica Player Enters China" *Harmonica Happenings* 7(3):7, 1973-1974. NE.

462. _____. "Writings of Peking Opera Actors" *Chinese Literature* 3:137-138, 1960. Reports new publications.

463. _____. "Ein wundervoller Einblick in Chinas Kultur" *Musik und Gesellschaft* 7:9-13, 1951. il. Report of Berlin festival performance of Chinese music.

464. _____. "Yiyang Opera Performed in Peking" *Chinese Literature* 9:140-141, 1959.

465. _____. "Performances for Peasants and Herdsmen in Tibet" *Chinese Literature* 11:108, 1973.

* * * * * * * * * *

466. Anosov, N. "Ha Gastrol'ah v Harodnom Kitae" [About the Stars in National China] *Sovetskaya Muzyka* 10: 127f., Oct 1958. NE.

467. _____. "Kitaiski Dirizher" [Chinese Conductor] *Sovetskaya Muzyka* 6:120f., June 1956. NE.

468. Apel, Willi. "Chinese Music" in *Harvard Dictionary of Music*. (Cambridge: Harvard University Press), 1946, p.136-138. mus. A brief though not misleading distillate of secondary sources. Replaced in the second edition by an article by Rulan Chao Pian.

468.1. Appleton, Charles L. "New York's Exotic Chinese Theatre" *Theatre Magazine* 47:18-19, 68, May 1928. il. Superficial. [RR]

469. Arlington, Lewis Charles. *The Chinese Drama from the Earliest Times Until Today, A Panoramic Study of the Art in China, Tracing Its Origin and Describing the Accompanying Music and Musical Instruments*. Shanghai: Kelly and Walsh, 1930. xxxi+177p. il. Reviewed by Theo Rühl in *Monumenta Serica* 2: 220-222, 1936-1937. French translation by G. Uhlman, *Le Théâtre Chinois depuis Origines jusqu'a nos jours*. Peiping: Henri Vetch, 1935. 184p. il. (115 plates), bibliography, index.

470. Arlington, L.C. and Harold Acton. *Famous Chinese Plays*. Peiping: Henri Vetch, 1937. 443p. mus.

471. [Arnaud, L'Abbé François and J.B.A. Suard]. *Variétés Littéraires, ou Recueil de Pièces Tant Originales que Traduites, Concernant la Philosophie, la Littérature, et les Arts.* Paris: Chez le Jay, 1770. 4 vols.   See I, 472-502, "Mémoire sur les danses chinoises, d'après une traduction manuscrite de quelques ouvrages de Confucius." Also see II, 309-353, "Traduction manuscrite d'un livre sur l'ancienne musique chinoise, composé par Ly-Koang-Ty, docteur et membre du premier tribunal des lettres de l'empire, ministre, etc." This important article derives from Amiot's manuscripts, and appeared prior to Amiot's major work on Chinese music. The question of Amiot's manuscripts will be dealt with in a future volume of Asian Music Publications, which will contain a translation of Amiot's work. Three editions were published of the collection *Variétés Littéraires*:   1) Paris: Lacombe, 1768-1969; 2) Paris: Le Jay, 1770; 3) Paris: Deterville, 1804. All were in four volumes.

472. Aslanov, A.P. "Koe Čto o Sovremennoi Yaponskoi i Kitaiskoi Muzyke" *Biblioteca Teatra Iiskusstva* Oct 1907. NE.

473. Association des Amitiés Franco-Chinoises, ed.   *Le Théâtre Chinois.* Paris: Paris-Pékin [1953 or 1954 ?]. (Supplement 3 to *Paris-Pékin*), 63p. il.   Pamphlet includes the following short articles: "Préface" by Claude Roy.   "Deux Voyageurs Français à l'Opéra de Pékin. I. Le Théâtre Chinois" by Jean-Jacques Mayoux.   II. "Les Yeux Ouverts sur le Théâtre Chinois" by Alice Ahrweiler.   "Festival International d'Art Dramatique de Paris: l'Opéra de Pékin" by Robert Ruhlmann (program notes for 6 plays). "Mei Lan-fang" (brief biographical note). "Art d'hier, art de Demain" by Mei Lan-fang. "Introduction au Théâtre Chinois: Quelques Précisions sur l'Ancien Théâtre Classique Chinois." "Les Théâtres Chinois de Province" by Jack Chen.

474. Astley, Thomas. *A New General Collection of Voyages and Travels.* London: 1745. See IV, 179. NE.

475. Aubry, Pierre. "La Musique Chinoise (extrait du Li-Ki)" *Revue Musicale* 6(19/20):470-471, 1906. NE.

* * * * * * * * * *

476. Bachmann, Werner. *Die Chinesischen Musikinstrumente der T'ang-Zeit.* [In preparation] cited in Bachmann, *Origins of Bowing,* p.69, Note 287. NE.

477. _____. *The Origins of Bowing: And the Development of Bowed Instruments Up to the Thirteenth Century*. London: Oxford University Press, 1969. xvi+178p., plates, bibliography, index. Translated by Norma Deane. A thorough examination of archeological, textual, and iconographic evidence on early bowed strings. Discussion of Chinese materials in chapter "Eastern Asia," p.64-70, and *passim*.

478. Bachy, Charles. "Observations sur le tam-tam des Chinois" *Mémoires, Société des Sciences de l'Agriculture et des Arts de Lille* 3s 8:45-52, 1870. NE.

479. Baglioni, S. "Beitrag zur Kenntnis der Natürlichen Musik" *Zeitschrift für Ethnologie* 46:591-614, 1914. NE.

480. Bagramian, Elleanor C. "Drama?" *Dodder* 2:53-55, Jan 1970. Analysis of a Yüan opera "Hsiao Shu-lan" which seems to lack dramatic qualities.

481. Baldwin, S.L. "Hymns and Music in Chinese" *Chinese Recorder* 19(10):489, Oct 1888. Short letter asking for information on hymns in China and use of native music.

482. Bali. "The White-Haired Woman, A New Approach to Chinese Drama" *China Digest* 4(5):16-18, July 13, 1948. Review with synopsis.

483. Ball, James Dyer. "Music (Chinese)" in *Encyclopedia of Religion and Ethics*, edited by James Hastings. (New York: Scribner's, 1917), IX:16-19.

484. _____. *Things Chinese*. 5th ed. Revised by E. Chalmers Werner. Shanghai: Kelly and Walsh, 1925. See p. 408-413 and *passim*.

485. Bancroft, Hubert Howe. *Essays and Miscellany*. Vol.38 of *The Works of Hubert Howe Bancroft*. 39 vols. San Francisco: History Co., 1890. Among Bancroft's detailed observations on San Francisco's Chinese are notes on music in living quarters (326-327), in restaurants (332, 334), for the Chinese New Year (362), in the theatre (366-377: much attention to instruments), in gambling houses (377-378), for funerals (392), and for religious ceremonies (411). Bancroft is a careful, if sometimes ethnocentric, observer. [RR]

486. Bantok, Granville. "Confucianism and Music" *New Quarterly Music Review* 3:157-164, Feb 1896. NE.

487. Barbeau, Marius. "Asiatic Survivals in Indian Songs" *Musical Quarterly* 20(1):107-116, Jan 1934. il., mus. On aural identification by a Chinese colleague, Barbeau posits a relationship between Northwest Amerindian dirge styles and Chinese music. Interesting, if somewhat naive hypothesis, but not well-supported here.

488. Barber, Sue E. [Sue E. Dunn]. "Music and Ideology: The Philadelphia Orchestra Experience" *In Theory Only* (Ann Arbor) 1:53-76, Feb-March 1976. A condensation of the author's M.A. thesis sparked discussion in later issues of *In Theory Only*. See also entries under M.A. Guck, E. Hantz, D.L. Harwood and M. Beebie.

489. _____. *Music and Politics: The Philadelphia Orchestra in the People's Republic of China.* M.A. (music), University of Michigan, 1977. viii+139p. Many photos, bibliography. A thorough and stimulating study of this important event in the Cultural Revolution of the mid-70s.

490. Barinova, G. "V Novom Kitae" [In New China] *Sovetskaya Muzyka* 4:89f., April 1950. NE.

491. Barker, E.H. "Music" *China Review* 15:54. NE.

492. _____. "Notation" *China Review* 15:188. NE.

493. Barnes, Clive. "The Ballet Nixon Saw in Peking" *New York Times*, Section 2, 23:2, March 19, 1972. NE.

494. Barrow, John. *Mémoires Concernant les Chinois.* See II, 86. NE.

495. _____. "Musique Chinoise" *Journal Asiatique*, 2s, 10:100. NE.

496. _____. *Travels in China.* London: Cadell and Davies, 1804. French translation by J. Castera. *Voyage en Chine.* Paris: 1805. See p.81, 313-323, 483. Musical passages excerpted in Frank Harrison, *Time, Place and Music* (q.v.).

497. Batchelder, Marjorie H. *Rod-Puppets and the Human Theatre.* Columbus: Ohio State University Press, 1947. xxiv+372p., 48 plates. See p.37-45, "Rod-Puppets in China" for description and historical survey of Chinese puppetry.

498. Bates, Alfred, ed. "Oriental Drama" Vol. 3 of *The Drama: Its History, Literature and Influence on Civilization.* London: Athenian Society, 1903. NE.

499. Bause, Renate.   "Eindrücke vom Festival 1964" *Neue Zeitschrift für Musik* 9:401-403, 1964.   NE.

500. Baxter, Glen William.   *Hua-Chien Chi: Songs of Tenth-Century China*.   Ph.D., Harvard, 1952.   Study of early collection of *tz'u* poems.

501. _____.   *Index to the Imperial Register of Tz'u Prosody*.   Cambridge: Harvard University Press, 1956. "... a guide to the titles and general shape of hundreds of tune patterns, insofar as these can be indicated by the poetry texts only." [Author]

502. _____.   "Metrical Origins of the Tz'u" *Harvard Journal of Asiatic Studies* 16(1/2):138-145, June 1953. Detailed scholarly study of this music-dependent poetic form, drawn from the author's Ph.D. dissertation.

503. Bayless, Gertrud R. "The Curious Lore of Chinese Music" *Étude* 48(9):617-618, Sept 1930.   il.   Author thinks well of China and has good grasp of musical situation, but information on scales inaccurate and misleading.

504. Bazin, Antoine Pierre Louise.   *Théâtre Chinois: ou choix de Pièces de Théâtre Composées sous les Empereurs Mongols Traduites pour la Première fois sur la texte Original, Précédées d'une Introduction et Accompagnées de notes ...*   Paris: Imprimerie Royale, 1838.   409p.

505. Beauclair, Inez de.   "Marginalia to Franz Heger's 'Alte Metalltrommeln aus Süd-ost-Asien'" *Studia Serica* 4:87-110, 1945.   NE.

506. Becker, Babette Minnie. *Music in the Life of Ancient China as Reflected in the Ceremonial Books: The I Li, the Chou Li, the Li Chi*. M.A. thesis (Oriental Languages and Literature), University of Chicago, 1954.   39p.   Collation and brief study of musical references.

507. _____. *Music in the Life of Ancient China: From 1400 B.C. to 300 B.C.*   Ph.D. dissertation (Oriental Languages and Literature), University of Chicago, 1957.   98p.   Chou and pre-Chou music approached through literature.   Early inscriptions and the classics combed for musical references.

508. Beebie, M. "Musicology, Social Sciences and Cultural Analysis" *In Theory Only* (Ann Arbor), 2:21-26, June-July 1976.   Comments on Sue Barber's article on the Philadelphia Orchestra in China.

509. Bellaigue, Camille. "La Musique chinoise" in *Notes Brèves*. Paris: Delagrave, 1911, p.176-184. NE.

510. Belpaire, Bruno. *T'ang Kien Wen Tse: Florilège de Littérature des T'ang*. Paris: Editions Universitaires, 1957. 2 vols., 412 and 432p. An anthology of T'ang literature in translation, with brief introductions. Music in T'ang life and culture illustrated by four short stories, I, 105-121. Three essays on music appear in full: 1) "Siao Tche: l'art de la vocalise," II, 250-263. 2) "Yo-fou-tsa-lou: Notes diverses sur les mélodies," par Toan An-tsie, II, 287-315. [A fully annotated translation of this important treatise may be found in the work of Martin Gimm listed below.] 3) "Notes sur les tambours à peau de bouc (Kie-kou-lou)," II, 357-371.

511. Benchley, Robert. "Foreign Correspondence from New York" *Life* 88:21, Aug 26, 1926. On New York's Chinese theatre. Fatuous. [RR]

512. Benedetti, Robert L. "What We Need to Learn from the Asian Actor" *Educational Theatre Journal* 25(4): 463-467, Dec 1973. Movement, timing, and other lessons to be learned from Asian drama, based on demonstrations by two Chinese actresses.

513. Berg-Pan, Renata. *The Chinese Influence on the Dramaturgy of Bertolt Brecht*. Ph.D. dissertation, Harvard University, 1971. 4+218p. NE.

514. Berl, E.D. *A Chronological Outline of Music in History (China, Arabia, Palestine, Greece)*. [n.c.]: O. Pagani, [n.d.], 95p. NE.

515. Berlioz, Hector. "Moeurs Musicales de la Chine" in his *A Travers Chants*. (Paris: Levy, 1862), p.252-258. English translation by Fredric Lieberman and Nguyen Kim-Oanh, "Chinese Musical Customs" *East-West Center Review* 1(1):1-6, June 1964. A short, biting satire directed against European musical society, using China as a foil. Reveals state of European popular knowledge of Chinese music in this period—which was not very great.

516. Bernard, Henri S.J. "Catalogue des Objets Envoyés de Chine par les Missionnaires de 1765 à 1786" *Bulletin de l'Université l'Aurore* (Shanghai) 3s, 9 (33-34):119-206, Jan-April 1948. Detailed, indexed, and annotated list, with extracts from letters accompanying the shipments.

45

GOSHEN COLLEGE LIBRARY
GOSHEN, INDIANA

517. _____. "Ricciana II. La Musique Européene en Chine" *Bulletin Catholique de Pékin* 21:40-43, 78-94, 1934. NE.

518. Bertin, Monseigneur de. *Mémoire sur la Musique des Chinois*, 1776. Ms. in the Bibliothèque Nationale, Paris. This is a doubtful citation. Probably refers to the Amiot Ms. in the Bertin collection. NE.

519. Bertuccioli, G. "The Ch'in: The Chinese Lute" *Eastern World* 3:33-35, 1952. NE.

520. Betz, B. "Be-Bop, BG, and a Box of Bubble-Gum" *Downbeat* 16:2, Aug 26, 1949. NE.

521. Biallas, F.X. *Konfuzius und sein Kult* Peking: Pekinger Verlag, 1928. See p.100-113, "Die Opfer. Nachwort." NE.

522. Billert, C. "Chinesische Music" in *Musikalisches Conversations-Lexicon*, 2nd ed., by Mendel-Reissman. (Berlin: Oppenheimer, 1880), II, 394-415. il., mus. NE.

523. Bingham, Woodbridge. "The Rise of Li in a Ballad Prophecy" *Journal of the American Oriental Society* 61:272-280, Dec 1941. Study of the influence of a popular song on the success of Li Yüan in founding the T'ang Dynasty.

524. Birch, Cyril. "Translating and Transmuting Yüan and Ming Plays: Problems and Possibilities" *Literature East and West* 14(4):491-509, 1970. NE.

525. Bitton, W. Nelson. "A Symposium of Opinion upon Church Music in China" *Chinese Recorder* 40(4): 195-213, April 1909. Several questions on church music discussed by both Western and Chinese Christians.

526. Bloch, Stella. "Dancing and Drama: East and West" *Orient* 1(3):7-12, Aug-Sept 1923. il.

527. Bodde, Derk. "The Chinese Cosmic Magic Known as Watching for the Ethers" in *Studia Serica Bernhard Karlgren Dedicata*, edited by Søren Egerod and Else Glahn. (Copenhagen: Ejnar Munksgaard, 1959), p.14-35. Fascinating study of a curious outgrowth of the Han preoccupation with cosmic interrelatedness and numerology. *Lü*-tubes were used to indicate the "arrival of the ether" of each month; varying opinions on the success of this method.

528. Bois, Georges.   "À propos des Idées de l'Ancienne
Chine sur la Musique" *Bulletin de la Société
d'Études Indochinoises* ns, 11(2):53-67, 1936. NE.

529. Boltz, Judith Magee. "Divertissement in Western Han"
Early China 1:56-63, il. Discussion of an unusual
pottery group of musicians, acrobats, and dancers
discovered in 1969.

530. Bonavia, David.   "Peking Attacks Beethoven the Capi-
talist" *London Times*, p. 6g, Jan 15, 1974. NE.

531. Bonner, Aletha M. "Musical Messages from Many Lands.
III: The Music of China and Japan" *Music and Youth*
4:--, June 1929. NE.

532. Bonosky, Phillip. *Dragon Pink on Old White* New York:
Marzani and Munsell, 1963. Report, generally sympathetic, of a 1959 trip to the People's Republic.
See especially "Chinese Opera" (p.17-27), an introduction to the tradition, revolutionary changes
under leadership of Mei Lan-fang, a visit to an
opera school; "Beethoven and Ballet" (p.104-110),
details a performance of the Ninth Symphony under
Yen Liang-kun, and the modern dance-drama "Red
Cloud."

533. Bonsey. A. "Chinese Hymnology and Church Music" *Chinese Recorder* 40(5):283-286, May 1909. Letter to
the editor, with various suggestions; nothing
valuable.

534. Borch, H. von.   "Das Chinesische Theater" *Sinica* 6:
89-90, 1931. NE.

535. Borde, Jean Benjamin de la. *Essai sur la Musique Ancienne et Moderne*. Paris: 1780. 4 vols. See Vol.
I, Chap. 15: "De la musique des Chinois." NE.

536. Borel, Henri. *Wijsheid en Schoonheid uit China*. 2nd
ed. Amsterdam: Van Kampen and Zoon, 1898. 163p. NE.

537. Bose, Fritz. "Chinesche Musik" *Riemann Musik Lexicon*
W. Gurlitt, ed. 12th ed. (Mainz: B. Schott's Sohne,
1967). Sachteil, p.160-162. Bibliog. Brief survey.

538. _____.   "Western Influences in Modern Asian Music"
Journal of the International Folk Music Council
11:47-50, Jan 1959. Brief survey mentions Westernized forms in India, Indonesia, and China.

47

539. Bovet, Jeanne. *La Musique Primitive en Chine*. Lausanne: Versonnet, 1961. [Comment Augustin découvrit la musique: série de langage du musicien.] Introduction to Chinese music for children, with 7-inch record.

540. Bowers, Faubion. "Chinese Theater" *Encyclopedia International* IV:380-381, 1969 ed.

541. _____. "For the Nixons, a Maoist Ballet" *New York Times* 15:1, Feb 23, 1972. NE.

542. _____. *Theatre in the East: A Survey of Asian Dance and Drama*. New York: Nelson, 1956; Grove Press, 1960. x+374p. il. A sympathetic, enthused, informed, reliable and tourist's-eye view of Chinese and other Asian dramatic and dance forms, both classical and modern.

543. _____. "Unity and Diversity Within Asia's Theater Arts" *Yearbook of Comparative and General Literature* 15:198-203, 1966. NE.

544. Brewer, William Henry. *Up and Down California in 1860-1864. The Journal of William H. Brewer, Professor of Agriculture in the Sheffield Scientific School from 1864-1903*. Edited by Francis P. Farquhar, with a preface by Russell H. Chittenden. New Haven: Yale University Press, 1930. Describes Chinese theatre in San Francisco, p.366-367.[RR]

545. Brezette, Majel C. *The Music of China, Korea and Japan in Relationship to the Rest of the World*. M.Ed. thesis, Wayne State University, 1951. NE.

546. Britt, Ernest E. *La Lyre d'Apollon*. Paris: Véga, 1931. 105p. mus. See p.97-105. NE.

547. Brooks, E[rnest] Bruce. *Chinese Aria Studies*. Ph.D. (Speech-Theater), University of Washington, 1968. x+178p. Available from University Microfilms, Ann Arbor, Michigan, Order No. 68-12678. Investigations of the formal, stylistic, and dramatic functions of arias and aria sequences in Yüan opera.

548. Bröring, Theodor. *Laut und Ton in Südschantung*. Hamburg, Germany: 1927. NE.

549. Brown, M.E. and W.A. *Musical Instruments and Their Homes*. New York: 1888. Includes 270 pen-and-ink drawings of instruments, among which are specimens from the Far East.

550. Buchler, Walter. "Native Musical Highlights in China and Japan" *Étude* 49(7):473-474, July 1931. Superficial notes.

551. Buchner, Alexander. *Musikinstrumente der Völker.* Hanau/Main: Verlag W. Dausien, 1968. 295p. il. German translation by O. Guth. Survey of folk and non-Western instruments with numerous large plates, some in color. Several good pictures of Chinese instruments; also useful for pictures of many minority-group instruments in Mongolia and Soviet Central Asia. Many plates show instruments being played. Text generally poor.

552. Budd, Josephine E. "The Philosophy of Chinese Music" *Musical Courier* 108(11):6, March 17, 1934. Incompetently done.

553. Budzyk, Kazimierz. "O Chińskiej Operze Narodowej" [On the Chinese National Opera] *Pamietnik Literacki* 46(4):305-342, 1955. NE.

554. Bührmann, Max. *Studien über das chinesische Schattenspiel: Erfahrungen aus einer Reise nach China.* Lüdenscheid: Volkshochschule, 1963. 53p. il. (Lüdenscheider Beiträge, Heft 10). NE.

555. Bulling, A. "Die Kunst der Totenspiele in der Östlichen Han-Zeit" *Oriens Extremus* 3(1):28-56, July 1956. NE.

556. [Burney, Charles]. "Chinese Music" *Cyclopedia...,* Abraham Rees, ed. (London: Longman, Hurst, Rees, Orme, and Brown, 1819). Vol. III, unpaginated, 11 cols. An interesting early account by a respected music historian, drawing on DuHalde, Amiot, reports from the Macartney Embassy, and letters from a correspondent in China.

557. Bushell, Stephan Wooten. "The Stone Drums of the Chou Dynasty" *Journal of the Royal Asiatic Society, North China Branch* 8:133-179, 1873. On a famous set of 10 drum-shaped stones with inscriptions said to be of great antiquity. Rubbings and translations are given, together with collated scoliast annotation.

558. Buss, Kate. *Studies in the Chinese Drama.* Boston: Four Seas, 1922. 77p. il. Limited edition of 1000 copies. 2nd ed. New York: Jonathan Cape and Harrison Smith, 1930. 97p. il. Introduction revised; some plates differ, texts same. See p.53-60 in first edition for discussion of music.

* * * * * * * * * *

559. Candlin, G.T. "Chinese Hymnology" *Chinese Recorder*, p.167-173, April 1893. NE.

560. Capellen, Georg. "Chinesische Lyrik vom dichterischen und musikalischen Standpunkt" *Blätter für Haus- und Kirchenmusik* 18:100-103, 1914.

561. Capron, E.S. *History of California from its Discovery to the Present Time ... with a Journal of the Voyage from New York, Via Nicaragua, to San Francisco, and Back, Via Panama.* Boston: John P. Jewitt & Co., 1854. il. Describes a "Chinese Dancing Saloon" in San Francisco (p.152-154). [RR]

562. Carawan, Guy and Candie. "Music for the People: A Trip to China" *Sing Out!* 25(2):25-27, July-Aug, 1976. il., mus.

563. Carroll, Thomas D. "The Origin, Development, and Diffusion of Musical Scales: An Index to Cultural Contacts" in *Proceedings of the 2nd Conference of the International Association of Historians of Asia.* (Taipei: 1963), p.149-178.

564. Carter, E.C. "Mei Lan-fang in America" *Pacific Affairs* 3:827-833, 1930. NE.

565. Castren, David Charles. *Philosophical and Historical Observations Concerning Chinese Musical Phenomena.* M.A. thesis (music), University of Minnesota, 1959. 52p. text, 38p. bibliog. and tables. NE.

566. Cavanagh, Marjorie Spickler. "Origin of Chinese Music" *Chinese Recorder* 52:462-469, 1921. NE.

567. Cerdannes, M. "La Musique Chinoise" *Comaedia Illustré*, p.487-488, Sept 1, 1909. NE.

568. Cerezal, Pedro. "Breve Estudio Sobre la Música China" *España y America* 12(1):120-136, 392-401, 495-502, 1914. NE.

569. Cervelli, Luisa. *Mostra di strumenti musicali dell' Estremo Oriente della Collezione Gorga. Catalogo.* Roma: 1965. 14p., 5 plates. Lists Chinese instruments, with description. One color plate of *yüeh-ch'in* and *p'i-p'a*, with musical scenes painted on soundboards.

570. Cha Fu-hsi. "Chin: The Chinese Lute" *Eastern Horizon* 1(5):47-50, 1960. The same text which appears in *Chinese Literature* as "The Chinese Lute," with a few minor editorial changes. No photos or music.

571. _____. "The Chinese Lute" *Chinese Literature* 3:128-135, March 1960. il. History of the *ch'in*; includes Western notation of Movement 18 from the tune "Kuanglingsan," story of the renaissance of the *ch'in* in Communist China.   Reproduction of scroll depicting *ch'in* construction, and photo of *ch'in* player Pu Hsueh-chai.

572. Chalmers, John.   "The Chinese Ch'ih Measure" *China Review* 13:332-336, 1884. NE.

573. _____.   "The Theory and Practice of Tuning Pipes" *China Review* 14:36-39, 1885. NE.

574. _____.   "Wind Instruments" *China Review* 13:402-405, 1884. NE.

575. Chamberlain, Ida Hoyt. "Magic Writing" *China Monthly* 2(11):9-12, 17-21, Nov 1941. il. During several years in China the author studied Chinese music, attempted to write compositions for Western orchestra, using Chinese materials.   This article describes her experiences studying and notating ("magic writing") the complete music for a Taoist service at the Temple Hou Men Huo Shen Miao, Peking, 1934.

576. Champness, C.S. "Hymnology in the Chinese Church,II" in *China Mission Year Book*, 1912. (Shanghai: Christian Literature Society for China, 1912), p.249-253. Historical notes on development of psalmody in China.

577. _____. "Music in China" *Chinese Recorder* 48:489-497, 1917. mus. NE.

578. _____.   "Problems of Chinese Psalmody" *Chinese Recorder* 51(4):265-271, April 1920.

579. _____. "Psalmody in Foochow" *Chinese Recorder*, p.674 -681, Dec 1906. NE.

580. _____.   "What the Missionary Can Do for Church Music in China" *Chinese Recorder* 40(4):189-194, April 1909. Learn how to teach Chinese groups efficiently.

581. Chan Chik.   "Chinese Dancers in Hong Kong" *Eastern Horizon* 3(2):5-8, Feb 1964. il. Photos only.

582. _____. "Peking Opera" *Eastern Horizon* 2(9):5-6, July 1963. il. Photos only.

583. Chan, Peter E. "The Chinese Scale" *Étude* 47(10):726, Oct 1929. Short letter more confusing than enlightening.

584. Chang Ch'i-yün. "Ch'i Ju-shan and the Chinese Opera" *Chinese Culture* 1:146-153, July 1957. Reprinted in his *The Essence of Chinese Culture.* (Taipei: China News Press, 1957), p.311-324, portrait. An appreciation of the life and work of this great modern scholar of Peking opera, written on the occasion of his 80th birthday.

585. Chang, Donald, John D. Mitchell, and Roger Yeu. "How the Chinese Actor Trains: Interviews with Two Peking Opera Performers" *Educational Theatre Journal* 26(2):183-191, May 1974. Transcribed interviews with two traditionally trained actresses.

586. Chang, Eileen. *The Rice-Sprout Song.* New York: Scribner's, 1955. 182p. NE.

587. Chang Feng. "Music: Biggest Shanghai Festival *Peking Review* 23:18-19, June 8, 1962. NE.

588. Chang Jen-hsia. "Historical Affinities Between Chinese and Indian Music" *Music Mirror* 1(2):24-27, Feb 1958. Good short review of cultural contacts in Sui-T'ang period.

589. _____. "India's Art—and China's" *China Reconstructs* 4(9):7-9, Sept 1955. il.

590. Chang, Joseph. "Shu Lai Pao (improvised rhythmical wording)—Its Origins and Practical Value" *Ching Feng* 12(2):29-47, 1969.

591. Chang Keng. "A Great Artist of Our Times" *Chinese Literature* 11:84-100, Nov 1962. On Mei Lan-fang.

592. _____. "My Recollection of the Production and First Performances of 'The White-Haired Girl'" *Chinese Literature* (9):99-105, 1977.

593. _____. "New Blossoms on an Old Tree" *China Reconstructs* 8(4):10-12, April 1959. il. On experimental adaptations of traditional and local operas.

594. _____. "Recollections of Mei Lan-fang" *China Reconstructs* 10(10):36, Oct 1961. il. Memorial tribute.

595. _____. "The Revival of Two Operas" *Chinese Literature* 8:64-69, 1960.

596. _____. "The Yangko Movement in Yenan" *China Recon-
     structs* 11(10):11-13, Oct 1962. Historical sketch
     from the beginnings to the "White-Haired Girl."

597. Chang Ling-chen. *Church Music in China*. B.A. thesis
     (music), University of Shanghai, April 1941. NE.

598. Chang, Paul Bao-hwa. *A Survey of Chinese Music*. [Mill
     Valley: Golden Gate Seminary], 1964. 36p., mus.
     NE.

599. Chang Pe-chin. *Chinese Opera and Painted Face*. Tai-
     pei: Mei-Ya Publications, 1969. viii+243p. il.
     This folio volume consists primarily of a large
     collection of color plates of facial designs.
     There is also a general introduction on Chinese
     opera and on face-painting techniques and styles.

600. Chang Shih-min. "Chants from the Shanghai Wharves"
     China Reconstructs p.32-34, July 1962. il., mus.
     Old work chants being recorded by the Shanghai
     Union of Musicians. Description, with some texts
     and a transcription.

601. Chang, T.C. "Drama of Shadows" *Free China Review* 15
     (3):36-39, March 1965. il. Popular articles on
     traveling shadow players still occasionally found
     in Taiwan countryside. Also in *China Today* 8(7):
     26-29, July 1965.

602. Chang T'ien-i. "A Critique on the Adaptation of
     'Lin's Shop'" *Selections from China Mainland Mag-
     azines* 491:37-43, Sept 27, 1965. From *Wen I Pao*,
     June 11, 1965. NE.

603. Chang Tien-lin. "Chinesisches Drama und chinesisches
     Theater" *Sinica* 13:225-240, 1938. NE.

604. Chang Tsui-feng. *My Life As a Drum Singer*. As told
     to Liu Fang, translated by Rulan Chao Pian. Cam-
     bridge, M.A.; privately printed, 1972. vi+119p.
     A draft translation, used by Pian in her Harvard
     classes. An important document by a modern
     master; supplements Catherine Steven's disserta-
     tion (q.v.) and the fictional *Drumsingers* by Lau
     Shaw.

605. Chang Wen-kang. "Two Pioneer Composers" *China Recon-
     structs* 4(12):27-29, Dec 1955. il. On Nieh Erh
     and Hsien Hsing-hai.

606. Chang Yun-ho. "Kunchu Actors Take the Stage Again:
     An Ancient Form of Chinese Opera Is Revived" *Peo-
     ple's China* (9):27-31, May 1, 1957. il.

607. Chang Yung-mei. "Create More Typical Proletarian He-
     roes" *Chinese Literature* 5:102-107, 1974.   Essay
     on the ideology behind writing of the new opera
     "Fighting on the Plain."

608. _____. "Fighting on the Plain" *Chinese Literature* 5:
     3-54, 1974. il.   July 1973 script of China Peking
     Opera Troupe production of this new model opera
     on revolutionary themes. Eight pages of color pho-
     tos from the stage production.

609. Chao Chung. *The Communist Program for Literature and
     Art in China*. Hong Kong: Union Research Institute,
     1967. Communist China Problem Research Series. NE.

610. Chao Feng. "Bartok and Chinese Music Culture" *Studia
     Musicologica* 5:393-401, 1963.   Bartok as viewed
     with Chinese eyes.   Study of Bartok in People's
     China and the Chinese doctrinaire interpretation
     of his work.

611. _____. "A Brief Introduction to Chinese Music" *China
     Digest* 1(1):12, 15-16, Dec 31, 1946.

612. _____ [Dschao Feng].   "China bildet junge Pianisten
     heran." *China im Bild* 14:18-19, July 20, 1959. NE.

613. _____. "Chinese Drama Goes on Tour" *People's China*
     18:25-27, Sept 16, 1955.   NE.

614. _____. "Chinese Folk Dances" *China Digest* 2(8):16-18,
     Sept 23, 1947.   il.

615. _____. "Envoys of Art and Peace" *People's China* (23):
     21-23, Dec 1, 1954.   il.   Cultural troupes from
     several countries visit China and vice versa.

616. _____.   "Gastroli kitaiskogo teatra" [Stars of the
     Chinese Theatre] *Sovetskaya Muzyka* 5:164f.,   May
     1956. NE.

617. _____.   "Pesnya: Golos Serdtsa Kitaiskogo Naroda"
     [Song: Through Which the Chinese Folk Speaks From
     its Heart] *Sovetskaya Muzyka* 11:13-16, Nov 1949.
     il. NE.

618. _____.   "Uchimsa na Opyte Sovetskih Muzykantovni
     (Pis'mo iz Kitaia)" [We Learn from the Experience
     of Soviet Musicians (Letter from China)] *Sovet-
     skaya Muzyka* 3:97f., March 1952. NE.

619. Chao Feng and Ma Shao-po. "The Chinese Theatre in Eu-
     rope" *People's China* (7):36-40, April 1, 1956. il.
     Interview/report of 1955 opera tour.

620. Chao Hua. "Do Musical Works Without Titles Have No Class Character" *Chinese Literature* 4:89-94, 1974. Condensed from *Renmin Ribao*, "criticizing the erroneous view that a piece of music without a title has no class character."

621. Chao Mei-pa. "Chinese Music" *Chinese Mercury* 1:58-59, Fall 1937. NE.

622. _____. *A Guide to Chinese Music*. Hong Kong: Tai Hwa Printing Factory, 1969. x+177p. il. mus. A revised and enlarged edition of *The Yellow Bell* with much new material on history, folk songs, and theatre. A collection of folk songs in piano arrangements is added. Chinese terms are Romanized in Wade-Giles and Chinese characters are added.

623. _____. "The Trend of Modern Chinese Music" *T'ien-Hsia Monthly* 4(3):269-286, March 1937. Development of Western music education in China, with speculation as to possible modifications of traditional music.

624. _____. *The Yellow Bell*. Baldwin, Md.: 1934. French edition, *La Cloche Jaune*. Brussels: Comité Inter-Universitaire sino-belge, 1932. Also in *China Review* 3(2):15-20; 3(3):13-16; 3(4):13-16, 1934; *Annales Franco-Chinoises* 7(28):1-42, 1933. A concise popular survey from the traditional Chinese standpoint, by a well-known singer trained in Western music.

625. Chao, T.C. and Bliss Wiant. "Christian Fellowship Hymns" *Chinese Recorder*, p.745-746, Nov 1933. NE.

626. Chao Ts'ung. "Art and Literature in Communist China" in *Communist China, 1949-1959*. (Hong Kong: Union Research Institute, 1961), III, p.153-186. See p. 181-184 on music and musicians.

627. Chao Wei-pang. "Games at the Mid-Autumn Festival in Kuantung" *Folklore Studies* 3:1-6, 1944. NE.

628. _____. "Modern Chinese Folklore Investigation" *Folklore Studies* 1:55-76, 1942; 2:79-88, 1943. Report on folklore (and folk song) research and publications of the Peking National University and the Folk Song Research Society.

629. _____. "Yang-Ko: The Rural Theater in Ting-Hsien, Hopei" *Folklore Studies* 3:1-38, 1944. A form that the Communists have developed into a major internal propaganda organ. History, structure, function, plots.

630. Chao Yen-hsia. "I am All for Operas with Contemporary
     Revolutionary Themes" *Chinese Literature* 10:63-67,
     1964. il.

631. Chao Yuen-ren [= Chao Yüan-jen]. "Music" in *Symposi-
     um of Chinese Culture*, edited by Ch'en Hêng-chê.
     (Shanghai: China Institute of Pacific Relations,
     1931), p.94-111. il., mus.

632. _____. "A Note on Chinese Scales and Modes" *Oriens*
     10(1):140-143, 1957. "The main point of this note
     is that modern Chinese folk music is in a key with
     one sharp more than it sounds."

633. _____. "Seventeen Examples of Melodies for Chant-
     ing Poetry in the Ch'angchow (Kiangsu) Dialect"
     *Bulletin of the Institute of History and Philol-
     ogy, Academia Sinica.* Extra Vol. No. 4:467-471,
     1961. (Taipei: 'Studies Presented to Tung Tso Pia
     on His Sixty-Fifth Birthday.') A brief descriptive
     article in Chinese with English summary and trans-
     criptions of the music and text of 17 short poems
     chanted by the author in several styles.

634. _____. "Singing in Chinese" *Le Maître Phonetique*, 3s
     39(6):9-11, 1924. A brief note written in the in-
     ternational phonetic alphabet. 1924.

635. _____. "Tone, Intonation, Singsong, Chanting, Reci-
     tative, Tonal Composition, and Atonal Composition
     in Chinese" in *For Ramon Jakobson*. (The Hague:
     Mouton, 1956), p.52-59. mus. The best presentation
     of the various modes of dynamic relationship be-
     tween language and melody in Chinese.

636. Charpentier, Léon. "Chansons Chinoises" *Revue Blanche*
     23:161-175, Oct 1, 1933. mus. NE.

637. Chauvelot, Robert. "Choses d'Asie" *Revue Musicale de
     la Société Internationale de la Musique* 9(7-8):
     22-26, July-Aug 1913. Report of a trip; China re-
     port brief and very negative.

638. _____. "Choses d'Asie de quelques Musiques et danses
     d'Extrême-orient" *Mercure Musical*, 1913. NE.

639. Chavannes, Edouard. "Des Rapports de la musique grec-
     que avec la musique chinoise" in his *Mémoires His-
     toriques de Se-ma Tsien*. (Paris: Leroux, 1895-1905).
     III, p.230-319, 605-645.

640. _____. "Sur la musique chinoise" *Indian Antiquary*
     12:--, 1912. NE.

641. Che P'ing.   "Learn From Revolutionary Model Plays,
     Defend Revolutionary Model Plays" *Selections from
     China Mainland Magazines* 666:25-28, Oct 31, 1969.
     From *Hung-ch'i* 10, Sept 30, 1969.

642. Ch'en Ch'i-t'ung.   "Cheers for Revolutionary Peking
     Opera on Contemporary Themes" *Selections from Chi-
     na Mainland Magazines* 435:23-27, Sept 22, 1974.
     From *Hung-ch'i* 15, 1964. NE.

643. Chen Chien-hua. *A Collection of the Best Chinese Folk
     Songs*. Hong Kong: The Author, 1974.   [6]+128p.,
     mus. [Translated by Huang Fei-jan]. NE.

644. Chen Chien-tai. "Chinese Music: More Mellow Than
     Jazz?" *The Instrumentalist* 30:73, June 1976. NE.

645. Chen Chin-hsin Yao and Chen Shih-hsiang. *The Flower
     Drum and Other Chinese Songs*. New York: John Day,
     1943. 64p. il., mus.   Arrangements of 17 songs
     using heterophonic settings trying to approximate
     Chinese feeling. Short essays introduce each type
     of song with valuable information. Chinese text,
     transliteration, and translation.

646. Chen Chung-hsien. "Across the Grasslands with a Mo-
     bile Theatre" *China Reconstructs* 15(2):20-24, Feb
     1966. il. On a Mongolian traveling troupe. Good
     color photos.

647. _____. "'The East Is Red': A Song and Dance Epic of
     the Chinese Revolution" *China Reconstructs* 14(1):
     17-23, Jan 1965. il.

648. _____. "The Making of a Pianist" *China Reconstructs*
     11(1):38-39, Jan 1962. il.   About Hung Teng, a
     young pianist trained at the Shanghai Conservatory.

649. _____. "Soochow Storytelling" *China Reconstructs* 19-
     21, Oct 1961. il. [cover]. Survey of the *ping-tan*
     ballad style.

650. _____.   "They Sing and Dance for Friendship" *China
     Reconstructs* 11(10):20-23, Oct 1962. il. On a song
     and dance ensemble, led by Chang Chun, which stud-
     ies and performs dances of other countries.

651. _____.   "Young Innovator on an Ancient Instrument"
     China Reconstructs 12(9):26-28, Sept 1963.   il.
     About the *p'i-p'a* virtuoso Liu Teh-hai.

652. Chen Fu-yen. *Confucian Ceremonial Music in Taiwan with Comparative References to Its Sources.* Ph.D. (music), Wesleyan University, 1976. 486p. (76-23, 699).

653. _____. "A Hypothesis Concerning the Taiwanese Hsi Ch'u of the Past" *Asian Music* 5(1):40-55, 1973. Historical survey of the development of opera types in Taiwan. This article is a revised excerpt from the author's M.A. thesis, *A Study of Hsi Ch'ü.*

654. _____. "Principles of K'un-ch'ü Singing" *Asian Music* 8(2):4-25, 1977. An annotated translation, with original text, of Wei Liang-fu's 16th century "*Ch'ü Lü*," one of the basic texts in the early history of *k'un-ch'ü.*

655. _____. *A Study of Hsi Ch'ü in Taiwan—Its Tradition and Continuation.* M.A. thesis, Wesleyan University, 1971. iv+76p., il., bibliog. An introductory examination of the various types and styles of opera in Taiwan, their historical development, and staging characteristics. The music itself is not studied.

656. Ch'en Hao-jan. *Facial Types of Chinese Opera.* Taipei: I Hua, 1960. 38p., il. In English and Chinese. NE.

657. Chen Hsing. "The London Philharmonic Orchestra in China" *Chinese Literature* 6:99-101, 1973. il. Friendly review.

658. _____. "The Philadelphia Orchestra Performs in China" *Chinese Literature* 12:104-107, 1973. il.

659. Chen Hua. "How the Opera 'Half a Basket of Peanuts' Came to Be Written" *Chinese Literature* 5, 1973. Reprinted in *Literature and Ideology* 16:77-78, 1973.

660. Chen Hui Ming. "Some Aspects of Chinese Music, Past and Present" *China Weekly Review* 55:104, Dec 20, 1930. NE. [Same as No. 692 below.]

661. Chen, Jack [Chen I-fan]. *The Chinese Theatre.* London: Dobson, 1949. 63p., il., mus. Good short popular introduction, with chapters on "Western style" and the *yang-ko.*

662. _____. "Dancing Seen in Peking" *Eastern Horizon* 4(7): 26-32, July 1965. il.

663. _____. *Folk Arts of New China*. Peking: Foreign Lan-
      guages Press, 1954. 64p. text, 24p. plates. A col-
      lection of articles on music, drama, film, acro-
      batics, etc., many of which are reprinted from
      People's China. Good plates, some in color. Also
      published in German in 1955.

664. _____. "Peking's Many Stages" *People's China* (1):16-
      22, Jan 1, 1953. il. Surveys theatre world, tra-
      ditional and modern.

*   _____. See also Association des Amitiés Franco-Chin-
      oises, ed.

665. Chen, Karl Chia. "New Opera in China" *Theatre Arts
      Monthly* 266:661-663, 1932. NE.

666. Chen Ko. "The Story of a Revolutionary Composer"
      China Reconstructs 13(11):34-37, Nov 1964. il.,
      mus. On Li Chieh-fu.

667. _____. "The Vienna Philharmonic Orchestra Comes to
      Peking" *China Reconstructs* 6:102-104, 1973. il.
      Chinese pianist Yin Cheng-chung joins orchestra
      under Claudio Abbado to perform the "Yellow River"
      piano concerto.

668. Ch'en Li-li. "Outer and Inner Forms of *Chu-kung-tiao*,
      with Reference to *Pien-wen*, *Tz'u* and Vernacular
      Fiction" *Harvard Journal of Asiatic Studies* 32:
      124-149, 1972. Based on the surviving texts, a de-
      scription and study of the formal characteristics,
      structural and literary devices of the Sung med-
      ley.

669. _____. "*Pien-wen* Chantefable and *Aucassin et Nicol-
      lette*" *Comparative Literature* 23(3):255-261, Sum-
      mer 1971. Comparison of structural similarities
      in these stories with interspersed song.

670. _____. "The Relationship Between Oral Presentation
      and the Literary Devices Used in Liu Chih-yüan and
      Hsi-hsiang Chu-kung-tiao" *Literature East and West*
      14(4):519-527, 1970.

671. _____. "Some Background Information on the Develop-
      ment of *Chu-kung-tiao*" *Harvard Journal of Asiatic
      Studies* 33:224-237, 1973. Surveys historical sour-
      ces, and discusses the few extant examples of this
      narrative chantefable medley genre of the Sung
      dynasty.

672. Chen Lin-jui. "Chinese Shadow-Plays" *China Recon-
      structs* 3(4):23-27, July-Aug 1954. il. Descrip-
      tive popular introduction.

673. _____. "Chou Hsin-fang, Creator of Great Opera Roles" *China Reconstructs* 11(6):16-19, June 1962.   il. [cover]. Biographical sketch of this leading *lao sheng* singer, and description of his most famous roles.

674. _____. "Folk Art Festival" *China Reconstructs* 2(4): 48-52, 1951. il.

675. _____. "Kuan Han-ching in 1958" *China Reconstructs* 7(8):6-8, Aug 1958. il. Fantasy on works of China's greatest dramatist.

676. _____. "The Language of the Chinese Theatre" *China Reconstructs* 12(11):28-31, Nov 1963. il. Popular survey of opera conventions.

677. _____. "Minority Peoples Song and Dance Show Socialist Advance" *China Reconstructs* 14(2):7-10, Feb 1965.   Report of song and dance festival held in Peking, Nov-Dec 1964. All song texts praise various Socialist innovations and glorious Chairman Mao.

678. _____. "The Peking Opera" *China Reconstructs* 7:Supplement, 1956. 22p., il. NE.

679. _____. "A Popular Folk-Drama" *China Reconstructs* 1 (6):23-25, Nov-Dec 1952. il. On "Liang Shan-po, Chu Ying-tai" as a popular Shaohsing opera.

680. _____. "Puppets Come to Town" *China Reconstructs* 4 (7):14-15, July 1955. Popular introduction, color photos.

681. Chen, Marjory Liu.   "Music Education and Community Life in Taiwan China" *Musart* 20(5):38-39, April-May 1968. il. mus. NE.

682. Chen Shih-chuan. "The Rise of the Tz'u, Reconsidered" *Journal of the American Oriental Society* 90(2): 232-242, April-June 1970.

683. Ch'en Sho-yi. "The Chinese Orphan: A Yüan Play" *T'ien-Hsia Monthly* 3(2):89-115, Sept 1936. Influence of this opera on European drama of the 18th century.

684. Chen, S.Y. "The Chinese Pipe Organ" *Asia* 30(7):507, July 1930. il. Brief note on the sheng.

685. Chen Shu-fang. "Szechuan Opera Is Reborn" *China Reconstructs* 8(7):14-16, July 1959. il. Description by leading actors.

686. Chen, Susan. "Beloved Critic of Chinese Opera" *Free China Review* 15(4):30-34, April 1965. il. Eulogistic biographical note on Chi Ju-shan, respected critic and scholar of Chinese opera who died in Taiwan in 1962.

687. Chen Ta. "The Lion Dance" *China Reconstructs* 12(12):35-36, Dec 1963. il. Surveys types and styles of this ubiquitous festival dance.

688. Chen Ying-chieh. "Warriors and Coquettes" *Free China Review* 23(8):16-19, Aug 1973. il. NE.

689. Cheng Chen-to. "Kuan Han-ching, a Great Thirteenth Century Dramatist" *Chinese Literature* 3:136-141, May-June 1958.

690. Cheng, Hawthorne. "Chinese Drama Since Pearl Harbor" *China At War* 11:45-47, Aug 1943.

691. _____. "Girl in Blue Gown" *The China Magazine* (N.Y.: Chinese News Service) 17(2):30-43, Feb 1947. il. On Chungking opera.

*   Ch'eng Hsiu-ling. See Zung, Cecilia S.L.

692. Cheng Hui Ming. "Some Aspects of Chinese Music, Past and Present" *China Weekly Review* 55:104, Dec 20, 1930. NE. [Same as No. 660 above.]

693. Cheng, Philip Hui-ho. *The Function of Chinese Opera in Social Control and Change*. Ph.D., Southern Illinois University, 1974. 151p. (75-13,266). NE.

694. Cheng, Stephen. "China and America Harmonize" *Music Journal* 30(8):26-27, Oct 1972. il. NE.

695. Chi Chul-young. *The Influence of Chinese Music on Korean Music*. Ed.D. dissertation (music), University of Northern Colorado, 1975. 171p. NE. Abstract in *Dissertation Abstracts* 36:589A-590A, Aug 1975.

696. Chi Ju-shan. "A Brief Consideration of the Outstanding Peculiarities of the Old Chinese Drama" in Ernest K. Moy, ed. *Mei Lan-fang: Chinese Drama* (New York: China Institute in America, 1930), [12-14]. Concise but informative notes on some stage conventions in singing and declamation.

697. _____. "The Chinese Drama" *China Today* 2(4):51-59, April 1959. Translated by Josephine Huang Hung.

698. _____. "Development of the Chinese Theatre" *China Arts and Handicrafts* 1(3):44-52, 1932. NE.

699. _____. [J.S. Chi] *The Essentials of Chinese Drama.* Peiping: 1935. NE.

700. _____. *Important Chinese Stage Costumes and Properties.* Peiping: 1954. 40p. il. NE.

701. _____. "Mei Lan-fang" *China Arts and Handicrafts* 1(4):11-13, 1932. NE.

702. _____. "Reflections on the Peking Drama" *Modern China Monthly* 5:56-59, Feb 1951.

703. _____. "Some Outstanding Characteristics and Conventions of the Chinese Theatre" *Orient et Occident* 1(10):34-40, May 1935. NE.

704. Chi Szu. "New Items on the Peking Stage" *Chinese Literature* 2, 1973. Reprinted in *Literature and Ideology* 16:61-66, 1973.

705. Chi Ti. "'The East Is Red' Rings Out Over Shanghai" *China Reconstructs* 16(2):10, Feb 1967. A great accomplishment of the Cultural Revolution: the decadent chimes of the clock in Shanghai's old Custom House are changed to ring out the music of "The East Is Red."

706. Chi Ti-wen. "The North China Theatrical Festival" *Chinese Literature* 5:108-120, 1974. il. Report of the festival held in Peking, January-February 1974, which included 15 varieties of opera and drama, and many song and dance performances and *chuyi* (ballad singing).

707. Chi Wen-hua. "Achievements of Chinese Modern Drama" *Chinese Literature* 10:94-100, 1965. NE.

708. Chi Yen-lang. "Recovering the Lost Lute Airs" *Journal of the International Society of Music Educators* 7:238, April 1963. il. NE.

709. _____. "Wiedererweckung alter chinesischer Lautenmusik" *Neue Zeitschrift für Musikwissenschaft* 123(2):71, 1962. il. Short note on activities of Peking Ch'in Study Group. Photo of Kuan Ping-hu.

710. Chi Yu-liang. "My Ambition" *Chinese Literature* 10:76-79, 1964. il. On modernized Peking Opera.

711. Chiang Ching [Mrs. Mao Tse-tung]. "On the Revolution in Peking Opera" *Chinese Literature* 8:118-124, 1967. il. Also in *China Reconstructs* 16(8):34-35, Aug 1967. German translation in *Peking Rundschau* No. 21, 1964.

712. _____. *On the Revolution of Peking Opera*. Foreign Languages Press: Peking, 1968. vi+65p. Chiang's keynote article is followed by several others amplifying the same topic. A significant source for the early development of the approved works of the Cultural Revolution.

713. Chiang Ling-chih, Li Shan-yuan, Sung Teh-lan, Fang Hsiung. "Comments on the Ballet 'The White-Haired Girl'" *Chinese Literature* 8:133-140, 1966.

714. Chiao Ch'eng-chih. *Le Théâtre Chinois d'Aujourd'hui*. Paris: Droz, 1937. 182p. il. NE.

715. Chieh Fu. "Let us Write Songs in Praise of the Heroic Workers, Peasants and Soldiers" *Chinese Literature* 11:108-120, 1967. Reflects the anti-Chou Yang hysteria of the Cultural Revolution; Chieh tells of his songs written for "workers, peasants and soldiers," and how they succeed only because of Mao's thought.

716. Chien Chi-hua. "The Singer of the 'Kone Nakha'" *Chinese Literature* 8:113-119, 1963.

717. Chien Chu. "Training Ground for Future Players in Chinese Opera" *Free China Review* 8:33-38, April 1958. il.

718. Ch'ien Chung-shu. "Tragedy in Old Chinese Drama" *T'ien-Hsia Monthly* 1(1):37-46, Aug 1935. NE. Discusses in particular two Yüan Dynasty tragedies: *Han Palace in Autumn* and *Rain in the Oil Trees*, and compares them unfavorably with Western classical tragedies. Remarkably well written (L.C.G. in *Bulletin of Far Eastern Bibliography* 1(1):3, Feb 1936).

719. Chin Hsiang-ling. "Music Chronicle" *T'ien-Hsia Monthly* 10:373-376, April 1940. NE.

720. Chin Ming. "The Creation of the 'Red Silk Dance'" *Chinese Literature* 4:102-105, 1975. On the revised version of a *yangko*-based dance presentation.

721. _____. "How the Peacock Dance Reached the Stage" *China Reconstructs* 12(3):10-11, March 1963. il. Stage version of a Tai folk dance from Yunnan.

722. Chin Shou-shen. "Peking Storytellers" *China Reconstructs* 11(5):6-9, May 1962. il. Popular introduction to traditional and modern genres of storytelling, mostly to musical accompaniment.

723. China Reconstructs. *Special Issue in Commemoration of the 25th Anniversary of Chairman Mao's 'Talks at the Yenan Forum on Literature and Art.'* 16(8): Aug 1967. 68p., il. Text of Yenan speech and other related short works of Mao; numerous comments and appreciations.

724. _____. *Taking Tiger Mountain by Strategy.* 19(2):1-44, 1970. A special issue with full text of this modern Peking Opera from the Cultural Revolution, numerous photos, and some description of its writing and production.

725. Ching Chung-hwa. "The Chinese Theatre in Western Europe" *China Reconstructs* 13(12):16-18, Dec 1964. il. Report of 1964 opera tour.

726. Chinn, Thomas W., H. Mark Lai, Philip P. Choy. *A History of the Chinese in California: A Syllabus.* San Francisco: Chinese Historical Society of America, 1969. Notes on Chinese theaters, p.71-73. [RR].

727. Chinnery, John. "Chinese Folk Music" *Recorded Folk Music* 2:1-6, March-April 1959. Discography.

728. Cho, Kevin. "Chinese Opera" *Hemisphere* (North Sydney) 12(10):24-27, Oct 1968. il. NE.

729. Chou Ch'ing-hua. "The Art of Make-Up in Chinese Opera" *West and East* 13:10-12, Feb 1968. NE.

730. Chou Hsin-fang, et al. "Peking Opera Enters a New Era: A Discussion by Nine Artists" *China Reconstructs* 13(9):2-11, Sept 1964. il. A symposium held in connection with the Festival of Peking Opera on Contemporary Themes. Includes the following articles: Chou Hsin-fang "For Workers, Peasants, Soldiers"; Ma Lien-lang "For the First Time, a Living Man"; Hsu Lan-yuan "Hundred Flowers Bloom"; Li Yu-ju "New Characters, New Audience"; Kao Yu-chien "Growing Up to a Role"; Chao Yen-hsia "Drama of an Underground Communist"; Kuan Su-sheng "Portraying the Minority Peoples"; Li Jung-wei "What the Dockers Want to See"; Chang Hsueh-chin "Opera for Today's Youth."

731. Chou Liang. "Peking People's Art Theatre" *Chinese Literature* 1:101-108, 1964. il. NE.

732. Chou, Lily Oan-Shau.   *The Ming Ch'uan-ch'i Drama: Anatomy of a Popular Theater*. Thesis, Harvard University, 1964. NE.

733. Chou, Philip. "What They Sing Along in Chinese" *Free China Review* 14(4):21-37, April 1964. il., mus. On contemporary popular songs and their composers. Also in *China Today* 8(6):31-34, June 1965.

734. Chou Tsung-han. "Some Popular Chinese Wind Instruments" *Chinese Literature* 4:106-111, 1975. il. Notes on the *shêng*, *ti-tzu*, and *so-na*, with description of current repertoire.

735. Chou Tzu-ch'iang. "Maoist Struggle on the Musical Arena" *Issues and Answers* 10(8):30-40, May 1974. NE.

736. Chou Wen-chung. "Asian Concepts and Twentieth-Century Composers" *Musical Quarterly* 57(2):211-229, April 1971. Surveys styles which synthesize various cultural elements; general coverage, special attention to John Cage.

737. _____. "China: Music" *Encyclopedia Americana* (1971 ed.) VI,587-589. il.

738. _____. "Chinese Historiography and Music: Some Observations" *Musical Quarterly* 62(2):218-240, April 1976. il. Surveys the literature on Chinese music in Western languages, and concludes that, except for a handful of scholars, it is an "underproductive field, which is inhibited by the lack of scholarly communication with China and of the opportunity for field work." A detailed examination of several problems demonstrates the need for access to primary sources in order to produce reliable studies. Argues that the student must be proficient both in sinology and musicology.

739. _____. "East and West, Old and New" *Asian Music* 1 (1):19-22, 1968-1969. A brief discussion of some musical elements of Chinese, Japanese, and Indian music, and their potential for use in contemporary music. Another version, in José Maceda, ed. *The Musics of Asia* (Manila: National Music Council, 1971) p.143-146.   This version concentrates more on Chinese music, particularly the *ch'in*.

740. _____. "A Plea for Technical Accuracy" *Translation 73* (Columbia University) 1(1):62-65, 1973. Brief comments deploring the dearth of accurate translations of texts on Chinese music, or texts using musical terms. Suggests some collaboration.

741. _____. "To Create a New Chinese Musical Idiom" *New York Times*, Sept 9, 1973. Portrait. Mostly positive report of the author's visit to the People's Republic.

742. _____. "Towards a Re-Merger in Music" in *Contemporary Composers on Contemporary Music*, edited by Elliot Schwartz and Barney Childs (New York: Holt, Rinehart and Winston, 1967), p.308-315. On the application of traditional Chinese aesthetic concepts in a contemporary context.

743. Chou Yang [Chow Yang]. "China's Dramatic Heritage" *People's China* (7):13-19, April 1, 1953. il. Historical survey.

744. _____. *China's New Literature and Art*. Peking: Foreign Languages Press, 1954. 156p. il. Collection of lectures and essays by an authoritative exponent of Peking party line (before the Cultural Revolution), including "The Reform and Development of Chinese Opera," which suggests that actors have been victims of feudal society and should therefore join with the new people's government in ridding their plays of any vestiges of feudalism.

745. _____. "For More and Better Works of Literature and Art" *People's China* (21):3-10, Nov 1, 1953. il. (portrait). Ideological essay.

746. _____. "New Folk Songs Blaze a New Trail in Poetry" *Chinese Literature* 6:8-16, 1958. Political harangue based on conveniently composed folk song texts.

747. _____. "The Reform and Development of Chinese Opera" *Chinese Literature* 2:23-37, 1953.

* Choutze, T. [pseudonym]. See Devéria, Gabriel.

748. Chow, Fong. "Han Dynasty Musicians and Instruments" *Journal of the American Musical Instrument Society* 1:113-125, 1975. il. Translation of extracts from the 1973 archaeological report on the Ma-wang-tui tomb discoveries: a *se*, a *yü*, a set of pitch pipes, and numerous figurines of musicians. Much detail is presented, demonstrating the strong possibility that the instruments were burial models only.

749. Chow, Grace C. "Chinese Folk Dance Opens a New Vista: Miss Mary Yui Pioneers it in Panama" *China Today* 5(7):41-44, July 1962. il.

750. Chow Sen-yung. "Gong, Drum and Cymbals in Red China: A Story of Tears and Broken Hearts Off Peking Opera Stage" *Free China Review* 8:21-24, Feb 1958.

751. Chu, C.T. "An Anatomy of Yuan Drama" *Chinese Culture* 11(1):67-81, March 1970.

752. Chu Chia-chien [also: Tchou Kia-kien]. *The Chinese Theatre*. London: Bodley Head, 1922. 36p. il. Translation of *Le Théâtre Chinois* (Paris: 1922) by James A. Graham, with paintings by Alexandre Jacovleff.

753. Chu Chung-mou. "Dark Before Dawn: Recollections of a Singer" *China Reconstructs* 11(12):36-37, Dec 1962. il.

754. Chu Fang. "An Ode on the Lute" *Eastern Horizon* 8(6): 60-62, 1969. A critical review of Van Gulik's *Hsi K'ang*, pointing out typographical, translation, and interpretation errors, and bristling at traditionally 'dead' scholarship, asking, "Will Sinology be content just to remain a pleasant nostalgic escapism from realities in its self-hypnotic ivory tower?"

755. Chu Fei and Hsi Sha. "Fukien Puppet Show" *People's China* (24):34-37, Dec 16, 1957. il. Introductory survey of several genres.

756. Chu Hsi-hsien. "They Write Their Own Music" *China Reconstructs* 8(4):42-43, April 1964. il., mus. Idyllic story of authoress' visit to peasant composer Shih Chan-yuan of Shansi.

757. Chu Hsi-hsien and Ko Hsing-chien. "Birth of a Song" *People's China* (8):28-31, April 16, 1954. il. Correspondence between worker (Ko) and composer (Chu) leading to new song, "The Prospectors."

758. Chu Lan. "Comments on the Shansi Opera 'Going Up to Peach Peak Three Times'" *Chinese Literature* 7:79-85, 1974. Condensed from *Renmin Ribao*, Feb 28, 1974. This opera about a horse is analyzed and repudiated as counter-revolutionary.

759. _____. "A Decade of Revolution in Peking Opera" *Chinese Literature* 9:85-94, 1974. An ideological survey, summing up achievements of the model revolutionary works, and encouraging further consolidation and development. Excerpted from *Hung-ch'i* (Red Flag) 7, 1974. Reprinted in *Literature and Ideology* (Toronto) 18:1-16, 1974.

67

760. _____. "A Discussion of Western Music" *China Reconstructs* 23(7):37-39, July 1974. Condensation of article from *Red Flag* 4, 1974, "Deepen the Criticism of the Bourgeois Theory of Human Nature." Rejects idea of absolute music, holding that "All works of music, rather than expressing personal feelings that stand above class, invariably reflect the interests and aspirations of a given class." See also *Survey of China Mainland Magazines* (4):63, 1974.

761. _____. "Keep to the Correct Orientation and Uphold the Philosophy of Struggle" *Chinese Literature* 8:68-75, 1974. Essay on current applications of Chairman Mao's *Talks at the Yenan Forum*. From *Peking Review* 22, May 31, 1974. Reprinted in *Literature and Ideology* (Toronto) 17:9-16, 1974.

762. Chu Liu-yi. "Folk Opera Flowers Among National Minorities" *China Reconstructs* 11(9):37-39, Sept 1962. il. Folk operas from Tai, Chuang, Pai, Yi minorities encouraged by government and presented at Kunming festival.

763. Chu, Peter and Lois N. Foster. *Chinese Theatres in America*. San Francisco: Federal Theatre Project, 1936. 303p. typescript. Copy in University of Washington Drama Library. Many on theatre activity during the late 19th century in gold-rush country.

764. Chu Yuan. "Theatre of Peking" *Pacific* 4:8-11, April-June, 1955. NE.

765. Chua Jao. "O Pisnich Nové Ciny" [On Song on New China] *Hudebni Rozhledy* 5(18):25-26, 1952. NE.

766. Chuang Pen-li. "Ch'ih: The Ancient Chinese Flute" *Bulletin of the Institute of Ethnology, Academia Sinica* 19:191-203, Spring 1965. English summary of article in Chinese. Thorough survey of literature on *ch'ih*, methods of reconstruction, tuning and scales.

767. _____. "Chinese Traditional Music for Birthday Celebration" in Fritz A. Kuttner and Fredric Lieberman, eds. *Perspectives on Asian Music: Essays in Honor of Dr. Laurence E.R. Picken* (New York: Society for Asian Music, 1975) p.7-12. mus. Survey of the musical styles and compositions commonly performed for birthday well-wishing; an auspicious, appropriate Festschrift contribution.

768. _____. "Chime Stones of Ancient China (Part I)" *Bulletin of the Institute of Ethnology, Academia Sinica* 22:97-137, Autumn 1966. il. English summary p.129-137. On the various types of chime-stone, materials, methods of reconstruction.

769. _____. "A Historical and Comparative Study of *Hsün*, the Chinese Ocarina" *Bulletin of the Institute of Ethnology, Academia Sinica* 33:177-253, Spring 1972. 16 plates, il., mus. The text in Chinese is followed by an extensive English abridgement (p.233-253), and illustrations in the main text have English captions. A careful historical study, with information on playing techniques, music, and modern improvements; and a comparative study of globular flutes worldwide.

770. _____. *Panpipes of Ancient China.* Taipei: Academia Sinica Institute of Ethnology, 1963. vii+118p. 48 figs., mus., tables. (Monograph No. 4). English abridgement p.95-117. A thorough and detailed study, discussing history, reconstruction, performance, and comparisons with panpipes of other Pacific-area cultures. Reviewed by Fredric Lieberman in *Ethnomusicology* 9(3):333, Sept 1965.

771. _____. "A Study of Some Ancient Chinese Musical Instruments" in José Maceda, ed. *The Musics of Asia* (Manila: National Music Council, 1971) p.185-190. Concise summary of research conclusions on reconstructing ancient *p'ai-hsiao*, *hsün*, *ch'ih*, and *pien-ch'ing*.

772. _____. *A Study of the Chime Stones Preserved in the National Museum of History.* Taiwan: 1969. (Collected Papers on History and Art of China, Second Collection, No. 2) 20, 61p. 4 plates. Chinese text with many figures, diagrams, and tables, with substantial (20p.) abridgement in English. Acoustical and structural studies of surviving instruments are related to descriptions and prescriptions in classic books.

773. Chulaki, Mikhail. *V Novom Kitae* [In New China]. Moscow: Gos. Muz. Izd-vo., 1954. 44p. NE. Same title in *Sovetskaya Muzyka* 6:95f., June 1953. NE.

774. Chun Ching. "A Soul-Stirring Class Struggle" *Chinese Literature* 3:4-8, 1967. The improbable political history of the composition and performance of the "revolutionary symphonic music," *Shachiapang.*

775. Chung Chen-tung. "Promote the Singing of Revolution-
     ary Folk Songs to Serve the Three Great Revolu-
     tionary Movements" *Selections from China Mainland
     Magazines* 531:20-35, July 5, 1966. From *Min-chien
     Wen-hsüeh* April 4, 1966. NE.

776. Chung Cheng. "'The East Is Red': A Magnificent Pag-
     eant" *Chinese Literature* 12:86-95, 1964. il. NE.

777. Chung Ching-wen.   "The People Sing of Chairman Mao"
     People's China (1):24-26, Jan 1, 1954. il. On new
     folk songs, with texts.

778. Chung Ho Music Society.   "Chinese Music in Peking"
     China Journal of Science and Arts 21(2):59-60, Aug
     1934.

779. Chung Wen.   "On Lu Hsun's Essay 'Forgetting Meat and
     Forgetting Water'" *Chinese Literature* 9:16-19,
     1974. Commentary on 1934 essay, from the viewpoint
     of the current anti-Confucian campaign. See main
     entry under Lu Hsun.

780. Cibot, Pierre Martial. "Essai sur les pierres sonores
     de Chine" in *Mémoires Concernant l'Histoire, les
     Sciences, les Arts, les Moeurs, les Usages, etc.,
     des Chinois* (Paris: Nyon l'aîné, 1776-1814) VI,
     255-274. il. An interesting technical addition to
     the Amiot study.

781. Clack, Robert Wood. *Celestial Symphonies: A Study of
     Chinese Music*. New York: Gordon Press, 1976. [iv]
     +92p. Impressionistic jottings; not reliable.

782. Clark, Franklin S. "Seats Down Front!" *Sunset* 54:33,
     54, April 1925. il. Subheading: "Since Women Have
     Appeared on the Chinese Stage, Chinatown's Thea-
     ters Are Booming." Scene is San Francisco. [RR]

783. Clark, Helen F. "The Chinese of New York Contrasted
     with Their Foreign Neighbors" *Century* 53:104-113,
     1897. il. Brief notes on the Chinese theatre in
     New York. [RR]

784. Clarke, Samuel R. *Among the Tribes in Southwest China*.
     London: Morgan and Scott, 1911. xiv+315p.   il.,
     maps. See p.63-66 and *passim*. NE.

785. Clément, Adèle. "Quelques notes sur l'état actuel de
     la musique en Chine" *Courrier Musical* April 1,
     1932. p.193. NE.

786. Clementi, Cecil. *Cantonese Love-Songs*. Oxford: Clarendon Press, 1904. 2 vols., il., mus. "Chinese
text and English translations of songs by Chao
Tzi-yung, description and illustration of accompanying p'i-p'a notation." (Waterman).

787. Closson, Ernest. "La Musique Chinoise" *Flambeau*. NE.

788. Cochell, E.W. "Chinese Bronze Drums" *Connoisseur* 15:
39, 1914. NE.

789. Cohn, James. *The Construction of Chinese Music: A
Survey of Origin and Theory* ... *A Report for Musicology Seminar* ... New York: 1950. 18p. In New
York Public Library, Music Collection, *MFBR (China). NE.

790. Cohn-Antenorid, W. "Chinesische Musik-Aesthetic"
Monatsheft für Musikgeschichte 35:1-8, 30-32, 1903.
Unreliable.

791. Collaer, Paul. "China" in *Elsevier's Encyclopedie
van de Muziek* I:411.

792. _____. "Chinoise (Musique Populaire)" in *Encyclopédie
de la Musique*, edited by Michel (Paris: Fasquelle,
1958) I,530-532. il., bibliog. Short coverage of
theory and instruments.

793. Comby, Paul. "Le Théâtre chinois" *Le Vie Illustrée*
March 8, 1907. il. NE.

* Condit, Jonathan. See Rembrandt Wolpert, et al.

794. Confucius. *The Analects of Confucius*. Translated by
Arthur Waley. London: George Allen & Unwin, 1938.
Standard translation of the work central to Chinese thought. There are 22 references to musical
subjects: 3:3, 23; 7:9, 13, 31; 8:8, 15; 9:14;
11:1, 25; 13:3; 14:13, 42; 15:10, 41; 16:5; 17:4,
11, 20, 21; 18:4, 9.

795. Connely, M. "Taipei Theater" *Holiday* 46:16f., Nov
1969. NE.

796. Connor, J. Torrey. "Only John" *Land of Sunshine* 4:
111-116, Feb 1896. Tongue-in-cheek description of
Chinese opera performance in San Francisco. [RR]

797. Constant, Samuel V. *Calls, Sounds and Merchandise of the Peking Street Peddlers*. Thesis, California College in China, 1936. Peiping: Camel Bell, 1936. xiv+185p. il., mus. A beautiful book, with descriptions of many peddlers, their wares, their ways, their sounding adjuncts. Descriptions of music and instruments lack precision.

798. Coomaraswamy, Ananda and Stella Bloch. "The Chinese Theatre in Boston" *Theatre Arts Monthly* 9(2):113-122, Feb 1925.

799. Corbett-Smith, Arthur. "The Chinese and Their Music" *Musical Times* 53:573-575, 1912. mus.

800. _____. "The Chinese Drama, Yesterday and Today" *Fortnightly Review* 99:1200-1212, 1913. NE.

801. Cordier, Georges. "Folklore du Yunnan: Jeux d'enfants et chansons diverses" *Bulletin de l'Ecole Française de l'Extrême-Orient* 28:349-440, 1928. Includes children's games and songs, village songs, military songs. Many texts translated, but no music given.

802. Cordier, Henri. "Chine: Musique" in *La Grande Encyclopédie* (Paris: Lamirault, [n.d.]), II,118-119.

803. Cornaby, W. Arthur. "Notes on the Chinese Drama and Ancient Choral Dances" *New China Review* 1(1):57-70, March 1919. A careful compilation of references to dance and drama in Chinese classic books and historical sources.

804. _____. "Old-World Stories of Hanyang" *New China Review* 2(6):517-537, Dec 1920. Includes retelling of the story of *ch'in* player Yu Po-ya and his friend Tzu-chi.

805. Cost, Herbert W. "Music in China Has Delicate Polyphonic Nuances" *Musical America* 43(13):16, Jan 16, 1926. Enthusiastic report of trip to China by Dr. Arthur E. Bostwick, librarian of the St. Louis Public Library.

806. Costantini, Celso. "Musica Indigena e Litturgia Cattolica" *Il Pensiero Missionario* 12:120-131, 1940. NE.

807. Couling, Samuel. "Drama" in *Encyclopaedia Sinica* (Shanghai: Kelly and Walsh, 1917), p.148-149.

808. _____. "Music" in *Encyclopaedia Sinica* (Shanghai: Kelly and Walsh, 1917), p.385-387. Brief survey of theory.

809. _____. "Musical Instruments" in *Encyclopaedia Sinica* (Shanghai: Kelly and Walsh, 1917), p.387-390. Concise descriptive survey, following traditional eight categories of instruments, mainly abstracted from Moule.

810. Coupland, Laura Helen. "The General Wanted a Wedding March" *Étude* 62(7):395, 422, July 1944. il. The author is asked to play piano for the wedding of a Chinese warlord. Her firsthand experiences are amusingly recounted.

811. _____. "Music in the Chinese Theater" *Étude* 62(8): 441, 486, Aug 1944. il. Continuation of preceding article, describes theatrical entertainment after wedding ceremony. A short but interesting item.

812. _____. "Music in the Streets of Cathay" *Étude* 61(10): 635, 690-691, Oct 1943. Firsthand account of musical activity in Canton: beggars, peddlers, processions.

813. Courant, Maurice Auguste Louis Marie (1865-1935). "Essai historique sur la musique classique des Chinois" in *Encyclopédie de la Musique et Dictionnaire du Conservatoire*, edited by Lavignac (Paris: Delagrave, 1913-1931) Part One, I,77-241. il., mus., bibliog. Also issued as: Thèse pour le doctorat présentée à la Faculté des lettres de Lyon. Excellent survey solidly based on Chinese sources. Particularly strong in material drawn from the dynastic histories. Still a major source.

814. _____. "Le Théâtre en Chine" *Revue de Paris* 7(3): 328-350, May 15, 1900.

815. Courcy, Maria René R. *Marquis de l'Empire du Milieu*. Paris: Didier, 1867. xi+692p. mus. NE.

816. Couvreur, Séraphin. *Li Ki: ou Mémoires sur les Bienséances et Cérémonies*. Ho Kien Fu: Imprimerie de la Mission Catholique, 1913. 2 vols. See II:45-114 for "Yüeh Chi" chapter in characters, Romanization, translations into French and Latin.

817. Cowell, Henry. "Music of the Hemispheres" *Modern Music* 6(3):12-18, March-April 1929. Amusing, naive dialogue contrasting Chinese and Western musical systems.

818. _____. "Music: Oriental" in *Encyclopedia of Social Sciences* (New York: Macmillan, 1933), XI,152-155.

819. Craig, Dale A. *The Hong Kong Archives of Chinese Music: First Annual Report*. Hong Kong: Chung Chi College, Chinese University of Hong Kong, 1973. 4p., mimeo.

820. _____. "Lo Ka Ping—Cantonese Musician" *Arts of Asia* (Hong Kong) 1(6):23-29, Nov-Dec 1971. il., mus. Visit with a *ch'in* player and collector; photos of five antique instruments.

821. _____. "Macro-Rhythm and Melodic Figuration in P'i-p'a Variations" *Chung Chi Journal* 9(1):37-47, Nov 1969. mus. Transcription and analysis of "Hwan le ge" and four variations, learned from a San Francisco musician; includes discussion of *p'i-p'a* ensemble technique.

822. _____. "Towards an International Music" *Chung Chi Bulletin* 47:29-32, Dec 1969. On cross-cultural currents in modern composition; advocates strong hybrids.

823. _____. "Whither Chinese Traditional Music?" *The World of Music* 15(4):21-40, 1973. il. After a brief survey of resources in traditional music, Craig suggests that to keep it from dying out, performance, composition, analysis, and education must be sponsored and encouraged—in that order. Parallel texts in French, German, and English.

824. Craig, Dale A. and Cheung Sai-Bung. "The Orchestra in China" in *Hong Kong Arts Festival 1974* (HK:HK Arts Festival Society, 1974) p.74-75. il. Brief popular note.

825. _____. "Transcendental World Music" *Asian Music* 2(1): 2-7, 1971. Advocates sensitive hybridization in contemporary composition; there is some discussion of Chinese music as a source for new compositions.

826. Creel, Herrlee Glessner. *The Birth of China*. London: Cape, 1936. New York: Reynal and Hitchcock, 1937. 402p. il. See p.97, 101, 330-331 on musical instruments excavated at early Shang sites.

827. Crist, Bainbridge. "Oriental Music" *Musical America* 33:9, April 2, 1921. NE.

828. Crompton, F.L. "Music in Shanghai" *Musical Times* 45 (740):642-643, Oct 1, 1904. il. Western musical activities in the foreign enclave.

829. Crossley-Holland, Peter. "Chinese Music" in *Grove's Dictionary of Music*, 5th ed., edited by Eric Blom (New York: St. Martin's Press, 1954). II,219-248. mus., bibliog. Detailed survey from the philosophical/theoretical viewpoint, largely from secondary sources. Scale theories and instruments get more space than "practice."

830. _____. "Non-Western Music: China" in *Pelican History of Music I*, edited by Denis Stevens and Alec Robertson (Baltimore: Penguin Books, 1960), p.42-59. Shorter and less technical than the Grove's article. Excellent introduction for laymen.

831. Crump, James I. "The Conventions and Craft of Yüan Drama" *Journal of the American Oriental Society* 91(1):14-29, Jan-March 1971. Technical study of prosody, structure, and style with considerable attention to the requirements and influence of music.

832. _____. "The Elements of Yüan Opera" *Journal of Asian Studies* 17(3):417-434, May 1958. A scholarly article with rich information on sources, types, and structure of Yüan opera, for which no music is extant, though information as to the structural use of modes and mode relationship from act to act is known.

833. _____. "Giants in the Earth: Yüan Drama as Seen by Ming Critics" in J.I. Crump and William P. Malm, eds. *Chinese and Japanese Music Dramas* (Ann Arbor: 1975) p.1-63. Study, with extensive translations, of the main schools of Ming thought on Yüan *tsa-chü*. The discussion centers on problems of mode and text-setting.

834. _____. "Liu Chih-yüan in the Chinese 'Epic,' Ballad, and Drama" *Literature East and West* 14(2):154-172, 1970. NE.

835. _____. "Wang P'o Yüan-pen" *Dodder* 2:31-34, Jan 1970. Translation of an early dramatic genre, from a text imbedded in the *Chin-Ping-Mei*.

836. _____. "Yüan-pen, Yüan Drama's Rowdy Ancestor" *Literature East and West* 14(4):473-490, 1970. NE.

*   See also Dolezelova-Velingerova, Milena.

837. Crump, James I. and William P. Malm, eds. *Chinese and Japanese Music-Dramas*. Ann Arbor: Center for Chinese Studies, University of Michigan, 1975. viii+255p., glossary. Report of a 1971 conference. Includes papers on Chinese and Japanese music-dramas by J.I. Crump, Rulan Chao Pian, William P. Malm, Carl Sesar, and Roy E. Teele. Each paper is followed by transcription of the roundtable discussion. A stimulating, helpful contribution. The Malm, Sesar, and Teele papers deal with Nō drama, but refer to China occasionally; the discussions include frequent comparative comments. See individual entries for Crump and Pian papers.

838. Cuisinier, Jeanne. "L'Influence de l'Inde sur les danses en Extrême-Orient" *Revue des Arts Asiatiques* 7:8-14, 1931-1932. Concerns the Indianized states of Southeast Asia.

839. Cummings, Margaret (Kamm). "Chinese Theater in Hawaii" *Paradise of the Pacific* 61:80-82, 1949. NE. [Annotation from N.F. Young, *The Chinese in Hawaii*—compares Hawaiian-style Chinese plays with ancient China drama. Lists plays produced by Chinese in Hawaii.]

840. Cursham, A. St. W. "The Lute of Jade" *China Journal* 34:8-13, Jan 1941. il. NE.

841. Czeké, A. von. "Einiges über die Musik der Chinesen" *Neue Berliner Musikzeitung* 22:139-140, 1868. NE.

842. Czi, Liu. "Despre Muzica Populară Chineză" [On Chinese Folk Music] *Muzica* 4(10, Supplement):2-5, 1954. NE.

843. _____. "Rozwój Ludowej Kultury Muzyczney w Chinach" [The Development of Folk Music Culture in China] *Muzyka* 5(7):63-68, 1954. NE.

844. _____. "Muzykaln'aja Kul'tura Novogo Kitaja" [The Music Culture of New China] *Sovetskaya Muzyka* 4: 126-130, 1954. NE.

845. _____. "O Kitajsko Narodnoj Muzyke" [Chinese Folk Music] *Sovetskaya Muzyka* 11:62-65, 1953. NE.

846. Čzoy, Jan [Chou Yang?]. "Puti Razvitija Kitajskoj Opery" [The Development of Chinese Opera] *Sovetskaya Muzyka* 7:67-72, 1953. NE.

* * * * * * * * * *

847. Dabrowski, Miroslaw. "'Mazowsze' w Chinskiej Repub- lice Ludowej" ['Mazowse' in the Chinese People's Republic] *Muzyka* 5:3-13, 1954. NE.

848. Dai Shen-yu. "The Confucian Philosophy of Music: A Theory in Jurisprudence" *Chinese Culture* 4:9-24, 1962. NE.

849. Dall, Caroline H. *My First Holiday; or, Letters Home from Colorado, Utah, and California.* Boston: Rob- erts Bros., 1881. Tourist describes Chinese thea- tre in San Francisco (p.373-379). More sensitive to visual details than most. [RR]

850. Danckert, Werner. "Hirtenmusik" *Archiv für Musikwis- senschaft* 13(2):97-115, 1956. Analytic study of pastoral music-making, including the herding peo- ples of China's borderlands.

851. _____. "Musikgötter und Musikmythen Altchinas" *Zeit- schrift für Ethnologie* 88(1):1-48, 1963. NE.

852. _____. "Ostasiatische Musikästhetik" *Ostasiatische Zeitschrift*, ns 7:63-69, 1931. A short but orig- inal and stimulating paper dealing in general con- cepts which are more often than not fruitful. Avoids typical Confucian party line.

853. _____. "Der Tiger als Symboltier der Musik in Alt- china" *Zeitschrift für Ethnologie* 83(1):86-109, 1958. il. Examines symbolic nature of the tiger in Chinese music and culture. Important material for understanding and future study of Chinese aes- thetics.

854. _____. *Tonreich und Symbolzahl in Hochkulturen und in der Primitivenwelt.* Bonn: H. Bouvier & Co., 1966. xvi+360p. il., mus. "Chinesische Funftonmu- sik" p.151-161, and *passim.* A most important study in number symbolism and music aesthetics, a topic central to the traditional Chinese ideas on music and music theory.

855. Daniélou, Alain. "Cina" in *Enciclopedia della Musica* (Milan: Ricordi, 1963), I:484-485. il.

856. _____. "The Cycle of Fifths: The Musical Theory of the Chinese" in his *Introduction to the Study of Musical Scales* (London: India Society, 1943), Pt. III.

857. _____. "III. Le cycle de quintes. La théorie musicale des Chinois" in his *Traité de Musicologie
Comparée* (Paris: Hermann, 1959), p.67-90. Almost
exclusively devoted to a minute mathematical exposition of intervals, scales, and tuning systems.

858. Darrière, Jacques. "Le Théâtre en mission. Que faut-
il attendre du théâtre" *Collectanea Comm. Synodalis* 9:1072-1076, 1936. NE.

859. David-Neel, Alexandra. "Theater in China Now" *Asia*
44(12):559-560, Dec 1944.

860. Dawa. "Liberated Serfs Sing" *China Reconstructs* 14
(4):19-23, April 1965. il. About Tibetan contributions to the National Minorities Amateur Song
and Dance Festival in Peking, by the group's
leader. Good color photos.

861. Dawes, F. *Six Essays on the Ancients, Their Music
and Instruments. I. Chinese, Japanese, Hindoos.*
Oxford: Hart, 1893. 20p. Many distortions, errors
of fact. Prejudiced approach to the value of the
musics.

862. Dawes, Rose A. "Street Songs of China Throw a New
Light on the Nation's Music" *Musician* 35(10):11-
12, Oct 1930. il., mus. Transcriptions of five
work and merchant songs heard by the author.

863. Dean, Sam. "Singing Craftsmen of Peking" *Asia* 21:
669-675, 722-724, Aug 1921. il. Firsthand description of peddlars, laborers, craftsmen, and their
songs and instruments. Some song texts; mostly
contextual information.

864. Dechevrens, Antoine. "Étude sur le système musical
chinois" *Sammelbände der Internationalen Musikgesellschaft* 2:485-551, 1901. mus., tables. Carries
on in the tradition of Amiot, adding some examples of "popular music" to a lengthy discussion
of traditional scale and mode theory.

865. Delitsiev, S. "Dva Goda v Novom Shankhae" [Two years
in New Shanghai] *Sovetskaya Muzyka* 23:173-175,
Jan 1959. il. NE.

866. Delza, Sophia. "The Art of the Science of T'ai Chi
Ch'uan" *Journal of Aesthetics and Art Criticism*
25(4):449-461, Summer 1967. Form, function, and
composition of T'ai Chi examined from aesthetic
perspective; suggests it is an art of being, per-
ceived by the doer, while observer perceives only
the presence of art, not the artness of it.

867. _____. *Body and Mind in Harmony: T'ai Chi Ch'uan (Wu Style), An Ancient Chinese Way of Exercise.* New York: Donald McKay, 1961. 184p. il. A practical introduction to this dance-related gymnastic.

868. _____. "Chinese Theatre-Dance; The Actor's Art in the Classical Chinese Theatre" *ICHPER Asian Journal* 1 (2):29-32, Dec 1969.

869. _____. "The Classic Chinese Theater" *Journal of Aesthetics and Art Criticism* 15(2):181-197, Dec 1956. il. A good introduction to the total experience of Chinese opera.

870. _____. "The Classic Chinese Theatre" in E.T. Kirby, ed. *Total Theatre: A Critical Anthology* (New York: Dutton, 1969) p.224-242.

871. _____. "The Dance-Arts in the People's Republic of China: The Contemporary Scene" *Asian Music* 5(1): 28-39, 1973. A personal report of the dance scene based on observation during a trip to the People's Republic.

872. _____. "The Dance in the Chinese Theatre" *Journal of Aesthetics and Art Criticism* 16(4):437-452, 1958. il. NE.

873. _____. "The Exercise Art of T'ai Chi Ch'uan as it Functions for the Creative Art of the Actor" *Drama and Theatre* 8(1):1-13, May 1970.

874. _____. "Perspectives on the Aesthetics of Change: From the Classical Chinese Theatre to the Revolutionary Peking Opera" *CHINOPERL Papers* 7:22-48, 1977. il.

875. _____. "A Picture of the Art of Face Painting and Make-Up in the Classical Chinese Theater" *Journal of Aesthetics and Art Criticism* 30(1):3-17, Fall 1971. il. Description of face types and makeup techniques in various roles, based on personal experience.

876. _____. "T'ai Chi Ch'uan" *Dynamics* (New York) 1(8-9): 2-7, Jan-Feb 1972.

877. _____. "T'ai Chi Ch'uan: The Integrated Exercise" *The Drama Review* 16(1):28-33, March 1972.

878. Dennys, Nicholas Belfield.   "Short Notes on Chinese
     Instruments of Music" *Journal of the Royal Asiatic
     Society, North China Branch* n.s., 8:93-132, 1873.
     il.   An early attempt at a systematic catalog of
     Chinese instruments, with line drawings.   Super-
     seded by Moule.

879. Densmore, G.B.   *The Chinese in California*. San Fran-
     cisco, 1880.   il.   Information on San Francisco's
     Chinese theaters and description of a performance,
     p.54-58.   [RR]

880. Devéria, C.   "Response to 'Chinese Music' by W.G."
     Revue de l'Extrême-Orient 1(3):498.   NE.

881. Devéria, Gabriel.   "Essai nouveau sur la musique chez
     les Chinois" *Magasin Pittoresque* 53:234-238, 287-
     288, 327-328, 390-392, 1885.   il., mus.   NE.

882. _____.   *Un Mariage Impérial Chinois: Cérémonial*.
     Paris: Leroux, 1887.   186p.   il.   NE.

883. _____.   "Pékin et le Nord de la Chine" *Tour du Monde*
     31:305-368; 32:193-256, 1876.   il., mus.   See 32:
     200, 235, and *passim*.   NE.

884. Diény, Jean-Pierre.   "Chansons des Han" *France-Asie*
     n.s.   18(173):267-276, May-June 1962.   Exposition,
     text in characters, and French translations of 20
     little-known poems of the *yüeh-fu* genre.   Exposi-
     tions contextual rather than technical.

885. Dietz, Betty Warner and Thomas Choon Bai Park. *Folk
     Songs of China, Japan, Korea*. New York: John Day,
     1964. 48p. 7-inch record. Nine Chinese songs, with
     Chinese text, transliteration and English text,
     and tasteful, simple piano accompaniment. The en-
     closed record illustrates only Japanese and Kore-
     an songs.

886. Dioszegi, V.   "Schamanenlieder der Mandschu" *Acta
     Orientalia Academiae Scientiarum Hungaricae*   11:
     89-104, 1960.   NE.

887. Dobie, Charles Caldwell. *San Francisco's Chinatown*.
     New York: Appleton-Century, 1936. Sensitive notes
     on Chinese theatre, p.276-284.   Includes story of
     Paderewski's encounter with Chinese opera.   [RR]

888. Dobson, W.A.C.H.   "Linguistic Evidence and the Dat-
     ing of the Book of Songs" *T'oung Pao* 51(4-5):322-
     334.   Suggests a time-scale ordering: *Sung-Ta Ya-
     Hsiao Ya-Kuo Feng* from 11th to 7th centuries B.C.

889. Dolby, A.W.E. "Kuan Han-ch'ing" *Asia Major* 16(1-2): 1-60, 1971. A detailed biographical study of the leading author of Yüan opera. Rich in background information. Extensive bibliography.

890. Dolezelova-Velingerova, Milena and James I. Crump, Jr. *Ballad of the Hidden Dragon: Liu Chih-yüan Chu-kung-tiao*. Oxford: Clarendon Press, 1971. 10, 128p. Translation with extensive introductory materials on this early dramatic ballad genre.

891. Dols, J. "Het Chineesche Tooneel" *China* 3:13-14, 1927-1928. NE.

892. _____. "La Vie chinoise dans la province de Kan-sou (Chine)" *Anthropos* 10-11:68-74, 466-503, 726-757, 1915-1916. 12-13:236-262, 958-1013, 1917-1918. il. See 10-11:489-503 and *passim*. NE.

893. Doret, Christiane. "Le Rôle de la musique dans la pensée Chinoise traditionnelle" *Musée de Genève* 93:11-14, March 1969; 94:15, April 1969. il. NE.

894. Douglas, Robert K. *China*. London: Society for Promoting Christian Knowledge, 1882. 400p. il. See p.160-172, "Music." NE.

895. _____. "The Chinese Drama" *Contemporary Review* 37: 231-235, Jan 1880. NE.

896. Downer, G.B. and A.C. Graham. "Tone Patterns in Chinese Poetry" *Bull, School of Oriental and African Studies* 26(1):--, 1963. NE.

897. Drake, F.S. "The Nestorian 'Gloria in Excelsis Deo'" *Chinese Recorder* p.291-300, May 1935. NE.

898. Druskin, M. "V Kitae" [In China] *Sovetskaya Muzyka* 10:125-129; 11:135-140, Oct-Nov 1957. NE.

899. Du Bois-Reymond, Marie. *Tagebücher über Chinesische Musik. I, 1908-1909. II, 1909-1911*. Unpublished ms. 47, 21p. Original handwritten manuscript deposited in Curt Sachs Collection, Rutgers University Library. Xerox in Institute of Ethnomusicology Archives, U.C.L.A. Musical experiences in China, much quoted by Sachs; valuable as a mirror of musical life in China as recorded by a sympathetic observer.

900. Dubs, Homer H. *Hsüntze, the Moulder of Ancient Confucianism*. London: Probsthain, 1927. 308p. See p.161-168, "Discipline Through Music."

901. _____. "La Musica Nell'Antica Cina" *Quaderni de Ci-vilta Cinese* 6:415-418, Dec 1956. NE.

902. _____, trans. *The Works of Hsüntze*. London: Probs-thain, 1928. 336p. See p.247-258, "Discipline Through Music." Good translation of the essays of this early, influential Confucian philosopher whose views on music helped to shape the "party line" of Classical China.

903. Dufflocq, Enrico Magni. *Storia Della Musica.* Milan: Società Editrice Libraria, 1933. See I,31-38, "Cina." il., mus.

904. Du Halde, Jean Baptiste. *Description de l'Empire de la Chine*. Paris: Lemercier, 1735. 4 vols. il., mus. See III,265-267 and *passim*. The source for much early knowledge and speculation on things Chinese until the more complete Jesuit writings at the end of the 18th century. English transla-tion by R. Brookes (London: 1738, 1741). Excerpts on music quoted in Frank Harrison, *Time, Place and Music* (q.v.).

*   Dunn, Sue E. See Sue E. Barber.

905. Durdin, Peggy. "The Bitter Tea of Mao's Red Guards" *New York Times* 6:28, Jan 19, 1969. NE.

906. Durdin, Tillman. "China's Most Popular Ballet Has a Communist Message and a Plot Reminiscent of *Uncle Tom's Cabin*" *New York Times* 12:1, April 25, 1971. NE.

907. Dvorská, Xenia. "The Peking Opera" *New Orient* 1(5): 11-13, 1960. NE.

908. _____. "Pohled na vývoj hudby v čině" [A Look at Mu-sical Development in China] *Hudebni Rozhledy* 13: 60-63, 1960. NE.

909. Dwight, Alan. "The Chinese Organ" *Eastern Horizon* 5 (10):36-42, Oct 1966. Dwight studied the *sheng* in Hong Kong; here reports on the instrument and on his experiences.

910. _____. "The Sheng (Bamboo Mouth Organ)" *Canon* 16(1): 10-12, Aug 1962. il. Short introduction based on Amiot and Eastlake. Points out relative scarcity of *sheng* in South China.

911. Dyson, Verne. *The Land of Yellow Spring*. New York: Chinese Studies Press, 1937. 143p. il. See p.113-116. NE.   * * * * * * *

912. Eastlake, F. Warrington. "The Chinese Reed Organ (Sheng)" *China Review* 11:33-41, 1882-1883. il., mus. The only extensive article on this instrument, much relied on by later writers, but in need of revision.

913. Eberhard, Wolfram. *Cantonese Ballads (Munich State Library Collection)*. Taipei: Orient Cultural Service, 1972. (Asian Folklore and Social Life Monographs, Vol. 30) ii+361p. NE.

914. _____. *Chinas Geschichte*. Bern: 1948. See p.123, 194, 196, 294. NE.

915. _____. "Die soziale Welt der südchinesischen Volksballaden" in *Volksüberlieferung: Festschrift für Kurt Ranke zur Vollendung des 60 Lebensjahres*, edited by Fritz Harkort, Karel C. Peeters, and Robert Wildhaber (Göttingen: Otto Schwartz, 1968), p.429-444. NE.

916. _____. "Hieratssitten und Feste der Miaotse von Kueichou. Aus dem Chinesische des Yü Chu-lan übersetzt und eingeleitet" *Weltkreis* 2:114-121, 1931. NE.

917. _____. *The Local Cultures of South and East China*. Leiden: E.J. Brill, 1968. [vi]+520p. Bibliog. Index. Translated from German by Alide Eberhard. "A greatly revised version of the second volume of my *'Lokalkulturen im alten China'*" (p. v.). Includes detailed studies of the Yao, Thai, Yüeh, Liao, and Tungus cultures, with much information on music, instruments, and dance. Of particular interest is the section on Yüeh bronze drums (p. 363-374), which surveys many related drum types, technology, and cultural significance.

918. _____. *Lokalkulturen im alten China*. Leiden: Brill, 1942. Supplement to *T'oung Pao* 37. NE.

919. _____. "Orakel and Theater in China" *Asiatische Studien* 18-19:11-18, 1965. On the use of drama texts and well-known characters in oracle verses.

920. _____. *Studies in Chinese Folklore and Related Essays*. Bloomington: Indiana University Research Center for the Language Sciences, 1970. (Indiana University Folklore Institute Monograph Series, Vol. 23) ix+329p., bibliog., il. See "Pounding Songs from Peking," p.147-171. NE.

921. _____. *Taiwanese Ballads: A Catalogue*. Taipei: Orient Cultural Service, 1972. (Asian Folklore and Social Life Monographs, Vol. 22) ix+171p., il. NE.

922. Eckardt, Hans. "Chinesische Musik, vom Ende der Han-Zeit zum der Sui-Zeit. Der Einbruch Westlicher Musik" in *Musik in Geschichte und Gegenwart* II, 1195-1216. il., bibliog. Concise general coverage, large bibliography.

923. Eddy, Frederic W. "Chinese Music" *Music Life* p.117-119, 1903. NE.

924. Edelman, Lily. *Music in China and Japan: Classroom Materials*. New York: Service Bureau for Intercultural Education, [1940?]. Publication 0-23. NE.

925. Eder, Matthias. "Das Jahr im Chinesisches Volkslied" *Folklore Studies* 4:1-160, 338, 1945. Translations of several hundred folk songs from various districts, with characters and lengthy textual annotations. Arranged in yearly sequence of folk holidays and festivals. No discussion of music *per se* or music notations. Texts drawn from published Chinese and Japanese collections.

926. Edkins, Joseph L. "Hymn in Honor of Ancestors" *Chinese Recorder* 15:61-64, 1884. mus. NE.

927. _____. *The Miau Tsi Tribes*. Foochow: Rozario, 1887. 7p. NE.

928. Edney, Eric. "Recommended—Five Records." *China Reconstructs* 6(10):31, Oct 1957. Descriptive review of new releases of folk and traditional music.

929. Edwards, E.D. *Chinese Prose Literature of the T'ang Period A.D. 618-906*. London: Probsthain, 1937. 2 vols. xii+236, viii+433p. Volume I includes an essay on T'ang music (p.30-40) and detailed bibliographical information on, and contents of, 7 T'ang essays on musical subjects included in the *T'ang Tai Ts'ung Shu*.

930. _____. "The Establishment of Schools of Secular Music by Ming Huang of the T'ang Dynasty" in *Actes du XVIIIe Congrès International des Orientalistes, 1931*. (Leiden: Brill, 1932) p.121-122. Very short abstract.

931 _____. "Principles of Whistling—Hsiao Chih—Anonymous" *Bull, School of Oriental and African Studies* 20:217-229, 1957. A treatise from the T'ang dynasty, translated.

932. Eichler, R. "Some Hakka Songs" *China Review* 12:193-195, 1883-1884. NE.

933. Eigner, Julius. "The Chinese Female Impersonator" *China Journal* 30(1):19-21, Jan 1939. Ten photos. Good pictorial introduction to one of the most important facets of the Chinese theatrical arts.

934. _____. "The Pageant of China's Drama" *China Journal* 26(2):70-73, Feb 1937. il. Short note with eight pages of photos.

935. Eisenstein, Sergei. "The Enchanter from the Pear Garden" *Theatre Arts Monthly* 19(10):761-770, 1935. NE.

936. Eitel, Ernest John. "Ethnographical Sketches of the Hakka Chinese: Popular Songs of the Hakkas" *Notes and Queries on China and Japan* 1:113-114, 129-130, 145-146, 1867. NE.

937. EL. "Dr. Mei Lan-fang (Thoughts on the Chinese and Russian Art)—Two Meetings" *Feniks* (Shanghai) 3: 14-15, Sept 1935. NE.

938. Elia, Pasquale d'. "Musica e Canti Italiani a Pechino (Marzo-Aprile 1601)" *Revista Degli Studi Orientali* 30:131-145, 1955. Eight songs taught by Matteo Ricci to servants at court; texts in Italian and Chinese; no music.

939. _____. "La Passione de Gesù Cristo in un' Opera Cinese del 1608-1610" *Archivum Historicum Societatis Jesu* 22:276-307, 1953. NE.

940. Ellis, Alexander J. "On the Musical Scales of Various Nations" *Journal of the Society of Arts* 33(1688): 485-527, March 27, 1885. Section 14 on "China" gives interval measurements of *ti-tzu, so-na, pien-lo, yün-lo, san-hsien, p'i-p'a* (done with the help of visiting musicians), and *ch'in*, bell chime, from another source.

941. Elson, Louis C. *Curiosities of Music: A Collection of Facts not Generally Known, Regarding the Music of Ancient and Savage Nations.* Boston: Ditson, [1880]. vi+363p. See p.114-200 on Chinese music. NE.

942. Enders, Elizabeth Crump. *Swinging Lanterns.* New York: Appleton, 1923. xiv+358p. il., maps. See p.131-140. NE.

943. Engländer, Richard. "Musikalisch-theatralische Chinoiserie" *Musica* 12:525-528, Sept 1958. il., mus. On Western treatments of Chinese and pseudo-Chinese themes and stories.

944. Enjoy, Paul d'. "Le Théâtre en Pays Chinois" *Bulletins et Mémoires de la Société d'Anthropologie de Paris* 5s 8:353-363, 1907. NE.

945. Erda, B. "Chinese Shadow Theater" *Natural History* 84 (2):46-51, 1975. il. NE.

946. Ernst, Alice Henson. *Trouping in the Oregon Country: A History of Frontier Theatre*. Portland: Oregon Historical Society [1961]. Contains good account of Chinese theatre in Oregon and Washington in 19th and early 20th centuries, p.96-102. [RR]

* * * * * * * * * *

947. Faber, Ernst. "The Chinese Theory of Music" *Notes and Queries on China and Japan* ns, 4:2-4, 1870. NE.

948. _____. "The Chinese Theory of Music" *China Review* 1: 324-328, 384-388, 1872-1873. 2:47-50, 1873-1874. NE.

949. Fabre d'Olivet. "Système Musicale des Chinois" in *La Musique Expliquée comme Science et comme Art* (Paris: 1928), 3rd ed. NE.

950. Fairfax-Cholmeley, E. "Beryl Grey and the Peking Ballet" *Eastern Horizon* 3(6):30-33, June 1964. il.

951. Fan Chih-lung. "Sixty-Five Years on the Stage" *China Reconstructs* 10(11):40-42, Nov 1961. On Kai Chiao-tien, a veteran actor of *wu-sheng* roles.

952. Fang Ming. "Chang Hsiang-yu—Opera Singer and Patriot" *People's China* (23):30-33, Dec 1, 1954. il. Biographical sketch of leading female star.

953. Farmer, Henry George. "Reciprocal Influences in Music 'Twixt the Far and Middle East" *Journal of the Royal Asiatic Society* 2:327-342, 1934. Also in *Studies in Oriental Musical Instruments* (Glasgow: Civic Press, 1939) p.3-17. il. Identification of some migrating instruments.

954. Faurot, Albert Louis. "Culture Currents—East and West" *Clavier* p.9-13, Feb 1969. il. On various borrowings: *shēng*/harmonium, dulcimer, pipe organ, and others. A popularized account.

955. _____. *Music in the Chinese Church*. M.A. thesis
     (theology), Oberlin, 1940. 120p. NE.

956. _____. *Songs from China's Borderland*. Dumagete City,
     Philippines: Silliman Music Foundation, 1961. 42p.
     Chinese characters and English translation.   Ar-
     rangements vary in style, usually simple harmon-
     ies.

957. Fei Chu and Sha Hsi.   "Fukien Puppet Show" *People's
     China* Dec 16, 1957. NE.

958. Feng Mu.   "Let the Image of Revolutionary Workers,
     Peasants, and Soldiers Be the Masters on the Stage
     of Peking Opera" *Selections from China Mainland
     Magazines* 450:20-24, Jan 4, 1965. From *Wen I Pao*
     Sept 30, 1964.

959. Ferguson, John. *Two Bronze Drums*. Peiping: 1932. 7p.,
     8 plates.   On 2 Chou bronzes found in Shensi Pro-
     vince, 1929.

960. Fernald, Helen E.   "Ancient Chinese Musical Instru-
     ments" *Museum Journal, Philadelphia* 17:325-371,
     1926.   il.   Reprinted in *A Harp With a Thousand
     Strings* (London: Pilot Press, 1944), edited by
     Hsiao Ch'ien, p.395-440. Lengthy study of musical
     instruments represented on Wei votive stelae and
     T'ang mortuary figurines in the museum collection.
     Numerous line drawings helpful.

961. _____. "A Selection of Chinese Music and Songs" in *A
     Harp With a Thousand Strings* (London: Pilot Press,
     1944), edited by Hsiao Ch'ien, p.515f.

962. Fidler, Sharon. "Song-Interruption and Dramatic Unity
     in Yüan Drama" *Dodder* 2:24-27, Jan 1970.   On the
     device of inserted dialogue in arias.

963. Fink, Gottfried Wilhelm. "Chinesische Musik" in *All-
     gemeine Encyclopädie der Wissenschaften unf Künste*
     (Leipzig: 1827), edited by Ersch and Gruber, XVI,
     373-383.   il., mus. NE.

964. _____.   "Einiges über die Begründungsbeweise des äl-
     testen Zustandes der Tonkunst, insonderheit über
     den Werth geschichtlicher überreste der fruhesten
     gebildeten Völker, namentlich der Hindostaner und
     Chinesen" *Allgemeine Musikalische Zeitung* 33(48):
     785-793, Nov 30, 1831.

965. Finsterbusch, Kate. "Die Mundorgeln des Museums für Völkerkunde zu Leipzig und die Darstellung des Instrumentes in Ost- und Südostasian" in *Beitrag zur Völkerforschung, Hans Damm zum 65. Geburtstag* (Berlin: Akademie-Verlag, 1961). [Veröffentlichen des Museums für Völkerkunde zu Leipzig, Heft 11]. NE.

966. Fischer, Erich. *Beiträge zur Erforschung der Chinesischen Musik (aus dem Phonogrammarchiv des psychologische Instituts der Universität zu Berlin).* Leipzig: Breitkopf und Härtel, 1910. 56p. il., mus. Ph.D. dissertation, University of Berlin, 1910. Reprinted in *Sämmelbande der Internationalen Musikgesellschaft* 12:153-206, 1910-1911. Detailed modal-structural analyses of several tunes, made from recordings. Large body of transcriptions particularly valuable.

967. _____. "The Phonograph and Chinese Music" *Quarterly Magazine of the International Musical Society* Jan 1911. NE.

968. Fischer, Hans. "Die Musik in China" *Musikalisches Wochenblatt* 40:681-682, 693-694, 1910. NE.

969. Fischer, J.F. "Cinsky Zapisnik" *Hudebni Rozhledy* 15 (16):677-679, 1962. NE.

970. Fisher, Barbara E. Scott. "Folk Songs of the East" *Christian Science Monitor Magazine* 7:--, Sept 9, 1944. il. NE.

971. Fisher, Fred. *Circle Comment.* Denton, Texas: Privately published, [1971-1972]. A series of 54 newsletters "about the history and philosophy of the 12-note idea," informally gathering data and investigating the topic on a worldwide basis. Chinese theory is a main subject. Based mainly on secondary sources; nevertheless brings together much fascinating and disparate material.

972. _____. "The Yellow Bell of China and the Endless Search" *Music Educators Journal* 59(8):30-33, 95-98, April 1973. On the lü and the search for perfection in cyclic and tempered systems; not technical.

973. Fitch, George H. "In a Chinese Theater" *Century Magazine* 24(2):189-192, June 1882. Detailed impressions. Much attention to musicians. San Francisco is locale. [RR]

974. Fitch, G.R. "Hymns and Hymn Books for the Chinese" *Chinese Recorder* p.466-470, Oct 1895. NE.

975. Fitch, R.F.   "An Outburst of Song in China" *Chinese Recorder* p.544-546, Sept 1935. NE.

976. Florenz, Karl. "Formosanische Volkslieder nach Chinesischen Quellen" *Mitteilungen der Deutsche Gesellschaft für Volk- und Naturkunde des Orient* 7: 110-158, 1898. NE.

977. Foo, Timothy Wo-ping. *Survey Appraisal of Secondary School Music in Hong Kong.* D.M.A. dissertation, University of Oregon, 1973. 130p.   Abstract in *Dissertation Abstracts International* 34(9):March 1974. NE.

978. Forkel, Johann Nikolaus, ed. *Musikalische-Kritische Bibliothek.* Gotha: 1778. See "Nachrichten von dem Zustande der Musik bei dem Egypten und Chinesen, aus den philosophischen Untersuchungen des Hrn. von Paw." NE.

979. Foster, A.   "Better Hymns" *Chinese Recorder* p.487, Aug 1912. NE.

980. Foster, J. "A Nestorian Hymn" *Chinese Recorder* p.238-247, April 1930. NE.

981. Fournier, Charles.   "Le Théâtre en Chine" *Revue Mondiale* p.15-18, Aug 1933. NE.

982. Frankel, Ch'ung-ho Chang. "The Practice of *K'un-ch'ü* Singing from the 1920's to the 1960's" *CHINOPERL Papers* 6:82-92. A survey of important people and events by a former *k'un-ch'ü* actress.

983. Frankenstein, Alfred.   "Flying Dragons and Sounds of Silver and Fine Wood" *This World* (Sunday magazine section of *San Francisco Chronicle*),   p. 23, 30, March 7, 1943. il. On an opera club in San Francisco's Chinatown.   Intelligent discussion of instruments, notation, musical style. [RR]

984. Friedenthal, Albert.   "Der Gehörsinn der Chinesen" *Allgemeine Musikzeitung* 34(50):849-851, 1907. NE.

985. Fu Chi-feng. "Chinese Acrobatics" *Chinese Literature* 11:100-106, 1973. il. Survey of this spectacular genre, traditionally associated with music and dance.

986. Fu Lei.   "My Son Fu Tsung" *China Reconstructs* 6(4): 9-10, April 1959. il.   Brief eulogy on first internationally recognized Chinese piano virtuoso.

987. Fu Pei-mei. "Music Chronicle" *T'ien Hsia Monthly* 8 (3):256-259, March 1939.

988. Fujino, Iwamoto. "On Chinese Soul-Inviting and Fire-fly-Catching Songs: A Comparative Study" *Acta Asiatica* (Tokyo) 19:40-57, 1971. NE.

989. Fung, H.K. "'A Chinese Joan of Arc.' The Theft of the Golden Basket" *China Arts and Handicrafts* 1 (4):10, 1932. On a success of Mei Lan-fang.

990. Fung Kwok-Ying. "The Chinese Theatre Yesterday and Today" *Canton Univ Forum* 1:2-5, April 25, 1938. NE.

* * * * * * * * * *

991. G., W. "Chinese Music" *China Review* 2:257-258. NE.

992. Gaida, I.V. *Kitajskij tradicjonnyj tieatr hsi-ch'ü* [Hsi-ch'ü, the Traditional Chinese Theatre]. Moscow: 1971. NE. "A Survey of the theories concerning the origin of the Chinese theatre, followed by a very detailed account of many forms considered to be the earliest instances of performing art." (Zbikowski, 1970:16).

993. Gailhard, André. "Étude Technique de la Musique Chinoise et Transcriptions pour Piano" in *Théâtre et Musique Modernes en Chine*, by George Soulié (Paris: Guethner, 1926), p.98-184. il., mus.

994. Galpin, Francis W. "A Western Organ in Medieval China. II. Some Notes on the Original Form and Source of the Hsin Lung Sheng" *Journal of the Royal Asiatic Society* p.206-211, 1926. mus. It interprets the Chinese texts given by Moule (see 1733). Instrument presented to Kublai Khan perhaps from "Moslem Kingdoms." Technology of Western organ, but use of free reed pipes and decorations on case imply some sinicization.

995. Gamble, Sidney D. *Chinese Village Plays from the Ting Hsien Region (Yang Ke Hsüan): A Collection of Forty-Eight Chinese Rural Plays as Staged by Villagers from Ting Hsien in Northern China.* Amsterdam: Philo Press, 1970. xxix+762p., mus., il. NE.

996. Gardner, Bertha Ashton. "Music Means 'Joy' in Chinese" *Étude*. A short appreciation of Chinese music based on visit of Chinese theater group.

997. Gardner, C.T. "Chinese Verse" *China Review* 1:248-254, 1872-1873. NE.

998. Garfield, Bernard H. "The State of Bassoon Playing in Communist China" *Woodwind World* 12(5):7f., 1973. il. NE.

999. Gargi, B. "Chinese Opera" *Unesco Courier* 8(7):17-20, 1955. NE.

1000. Garnsey, Wanda. "Music and Porcelain" *Eastern Horizon* 5(4):29-34, April 1966. Enthused tourist report of visits to Peking Music Research Institute and Porcelain-Craft Center.

1001. Gaspardone, Émile. "Le Théâtre des Yüan en Annam" *Sinologica* 6(1):1-15, 1959. NE.

1002. Gautier, Judith. *Les Musiques Bizarres à l'Exposition de 1900*. Paris: Ollendorf, 1900. A series of handbooks. "La Musique Chinoise à l'Exposition de 1900" (23p.) includes a short introduction on traditional theory and instruments and impressionistic piano transcriptions of a song and two *ch'in* pieces.

1003. _____. *Les Peuples Étranges*. Paris: Charpentier, 1879. 33p. il. See p.17-42.

1004. Gebeschus, I. "Wie China singt und dichtet" *Musikwoche* 38. NE.

1005. Geoffrey-Dechaume, François. "Music" in his *China Looks at the World* (New York: Pantheon, 1967), p.145-161. Aesthetic musings on the Chinese character *vis-à-vis* the West.

1006. Gerhard, L. "Die Musik der Chinesen" *Deutsche Militär-Musiker-Zeitung* 27:535-536, 1905. NE.

1007. Gibson, H.E. "Music and Musical Instruments of Shang" *Journal of the Royal Asiatic Society, North China Branch* 68:8-18, 1937. il. An important study of musical terms found in oracle-bone inscriptions and other early sources. Variant character readings shown and chronological order suggested.

1008. Gignon, Fernand. "The Party Line and Classic Art of Red China" *Show* 2(3):42-49, March 1962.

1009. Gilbert, Will G. "Chinese Muziek" in *Algemene Muziekencyclopedie* (Antwerp, 1957), p.92f. NE.

1010. Giles, Herbert A. "Dance in Ancient China" *Adversaria Sinica* (Shanghai), 1906. NE.

1011. _____. "Echoes of Orpheus" *Adversaria Sinica* 2:45-47, 1906. NE.

1012. _____. *Glossary of Reference on Subjects Connected with the Far East.* 3rd ed. Shanghai: Kelly and Walsh, 1900. 382p. See p.188-189. NE.

1013. _____. "Mr. Waley and 'The Lute-Girl's Song'" *New China Review* 3(4):281-288, Aug 1921. Rejoinder to Waley's critique of Giles' translation of Po Chu-yi's poem (See Waley #2225 below.).

1014. Gilman, Benjamin Ives. "On Some Psychological Aspects of the Chinese Musical System" *Philosophical Review* 1(1):54-78, Jan 1892; 1(2):154-178, March 1892. Tables, mus. Study of tuning, scale, and mode based upon performance by Chinese from New York's Chinatown, with transcriptions.

1015. Gimm, Martin. "Historische Bemerkungen zur chinesischen Instrumentenbaukunst der T'ang" *Oriens Extremus* 17(1-2):9-38, Dec 1970; 18(1):123-133, July 1971. il. Detailed historical study focusing on the famous Lei family of *ch'in*-makers. An abstract of this article appears in Fritz A. Kuttner and Fredric Lieberman, eds. *Perspectives on Asian Music: Essays in Honor of Dr. Laurence E.R. Picken* (New York: Society for Asian Music, 1975), p.13-14.

1016. _____. "Nan Cho [d. 854]. Notizen zu seinem Leben und Werk" *Oriens Extremus* 14(1):43-58, Aug 1967. Detailed bio-bibliographical study of T'ang scholar best known for his *Chieh-ku-lu*, an important early essay on drumming.

1017. _____. *Das Yüeh-fu Tsa-lu des Tuan An-chieh. Beiträge zur Kulturgeschichte und Terminologie vom Musik, Schauspiel, und Tanz in der T'ang-dynastie, I.* Wiesbaden: Harrasowitz, 1966. 600p. (Asiatische Forschungen, 19). An excellent, extensively annotated translation of this important source. Information on music, dance, and theatre genres, musical instruments, specific compositions, and music theory. Review by D.C. Twitchett in *Asia Major* 16(1-2):210, 1971; review by Eta Harich-Schneider in *Sinologica*, 1970.

1018. Girton, Gloria. "Notes on the Kong Hou or Chinese Vertical Harp" *The American Harp Journal* 5(2):3-7, Winter 1975. il., with photo and notes on a Japanese harp by Alice Lawson Aber. Survey distilled uncritically from secondhand sources.

1019. Glasgov, N. *Kitaijskie narodnye pesni* [Chinese Folk Songs]. Moskva: 12d. Inostr. Lit., 1960. 95p. NE.

1020. Goldberg, Isaac. "John Hazedel Levis and the Music of China" *Musical Record* 1(11):396-401, April 1934. NE.

1021. Goldschmidt, Harry. "Über das neue chinesische Musikschaffen und seine Perspektiven" *Musik und Gesellschaft* 6(11):409-413, Nov 1956; 6(12):449-453, Dec 1956. mus. A good examination of contemporary composition in Red China.

1022. Gol'dšmit, G. "Stanovlenie Nogovo" *Sovetskaya Muzyka* 2:198-205, 1957. NE.

1023. Golomshok, Eugene A. "Chinese Dancers" *Theatre Arts Monthly* 20:392-396, 1936. NE.

1024. Goloubew, Victor. "Sur l'Origine et la diffusion des tambours métalliques" *Pre-Historia Asia Orientalis* 1:137f., 1932. NE.

1025. Goodrich, Chauncey. "Chinese Hymnology" *Chinese Recorder* p.221-226, May–June 1877. NE.

1026. Goodrich, Joseph King. "Chinese Music" *Musical Observer* 19(2):31, 59, Feb 1920. NE.

1027. Goodrich, Luther Carrington. "The Chinese Sheng and Western Musical Instruments" *China* 17(1):10-11, 14, Jan 1941. I. NE.

1028. Goodrich, L.C. and Ch'ü T'ung-tsu. "Foreign Music at the Court of Sui Wen-ti" *Journal of the American Oriental Society* 69:148, 1948. NE.

1029. Gordon, Beate and Joseph. *An Introduction to the Dance of India, China, Korea, Japan.* New York: The Asia Society, 1965. iv+8p. Whirlwind tour, non-technical.

1030. Gorodinski, V. "Kniga o kitaiskom musyke" [Book About Chinese Music] *Sovetskaya Muzyka* 12:95f., 1952. NE.

1031. Gottschall, Rudolf von. *Das Theater und Drama der Chinesen*. Breslau: Trewendt, 1887. 210p. See p.28, 34-35, 68-81.

1032. Grady, Sandy. "China Limits Orchestra Concerts" *Philadelphia Bulletin* Sept 11, 1973, p.37. NE. [Philadelphia Orchestra trip report.] Grady sent back a series of reports from China during this period; for full list, see Sue Barber *Music and Politics*.

1033. Graf, Walter. "Zu den west-östlichen Parallele in den frühen Reflexionen über Musik" in *Essays in Ethnomusicology: A Birthday Offering for Lee Hye-Ku* (Seoul: Korean Musicological Society, 1969), p.301-338. On similarities between early Chinese musical concepts and those from various West Asian and Greek sources.

1034. Graham, David Crockett. "The Ch'uan Miao of Southern Szechuen" *Journal of the West China Border Research Society* 1:56f., 1922-1923. NE.

1035. _____. *Songs and Stories of the Ch'uan Miao*. Washington: Smithsonian, 1954. Texts only; no music.

1036. Graham, Mrs. Goodwin Price. "Amateur Theatricals in China" *Quarterly Journal of Speech Education* 10: 162-165, 1924. NE.

1037. Granet, Marcel. *Danses et Légendes de la Chine Ancienne*. Paris: Alcan, 1926. 2 vols. 210p. NE.

1038. _____. *Danses et Légendes de la Chine Ancienne*. Paris: Presses Universitaire de France, 1959. 2 vols. 711p. [Annales du Musée Guimet, Bibliothèque d'Études, 64]. NE. Review by J. Gernet in *Journal de Psychologie Normale et Pathologique* 58(1):114-117, Jan-March 1961.

1039. _____. *Fêtes et Chansons Anciennes de la Chine*. Paris: Leroux, 1919. x+301p. A major sinological study, interpreting many of the *Shih Ching* odes as harvest and festival songs. Slightly emended English translation: *Festivals and Songs of Ancient China* (New York: Dutton, 1932).

1040. _____. *La Pensée Chinoise*. Paris: La Renaissance du Livre, [n.d.]. xxiii+614p. See p.209-249, "Nombres et rapports Musicaux" and p.408-415, "L'etiquette (musicale)."

1041. Graves, Stella Marie and Malcolm F. Farley. *Min River Boat Songs*. New York: John Day, 1946. 48p. Original melody given for 29 tunes collected *in situ* by Farley, together with modern settings by Graves. No Chinese texts.

1042. Gray, Zelda. "The Origin of Chinese Music: A Beautiful and Fanciful Legend" *Tempo* 1(12):23-25, Dec 1934. il. NE.

1043. Green, Mrs. E.M. "The Chinese Theater" *Overland* 41: 118-125, Feb 1903. A detailed description of a Chinese theatrical performance in an American city (San Francisco?). Good attention to instruments and role of orchestra. [RR]

1044. Green, G.P. *Some Aspects of Chinese Music and Son Thoughts and Impressions on Art Principles in Music*. London: Reeves, 1913. 149p. il. Inconsequential romantic wanderings of a poetic mind without much attention to reality.

1045. _____. "Some Notes on Chinese Music and Instruments" *Musical Standard* 28:153-154, 1907.

1046. _____. *The Spirit of Music in Nature, Art and Legend from the East to the West*. London: Reeves, [n.d.].

1047. Green, Nan. "Music Wherever They Go" *China Reconstructs* 7(9):15-17, Sept 1958. il. On a traveling song-and-dance troupe.

1048. Greene, Felix. *The Wall Has Two Sides*. London: Cape, 1963. See Chap. 23, "Long Live the Dances," on the music and dance schools in Peking. NE.

1049. Grey, Beryl. *Through the Bamboo Curtain*. New York: Reynal, 1966. 127p. il. Unpretentious, unadorned account of the author's five-week tour of China in 1964, where she performed and taught ballet in Peking and Shanghai. Incidental information on music, opera, and traditional dance.

1050. Grosbois, Ch. "Introduction à la musique chinoise" *Bulletin de l'Université l'Aurore* 3s, 5(1):61-116, 1944. il., mus.

1051. Grosier, Abbé. *A General Description of China*. London: Robinson, 1795. 2 vols. Originally published in French. See II:492-506, "Music of the Chinese," based on and supporting Amiot's contention that Chinese musical culture antedated and influenced that of Greece.

1052. Guck, M.A. "Comment: On Avoiding Culture Shock" *In Theory Only* (Ann Arbor) 2:44-45, April-May 1976. Reply to Sue Barber's article on the Philadelphia Orchestra in China.

1053. Guiganino, A. "La Musica Nella Filosofia e Nella Poesia dell' Antica Cina" *Cina* 4:7-19, 1958. NE.

1054. Guimet, Émile. "Le Théâtre en Chine au XIIIe Siècle" in his *Conférences Faites au Musée Guimet* (Paris: Leroux, 1905), p.201-277.

1055. Gulik, Robert Hans van. "Brief Note on the Cheng, the Chinese Small Cither" *Journal of the Society for Research in Asiatic Music (Tōyō Ongaku Kenkyū)* 9:10-25, March 1951. Reprinted in Liang Tsai-Ping, *Chinese Music*. Excellent introduction to the *cheng*, covering structure, manner of playing, traditional Chinese theories of origin and history, social function, title listing of important tunes in the repertoire, and state of contemporary *cheng* music and research. No transcriptions or musical analysis.

1056. _____. "Chinese Literary Music and Its Introduction into Japan" in *18th Annals of the Nagasaki Higher Commercial School, 1937-1938*, p.123-160. NE. Dr. Van Gulik (in a personal communication) states that the content of this article has been incorporated into *The Lore of the Chinese Lute*.

1057. _____. *Hsi K'ang and His Poetical Essay on the Lute.* Tokyo: Sophia University, 1941. 90p. il. Monumenta Nipponica Monograph. Translation of an early prose-poem on the *ch'in*, with copious introductory data (biographical, historical, textual, bibliographical) and notes. New edition, revised and reset (Tokyo: Sophia University and Charles E. Tuttle Co., 1969. 133p.).

1058. _____. "Hsi Kang's Poetical Essay on the Lute" *T'ien-Hsia Monthly* 11:370-384, 1940-1941. NE.

1059. _____. *The Lore of the Chinese Lute: An Essay in Ch'in Ideology.* Tokyo: Sophia University, 1940. (Monumenta Nipponica Monograph) xii+224+13p. il. mus. Also issued serially in *Monumenta Nipponica* 1(2):94-146, July 1938; 2(1):75-99, Jan 1939; 2(2):77-104, July 1939; 3(1):127-176, Jan 1940. Thorough study of the philosophical and sociological values pertaining to the *ch'in*. History, symbolism, literature, and related areas are well treated. Music-theoretical questions are not discussed. Nevertheless remains one of the richest essays on any Chinese musical instrument or other musical subject. Required reading. New edition revised and reset (Tokyo: Sophia University and Charles E. Tuttle Co., 1969. xix+271p.). Incorporates addenda and corrigenda of 1951 (below) and makes other small corrections.

1060. _____. "The Lore of the Chinese Lute: Addenda and Corrigenda" *Monumenta Nipponica* 7:300-310, 1951. Adds some new material, but nothing of major significance.

1061. _____. "On Three Antique Lutes" *Transactions of the Asiatic Society of Japan* 17:155-189, Dec 1938. Included in an Appendix of *The Lore of the Chinese Lute*.

* * * * * * * * * *

1062. H., F.W.   "Oriental Music Considered, Essay the Third: On the Music of the Chinese" *Musical Record* 9:27-36, 1827. NE.

1063. H., H.   "A Letter from Peking: A Unique Song and Dance Performance" *Eastern Horizon* 8(3):31-33, 1969. Peasants rehabilitated by acupuncture sing and dance praises of Mao; good example of overwritten attempt at popular legend.

1064. Haberlandt, Michael. "Die Eingeborenen der Kapsulan-ebene von Formosa" *Mitteilungen der Antropologischen in Wien* 24:184-193, 1894. il. NE.

1065. Hadden, R.M. "Letters: Our Turn Next!" *Music Trades* 122:28f., Feb 1974. NE.

1066. Haenselman, Carl F. "Chinese Music: Some Characteristics of Its History, Theory, and Practice" *Appalachian Faculty Publications* (Appalachian State University), 1962. NE.

1067. Häger, Bengt.   "The Shackled Muse: Music in China Today" *High Fidelity* 17(10):93-98, Oct 1967. il. NE.

1068. Hall, William L.   "Chinese Opera" *Asia* 18(4):323-325, April 1918. Il. by Gertrude Emerson. Verse translations of some arias.

1069. Halliday, Michael. "Chinese Drama Festival" *Asian Horizon* 1(2):44-48, Summer 1948. NE.

1070. Halson, Elizabeth [Pseud.]. *Peking Opera*. Hong Kong: Oxford University Press, 1966. xx+92p. il., plates. An introductory handbook; well-rounded but superficial. Reviewed by Willem Adriaansz in *Ethnomusicology* 11:426-427, 1967.

1071. Hamada, Kosaku. *Sen-oku Sei-shô; Or the Collection of Old Bronzes of Baron Sumitomo: Part I, Bronze Vases, &c.* 2nd ed. with change in format. [Tokyo]: 1924. 4 vols. An outstanding descriptive catalog; the plates are collected in 3 volumes, with facing Japanese commentary, while an English text is given in a separate volume. Items 118-131, 135-139 and 156 are of musical interest. Particularly important is the unique large bronze drum Item 130, with 2 bronze drumheads cast as imitation crocodile skin, and unusual humanoid ornamentation.

1072. _____. *Ten Bronze Bells Formerly in the Collection of Ch'ên Chieh-ch'i: Being a Special Volume of the Senoku-Seishô, Or the Collection of the Chinese Bronzes of Baron Sumitomo.* 2nd ed., with change in format. [Tokyo]: 1924. 13p. English text, 36p. Japanese. il. General introduction to bronze bells, and a descriptive catalog of ten fine bells, with photographic plates and rubbings for each bell in the Japanese text. A chart compiled by musicologist Hisao Tanabe gives pitch measurements for each bell. The English text is extensive.

1073. Hamm, H. "Der Jaegerchor in Peking—Wandel des Musiklebens in China" *Musikhandel* (Bonn) 27(2):65-66, 1976. NE.

1074. Hammond, Louise Strong. "A Competition for Original Hymns" *Chinese Recorder* p.606-608, Sept 1929. NE.

1075. _____. "A New Plainsong" *Chinese Recorder* 51(3):179-184, March 1920. Describes a Mass written by Chiu Chang-nien using Chinese style; advocates Gregorian-Chinese fusion.

1076. _____. *Plum Blossoms: A Three-Movement Suite. An Old Chinese Melody Arranged for the Pianoforte.* Shanghai: Commercial Press, 1925. 6p. NE.

1077. _____. "The Tunes of Chinese Poetry" in *Yearbook of Oriental Art and Culture 1924-1925* (London: Benn, 1925), edited by Arthur Waley, I,114-129. mus. Study of mnemonic tunes for reciting poetry, with transcriptions and Western settings.

1078. Han Chi-hsiang. "A Blind Minstrel Sees the Light" *China Reconstructs* 13(5):32-34, May 1964. il. Autobiographical sketch by a *san-hsien* player and a ballad singer, telling of his reforms and modern themes.

1079. Han, Sophie. "Notes on Chinese Music" *Peabody Bulletin* 30s, 1:8-13, Dec 1933. mus. NE.

1080. Hanan, Patrick D. "The Development of Fiction and Drama" in Raymond Dawson, ed. *The Legacy of China* (Oxford: Oxford University Press, 1964; paperback GB352, 1971), p.115-143.

1081. _____. "The *Yün-men Chuan*: From *Chantefable* to Short Story" *Bull, School of Oriental and African Studies* 36(2):299-308, 1973. Investigation and description of a Ming *chantefable*; information on musical accompaniment and performance practice.

1082. Hansmann, Claus and Ludwig Krafft. *Schattenspiel aus Szetschuan*. München: Ehrenwirth Verlag, [1964]. 52p. il. NE.

1083. Hantz, E. "Comment: On the Orientation of Music and Politics" *In Theory Only* (Ann Arbor) 2:45-47, April-May 1976. Reply to Sue Barber's article on the Philadelphia Orchestra in China.

1084. Harich-Schneider, Eta. "The Earliest Sources of Chinese Music and Their Survival in Japan" *Monumenta Nipponica* 11(2):85-103, 1955. Thoughtful survey of some extant archeological, pictorial, and literary sources for the study of ancient Chinese music, with comments on possible parallels to contemporary musical phenomena in Japan.

1085. _____. *The Relations of Foreign and Native Elements in the Development of Japanese Music; A Case Study.* M.A. thesis (Political and Social Science), New School of Social Research, 1954. vii+ 112p. A comparative study of the introduction of Chinese music (T'ang, Sung) and Western music (Edo, Meiji) into Japan.

1086. Harrison, Frank. *Time, Place, and Music: An Anthology of Ethnomusicological Observation c. 1550 to c. 1800.* Amsterdam: Frits Knuf, 1973. viii+221p. 14 plates, music (Source Materials and Studies in Ethnomusicology, I). Stimulating collection of excerpts from varied reports by European travelers around the globe, with parallel English translation where necessary. Includes eight reports from 18th-century China.

1087. Harrison, Lou. "Some Notes on the Music of Mouth Organs" in *Essays in Ethnomusicology: A Birthday Offering for Lee Hye-Ku* (Seoul: Korean Musicological Society, 1969), p.371-382. On the tunings and musical styles of members of this instrument family from East and Southeast Asia.

1088. Harlez, Charles de. "Miscellanées Chinoises, Deux Traités de la Musique. I. Le Li-Yo dy Sung-li Tsing-i. II. Le Yo-Ki" *Giornale della Società Asiatica Italiana* 6:161-186, 1892.

1089. Hart, James. "The Discussion of the *Wu-i* Bells in the *Kuo-Yü*" *Monumenta Serica* 29:391-418, 1970-1971. Study and translation of an important early text bearing on music theory; persuasive alternate interpretations to Robinson and Needham's reading of this passage, but Hart fails to pay sufficient attention to tuning patterns.

1090. Hartner, Willy. "Some Notes on Chinese Musical Art" *Isis* 29(78):72-94, July 1938. il., mus. NE.

1091. Harwood, D.L. "Music and the Pragmatics of Revolution" *In Theory Only* (Ann Arbor) 2:26-28, June-July 1976. Comments on Sue Barber's article on the Philadelphia Orchestra in China.

1092. Hauser, Miska. *The Letters of Miska Hauser, 1853* (History of Music in San Francisco Series, Vol. 3). San Francisco, History of Music Project, Works Progress Administration of California, 1939. Reprinted: New York, AMS Press, Inc., 1972. In letters written on a concert tour, violinist Hauser comments *passim* on the Chinese in San Francisco. He describes their reactions to his playing of Chinese melodies (p.30) and makes note of Chinese music in a holiday parade (p.65), at the Chinese theatre (p.41), and in a funeral procession (p.68). [RR]

1093. Hawkes, David. "Reflections on Some Yüan Tsa-chü" *Asia Major* 16:69-81, 1971. About the theatrical effect of hanging criminals on stage.

1094. Hayashi, Kenzo. "Gogenhu and the Clue to its Interpretation" *Journal of the Asiatic Society of Japan* 2:--, 1940. NE. "Study of the notation for
the five-stringed lute, ... very important   not
only because it confirms the results that the
author obtained in his better known study of the
Tun-huang Codex of *p'i-pa* notation, but because
it gives us transcriptions of several eighth-
and ninth-century musical examples. Both studies
show certain practices in *p'i-pa* playing of the
T'ang period" (Rulan Chao Pian, in *Notes* 28(2):
229, Dec 1971).

1095. _____. "Study on Explication of Ancient Musical
Score of P'i-p'a Discovered at Tun-huang, China"
Bulletin of Nara Gakugei University 5(1):1-22,
Dec 1955. il., mus. A detailed study of possible
interpretations of the ancient notation.   Many
tables. Text of ancient score reproduced photo-
graphically, together with reconstructed transcription in Western staff notation. Fascinating
musicological deductions.

1096. Headland, Isaac Taylor. "Chinese Children's Games"
*Journal of the Royal Asiatic Society, North China
Branch* 37:150-184, 1906.   Descriptions of many
games, with texts of songs in English where relevant, but neither illustrations nor music.

1097. Hemming, R. "The Philadelphia in China—Eugene Ormandy Describes Some of His Musical Adventures
in the Far Eastern Wonderland" *Stereo Review* 33:
59-63, July 1974. il. NE.

1098. Henle, Hans. "Modern Opera in the Chinese Provinces"
Eastern Horizon 4(5):40-43, May 1965.

1099. Henschke, Alfred [Pseud. Klabund]. *Dumpfe Trommel
und Berauschter Gong: Nachdichtungen Chinesischer
Kriegslyrik.* Leipzig: Inselverlag, 1915. 45p.
(Inselbücherei 183). NE.

1100. Hermand, Louis. "Chronique Musicale" *Relations de
la Chine* p.46-51, Jan 1907. NE.

1101. Hickmann, Hans. "Notation Einstimmige Musik Ausser-
european" in *Musik in Geschichte und Gegenwart*
IX,1595-1667. An excellent article, with examples
and extensive bibliography.   Five illustrations
of Chinese and Japanese notations.

1102. Hiemenz, J.   "Taking Tiger Mountain by Strategy;
      Peking Opera Troupe of Shanghai Filmed Perfor-
      mance Version" *High Fidelity and Musical America*
      22:MA 11, Oct 1972. NE.

1103. Hightower, James Robert. *Topics in Chinese Litera-
      ture, Outlines and Bibliographies*. Rev. ed. Cam-
      bridge: Harvard University Press, 1965. x+141p.
      (Harvard-Yenching Institute Studies, Vol. 3).
      Introductory chapters—concise, informative—on
      all aspects of Chinese literature, including
      drama, poetry, song texts, classics, etc. Bibli-
      ographies of relevant materials in both Western
      and Oriental languages given for each genre.

1104. Hinchliff, Thomas Woodbine. *Over the Sea and Far
      Away, Being a Narrative of Wanderings Around the
      World*. London: Longmans, Green & Co., Ltd., 1876.
      Brief, negative account of Chinese theatre in
      San Francisco, p.211-212. [RR]

1105. Hinton, William. *Fanshen: A Documentary of Revolu-
      tion in a Chinese Village*.   New York: Vintage
      Books, 1968. Sympathetic firsthand narrative of
      events in the early years of the People's Repub-
      lic in rural China.   Chapter 34, "Drama in the
      Fields," describes performance and repertory of
      a touring opera troupe.

1106. Hirth, Friedrich. "Chinesische Ansichten über Bronze-
      trommeln" *Mitteilungen des Seminars für Orien-
      talische Sprache zu Berlin* 7(1):200-262, 1904.
      Also in book form, Leipzig: Harrassowitz, 1904.
      65p. Annotated translations of many Chinese ref-
      erences to bronze drums, with original texts.

1107. _____.   "Das Schattenspiel der Chinesen" *Keleti
      Szemele* 2:77, 1901. NE.

1108. _____. "Über Hinterindische Bronze-Trommeln" *T'oung
      Pao* 1:137-142, 1890.   Short discussion of some
      Chinese sources for bronze drum study.

1109. Hittell, John S. *A Guide Book to San Francisco*. San
      Francisco: A.L. Bancroft & Co., 1883. Notes for
      tourists on Chinese funerals, theatres, p.48-49.
      [RR]

1110. Ho Chi-fang.   "Chinese Folk Songs" *Chinese Litera-
      ture* 1:126-142, 1954. Partial German translation
      by Horst Hockendorf in *Aufbau* 13(3-4):283-296,
      1957.

1111. _____. "Guide for China's Revolutionary Literature and Art" *China Reconstructs* 11(5):2-5, May 1962. il. Mao's Yenan Forum seed blossoms into Yangko, new opera, music for the masses.

1112. Ho Chih-hao. "Chinese Choreography Under Renovation" *China Today* 6(2):16-23, Feb 1963. il.

1113. Ho Ching-chih. "How the 'White-Haired Girl' Was Written and Produced" *Chinese Literature* 2:110-114, 1953.

1114. Ho Ching-chih and Ting Yi. *The White-Haired Girl: An Opera in Five Acts*. Peking: Foreign Languages Press, 1954. xvi+98+[8], music, photos. Script of this important opera built on folk themes. Includes piano-vocal score for three songs. Includes above article by Ho on genesis of the opera. The script was previously published in *Chinese Literature* 2:38-109, 1953. The translation is by Yang Hsien-yi and Gladys Yang.

1115. Ho Lu-ting. "Problem Nacional'noj Formy v Kitayskoj Muzyke" [Problems of National Form in Chinese Music] *Sovetskaya Muzyka* 1:125-131, 1957. NE.

1116. _____. "What Kind of Music for China?" *China Reconstructs* 12:5-8, Dec 1956. Reprinted in *China in Transition* (Peking: China Reconstructs, 1957), p.377-382. Injunctions to use Western orchestra, make depth study of Western techniques, adapt traditional music.

1117. Ho Wang. "Small-Town Drama Troupe" *China Reconstructs* 12(1):28-29, Jan 1963. il. On an amateur local opera troupe of the *pangtze* style in Anhwei.

1118. Ho Yun. "Making Music With a Leaf" *China Reconstructs* 11(5):24-25, May 1962. il. The use of this simple *ad hoc* folk instrument in China, particularly among "National Minorities," is explained in this charming short article, with a revealing photo of an old bas-relief statue of a leaf-blowing musician.

1119. Hoa, Irene. "First Symphony in Peking" *China Reconstructs* 3(5):46-47, Sept-Oct 1954. il. The author relates her excitement at attending the first all-Western symphony concert by a Chinese orchestra.

1120. Hoffman, Alfred. *Die Lieder des li Yü 937-978, Herrschers der Südlichen T'ang-Dynastie*. Cologne: Creven Verlag, 1950. 274p. Poetry translations, *tz'u* form.

1121. Hogans, O.R. "Tick-Talking Around the World; Chinese Clock—200 Years Old" *Musical Box Society International* 16(3):118-123, 1970. NE.

1122. Holford, Franz. "Songs and Dances of China" *Canon* 15(9):4-6, April 1962. il. Brief survey of folk dances based on Red Chinese folk festivals.

1123. Holm, David. "Report on an Experiment with *Yangge* Dance and Music" *CHINOPERL Papers* 7:92-105. il., mus. On teaching *yang-ko* dancing to a British group; includes information on typical dance steps and music.

1124. Honegger, H. "Voyage musical en Chine populaire" *Schweizerische Musikzeitung* 113(5):299-300, 1973. NE.

1125. Hoose, Harned Pettus. *Peking Pigeons and Pigeon-Flutes*. Peiping: College of Chinese Studies, California College in China, 1938. 28p. NE.

1126. Hornbostel, Erich Maria von. "Ch'ao-T'ien-Tze. Eine chinesische Notation und ihre Ausfuhrungen" *Archiv für Musikwissenschaft* 1:477-498, July 1919. mus. Compares a basic Chinese tune notation with several embellished realizations.

1127. _____. "Chinesische Idiogramme in America" *Anthropos* 25:935-960, 1930. NE.

1128. Houn, Franklin W. "The Stage As a Medium of Propaganda in Communist China" *Public Opinion Quarterly* 23:223-235, Summer 1959. NE.

1129. Howard, Florence. *Lecture Recital on Chinese Music*. Washington, 1934. 4p. Program.

1130. Howard, Walter. "Chinesische und europäische Musik" in *Chinesische Musik*, edited by Richard Wilhelm (Frankfurt: China Institute, 1927), p.44-47. il. Also in *Sinica* 2:132-135, 1947. Compares aesthetics, form, context of music in the two cultures.

1131. Hrdlička, Zdeněk. "Old Chinese Ballads to the Accompaniment of the Big Drum" *Archiv Orientalni* 25(1):83-145, 1957. A detailed study based on Chinese sources and field research of the *ta-ku shu* genre; historical and textual orientation, but much musical information is given. No notations.

1132. _____. "Čínští Pěvci Balad k Velkym Bubnum" [Chinese Ballad Singers with the Big Drums] *Nový Orient* 11:131-132, 1956. NE.

1133. _____. "O Původu a vývoji Lien-chua-lao" [On the Origin and Development of Lien-.hua-lao] *Ceskoslovenská Ethnographie* 4(2):154-169, 1952. il. On a genre of narrative singing with acting and musical accompaniment. English summary; photos in color and black and white.

1134. _____. "O Původu 'Vyprávěni Smišených se Zpěvy'" [The Origin of 'Narration Combined with Songs'] *Nový Orient* 11:93-95, 1956.

1135. Hrdličková, Věna. *Čínští Vypravěči a Pěvci Balad.* Thesis, Universita Karlova, Prague, 1966. 220p. NE.

1136. Hrdličková, Venceslava. "The Chinese Storytellers and Singers of Ballads: Their Performance and Storytelling Techniques" *Transactions of the Asiatic Society of Japan* 3 ser, 10:97-115, 1968. NE.

1137. _____. "The Professional Training of Chinese Storytellers and the Storytellers' Guilds" *Archiv Orientálni* (Prague) 33:225-248, 1965. NE.

1138. _____. "Some Observations on the Chinese Art of Story-Telling" *Acta Universitatis Carolinae—Philologica 3 Orientalia Pragensia III*, p.61-62. NE.

1139. Hsia Nai. "New Archeological Discoveries" *China Reconstructs* 4:13-18, July-Aug 1952. Report on recent excavations, including 1950 Anyang find of *ch'ing* with tiger-figure carving (photo). Reprinted in *China in Transition* (Peking: China Reconstructs, 1957), p.384-391.

1140. Hsai, Paul. "A Summary of Tsang Mou-hsün's Two Prefaces to Selected Yüan Plays (Yüan-ch'ü Hsüan)" *Dodder* 2:39-40, Jan 1970. A Ming scholar's view of Yüan *tsa-chü*. NE.

1141. Hsiang Chiu-wen. "New 'Cheng' Music" *Chinese Literature* 1:120-124, 1974. il. Brief background on the *cheng* and technical improvements in its construction and performance practice, followed by discussion of revolutionary *cheng* piece, "Fighting the Typhoon," a "... successful example of the way in which our traditional instrumental music can make discriminating use of China's musical heritage to reflect... spirit of our socialist age."

1142. Hsiang Yen. "Peking Operan" *Musik-Kultur* 30(6):12-13, 1966. il. NE.

1143. Hsiang Yu. "Folk Music Finds Its Place" *China Reconstructs* 8(9):2-5, Sept 1959. il., mus. Broad descriptive survey of folk music performance and research in modern China.

1144. Hsiao Chang-hua. "Past and Present" *Chinese Literature* 11:132-139, 1959. il. Reminiscences of an old Peking opera actor.

1145. Hsiao Chang-hua, Chuan-sung Wang and Chi-ho Chou. "The Clown in Traditional Chinese Theatre" *Chinese Literature* 4:104-113, 1963. il.   Brief sketches by well-known practitioners.

1146. Hsiao Ch'ien, ed. *A Harp With a Thousand Strings*. London: Pilot Press, 1944. xxiv+536p. A miscellany of Chinese culture, including the Fernald articles cited above.

1147. Hsiao Ching-chang.   "Cradle for Future Musicians" *China Reconstructs* 12(4):20-21, April 1963. il. (cover). On the Shanghai Children's Music School.

1148. _____. "The Man with the Magic Flute" *China Reconstructs* 11(3):30-31, March 1962.   il. (cover). Biographical sketch of virtuoso *ti-tzu* player and teacher, Lu Chun-ling.

1149. Hsiao, Emi.   "Revolyutsionnye Kompozitory Kitaya" [Revolutionary Composers of China] *Sovetskaya Muzyka* 11:88-91, Nov 1940. il., mus. NE.

1150. Hsiao, K.C.   "Chinese Scale Theories" in *The Musician's Arithmetic*, by Max F. Meyer (Columbia: University of Missouri, 1929), Appendix 6, p.105-117. (The University of Missouri Studies, Vol. IV, No. 1). Unreliable.

1151. Hsiao Shu-fang, Hwang Yun-tze, Hsiao Shu-hsien, Chiang Yee, Hermann Scherchen. *Chinesische Kinderfreuden in Bild, Wort, und Musik*. Zurich: Büchergilde Gutenberg, 1946. 42p. il., mus. A children's book.   Pictures by Hsiao Shu-fang; poems by Hwang Yun-tze and Hsiao Shu-hsien; German text by Hermann Scherchen; and introduction by Chiang Yee. Chinese children's games and festivals are described.

1152. Hsiao Shu-hsien.   "La Chanson populaire chinoise"
      Sinologica 1:65-86, 1948. mus. Ten songs in tran-
      scription, numerous short examples, basic modal
      and melodic analyses. Clear presentation of mne-
      monic chanting, theorizing such chants may be
      origin of popular songs. Suggests that symmetri-
      cal melodicules are key elements of Chinese mel-
      ody. Short discussion of language tones. Histor-
      ically weak, no sources given.

1153. Hsiao Wen. "Drama for a Great Cause" *Chinese Liter-
      ature* 11:103-109, 1965.

1154. Hsiao, Yiu-mei Chopin. *Ein geschichtliche Untersu-
      chung über das chinesische Orchester bis zum 17.
      Jahrhundert.* Dissertation (philosophy), Univer-
      sity of Leipzig, 1919. NE.

1155. *Hsi-ch'ü Pao*.   "Criticism of 'Hai Jui Relieved of
      His Office' and 'Hsieh Yao-huan' Gradually Deep-
      ens" *Selections from China Mainland Magazines*
      528:47-50, June 13, 1966. From March 10, 1966.
      NE.

1156. Hsieh Wen-ping.   "A Fierce Struggle for Control of
      the Peking Opera Stage—The Production and Stag-
      ing of *On the Docks*, a Peking Opera on a Revolu-
      tionary Contemporary Theme" in Chiang Ching, *On
      the Revolution of Peking Opera* (Peking, 1968),
      p.27-33.

1157. Hsin Hua. "Grandmothers' Choral Club" *China Recon-
      structs* 23(11):35-37, Nov 1974. il. Group of re-
      tired women learn to sing Peking opera, and per-
      form excerpts from the model revolutionary works.

1158. _____.   "Tientsin Song and Dance Ensemble Visits
      Japan" *Chinese Literature* (11):122-126, 1977. il.
      Story about the June 1977 cultural exchange tour.

1159. _____. "Tsaidan Choma, Tibetan Singer" *Chinese Lit-
      erature* 12:101-103, 1973. Biographical sketch of
      a politically active folk singer.

1160. Hsin Ping. "New Children's Songs from a Peking Pri-
      mary School" *Chinese Literature* 6:104-109, 1975.
      il. The peanut gallery joins the fight to repud-
      iate Lin Piao and Confucius.

1161. Hsin Wen-chi. "Lui Tsun-Yuen the Prodigious Classi-
      cal Music of P'i-P'a" *West and East* 12(9):6-7,
      Sept 1967. Review of a concert in Taipei.

1162. Hsin Wen-tung. "Art Derived from the Life and Struggle of the Masses" *Chinese Literature* 8:76-86, 1974. il. Political sources of inspiration for the dances of the Tahsing County amateur art propaganda team.

1163. Hsin Wu. "Proletarian Art Blossoms on Socialist Stage" *China Reconstructs* 16(1):19-25, Jan 1967. il. Song and dance performances by various local groups; cultural revolution.

1164. Hsing Chi. *China's Klassieke Opera*. Amsterdam: Exotic Music Society, 1957. NE.

1165. Hsing Lien-chun. "Answers to Questions on Chinese Dramatic Art" *West and East* 14:9-12, Aug 1969. NE.

1166. Hsiung Shih-i. "Drama" in *China*, edited by Harley Farnsworth MacNair (Berkeley: University of California Press, 1946), p.372-385. A concise, authoritative survey of the historical development of Chinese drama, with some consideration of the musical element, by a recognized Chinese scholar in the field.

1167. Hsu Chien. "Ancient Lute" *Eastern Horizon* 4(4):29-31, April 1965. Short introduction to the *ch'in*, account of mainland publications and research in this genre.

1168. Hsu Chih. "Nieh Erh: People's Composer" *People's China* 2(2):12-14, July 1950. Biographical sketch.

1169. Hsu, Delores Menstell. "Musical Elements of Chinese Opera" *Musical Quarterly* 50(4):439-451, Oct 1964. il., mus. Introduction to modern opera music based on Western secondary sources.

1170. Hsu Fang. "Home of Folk-Songs" *Chinese Literature* 6:90-94, 1973. Folk songs of workers' brigades in Locheng, Anhwei Province. Texts only.

1171. Hsu, Francis L.K. *Americans and Chinese: Purpose and Fulfillment in Great Civilizations*. New York: Doubleday & Co., 1970, 493p. A sociologist reflects on differences between Chinese and Western musics and on the relative status of musicians, p.371-374. [RR]

1172. Hsu Hsia-lin. "Confucius' Reactionary Ideas About Music" *Chinese Literature* 8:94-98, 1974. Critical essay, in the spirit of "criticism of Lin Piao and Confucius," holding that "his wish to make music serve 'the right way' was part of his attempt to preserve the declining old order ..."

1173. Hsu, Vivian. "Monks and Nuns as Comic Figures in Yüan Drama" *Dodder* 2:10-12, Jan 1970.

1174. Hsu, Vivian C.W. Ling. "The Political Usage of Song in Ancient China" *Tamkang Review* 1(2):201-226, 1970. NE.

1175. Hsu Wen-ying. *Ku-Ch'in*. M.M. thesis, New England Conservatory, 1959. History, analysis, origin, music, transcriptions. NE.

1176. _____. *Origin of Music in China*. Taiwan: Wen-ying Studio, 1973. 24p. Pamphlet publication of a paper delivered in 1970 at the annual meeting of the Society for Ethnomusicology. Proposes idiosyncratic theory that "Emperor Shun was the originator of Chinese music, which was derived from a string of silk. He put the calculated tones of definite pitch on his five-string *ch'in* and pentatonic idiom was initiated." Questionable evidence, unwarranted inference, disregard of modern scholarship combine to invalidate the argument. Another version in *Chinese Culture* 13(3):43-66, Sept 1972.

1177. _____. "When Poetry Was Music" *Free China Review* 14(1):35-42, Jan 1964. mus. Short introduction to ancient Chinese music, based on old texts. Bad translations by author and very little textual criticism. Speaks in a non-scholarly fashion of the important sources, and gives characters for all names and terms.

1178. Hsueh Ching. "The Birth of the First Ballet with a Modern Revolutionary Theme" *Chinese Literature* 3:9-12, 1967. On "The Red Detachment of Women," a ballet instigated by Chiang Ching, opposed by Chou Yang.

1179. Hu Jui-chuan. "Uncle Huang Sees the Opera" *China Reconstructs* 10(3):32, March 1961. il. A moral fable.

1180. Hu Pin-chung. "Music Has More Than Charms" *Free China Review* 19(6):41-42, June 1969. Short popular article on serious significance of traditional Chinese music.

1181. _____. "Poetry That Sings" *Free China Review* 20(9): 19-21, Sept 1970.

1182. Hu Shih. "Mei Lan-fang and the Chinese Drama" in Ernest K. Moy, ed. *Mei Lan-fang: Chinese Drama* (New York: China Institute in America, 1930), [2].

1183. Huang de Lopez de la Camara, M. "L'Art Dramatique en Chine" *Sinologica* 1(3):246-257, 1948. il. NE.

1184. Huang Kang. "An Unforgettable Night in Yenan" *Chinese Literature* (9):91-98, 1977. Reminiscence and discussion commemorating the 35th anniversary of the *Talks at the Yenan Forum*.

1185. Huang Siu-chi. "Musical Art in Early Confucian Philosophy" *Philosophy East and West* p.49-60, April 1963. Abridged reprint in *Society for Asian Music Quarterly Newsletter* p.10-13, Summer 1964.

1186. Huber, E. "Die Chinesischen Gongs" *Erdhall* 2(2): 43-47, 1938. NE.

1187. Hübner, Wilhelm. "Die erste Konzertreise der Wiener Philharmoniker in die Volksrepublik China" *China Report* 11:20-29, 1973. NE.

1188. Hughes, E.R. *Chinese Philosophy in Classical Times.* London: Dent, 1942. 336p.

1189. Hughes, Richard. "Chinese Opera Walks the Party Line" *New York Times Magazine* p.62, 64, 67, 69, March 21, 1965. il. Popular account enlivened by translations from mainland papers and tongue-in-cheek approach to Socialist realism.

1190. Hummel, Arthur W. *Eminent Chinese of the Ch'ing Period (1644-1912).* Washington: U.S. Government Printing Office, 1943. xii+1101p., index. A staggering biographical encyclopedia; includes scholars of music and drama; indexed by subject.

1191. Hung Ch'eng. "Rezension der Oper: 'Mit taktischen Geschick den Tigerberg erobert'" *China, Zeitschrift für Politik, Wissenschaft und Kultur* 37: 14-15, 1970. NE.

1192. _____. "'To Find Men Truly Great and Noble-Hearted, We Must Look Here in the Present'—In Praise of the Heroic Image of Yang Tzu-jung Molded in the Revolutionary Model Play 'Taking the Bandits' Stronghold'" *Selections from China Mainland Magazines* 667:20-26, Nov 24, 1969. From *Hung-ch'i* 11, Oct 29, 1969.

1193. Hung, Josephine Huang. *Children of the Pear Garden: Five Plays from the Chinese Opera*. Taipei: Heritage Press, 1961. xvi+309p. il. General introduction to Peking opera, p.1-52, followed by translations of "The Faithful Harlot," "Two Men on a String," "Twice a Bride," "One Missing Head," and "The Price of Wine."

1194. _____. "Das chinesische Theater" in Heinz Kinderman, ed. *Fernöstliches Theater* (Stuttgart: Alfred Kröner Verlag, 1966). German translation by Ingrid Peschek. NE.

1195. _____. *Ming Drama*. Taipei: Heritage Press, 1966. vii+289p. il. mus., index, bibliog. P.25-41, "The Music of the Ming Theatre." Basically a history of *k'un-ch'ü*, this book includes sections on its predecessors and successors.

1196. _____. "The Unique Art of Chinese Opera" *Journal of China Society* 4:53-67, 1964. il. Introductory survey.

1197. Hung Ping. "A Fine Peking Opera on a Revolutionary Modern Theme" *Chinese Literature* 8:182-193, 1967. il. Eulogizes "Taking the Bandit's Stronghold" in light of Mao's thought.

1198. Hung Sheng. *The Palace of Eternal Youth*. Peking: Foreign Languages Press, 1955. Translated by Yang and Yang. Translation of a major play, in which music has important symbolic value. Includes 11 unnumbered pages of transcription of music for the Tan-tzu episode, with original Chinese text, as a concluding appendix (Bruce Brooks).

1199. _____. "What Is the Chinese Drama?" *China Journal of Science and Arts* 1(3):219-229, 1923.

1200. Hung Wen and Hsueh Ching. "Always Courageously Advance Along Chairman Mao's Revolutionary Line in Literature and Art" *Peking Review* 12(20):9-12, May 16, 1969. NE.

1201. Hung Yu. "Ah Chia on 'The Red Lantern'" *Chinese Literature* 5:98, 1965. NE.

1202. Hunter, William. "Music for the Chinese" *Chinese Recorder* 33(5):244-247, May 1902. NE.

1203. Huo Chu. "'Shachiapang'——A Beacon Fire" *Chinese Literature* 3:13-18, 1967. il. On this cultural revolution symphonic opera.

1204. Hurry, R.B. "A Far-Eastern Gateway" *Music and Letters* 3(4):372-377, Oct 1922. Western music in the Shanghai foreign enclave.

1205. Hüttner, Johann Christian. "Die Musik der Chinesen" *Journal des Luxus und der Moden,* Jan 1796. NE.

1206. _____. *Nachricht von der Brittischen Gesandschaftreise durch China und einen Theil der Tartarei.* Berlin: Voss, 1797. vii+190p. In French as *Voyage à la Chine.* Paris: Fuchs, 1799. Passages on music excerpted and translated in Frank Harrison, *Time, Place, and Music* (q.v.).

1207. _____. "Ein Ruderliedchen aus China mit Melodie" *Journal des Luxus und der Moden* 11:35-40, Jan 1796. mus. [Is this the same as Item 1205?] NE. Partly translated by Frank Harrison in his *Time, Place, and Music.*

1208. Huth, Arno. "Chinesische Musik in Frankfurt" *Auftakt* 7:214-216, 1927.

1209. Hwang, Lillian S.D. *The Growth and Use of Music in the Chinese Church.* B.D. thesis, Nanking Theological Seminary, June 1935. NE.

1210. Hwang Ti-pei, ed. *Chinese Musical Instruments.* Taiwan: National Taiwan Arts Hall, 1961. 40p. il., mus. A useful, descriptive handbook, generally non-technical, covering 61 instruments. Short texts in both Chinese and English for each instrument. Illustrations or photos, ranges on the staff, and the Chinese characters for each instrument are given.

1211. Hwang Yau-tai. "My Approach to a Modern Chinese Music" *Chinese Culture* 13(2):83-87, June 1972. NE.

1212. Hye-Kerkdal, K.J. "Tanz im alten China" in *Congrès International des Sciences Anthropologiques et Ethnologiques* (Paris: Musée de l'Homme, 1964), II,105. Brief abstract suggests that one must look to pictorial sources for determining if a characteristically "Chinese" dance style can be said to exist.

1213. _____. "Tanz im alten China, eine tanzkritische Untersuchung archäologischer Objecte aus der Prä-Han bis T'angzeit" *Archiv für Volkskunde* 16:31-48, 1961. NE.

* * * * * * * * * *

1214. Ikonnikov, A.   "Isskusstvo Kitayskikh Druzei" [The
      Art of Our Chinese Friends] *Sovetskaya Muzyka* 23:
      113-117, Feb 1959. il. NE. Also (a continuation?)
      1:134f., 1960. NE.

1215. _____. *Kitaiskii Teatr i "Kitaischina" v Detskom
      Sele* [The Chinese Theater and "Chinoiseries" in
      Detskoe Sele]. Moscow: Gos. Izd-vo Izobrazietel'
      nyleh Iskusstv, 1931. 39p. il. NE.

1216. _____.   "Šanchajkij Teatr Pekinskoi Muzykal'noi
      Dramy" *Sovetskaya Muzyka* 2:158-164, 1957. NE.

1217. Ing, Benjamin Z.N.   "Music Chronicle" *T'ien-Hsia
      Monthly* 4(1):54-60, Jan 1937.   On Western music
      activities and teaching.

1218. Irwin, Eyles. *Four Chinese Tunes Contributed with
      Brief Commentary to the Oriental Collections.*
      London: Cadell and Davies, 1797-1798. I,343; II,
      148. mus. NE.

1219. Irwin, Will.   "The Drama in Chinatown" *Everybody's
      Magazine* 20:157-169, 1909. il. Highly literate,
      with excellent descriptions. Subject treated in
      historical perspective. Instruments (with their
      Cantonese names) given good attention. Based on
      Chinese theaters in San Francisco and New York.
      Many first-rate photographs. [RR]

1220. Ishii, Shinji. "The Island of Formosa and Its Prim-
      itive Inhabitants" *Transactions and Proceedings
      of the Japan Society* 14:38-60, 1915-1919. NE.

              * * * * * * * * * *

1221. J.   "The Purification of San Francisco" *Blackwood's
      Magazine* 179:832-843, 1906.   Visit to Chinese
      theatre (post-earthquake) briefly described. [RR]

1222. J., J.C. "Notes on Chinese Music" *Chinese Recorder*
      17:363-474, 1886. NE.

1223. Jablonski, Witold. "Le 'Siao-ha (I-eu) l-yu' pékin-
      ois (chansons pour enfants)." *Bulletin Interna-
      tional de l'Académie Polonaise des Sciences et
      Lettres* 1-3:30-32, Jan-March 1936. French resumé
      of main paper in Polish.

1224. _____. *Les "Siaohua (I-eu) L-Yu" de Pékin: un Essai sur la Poésie Populaire en Chine*. Krakow: Nakladem Pojskiej Akademji Umiejyetnosci, 1935. 193p. il. (Polska Akademja Umiejetnosci: Prace Komisji Orjentalistycznej 19). NE. Reviewed by: John K. Shyrock in *Journal of the American Oriental Society* 56:375-376, Sept 1936. Text in French with Polish summary. Contains about 800 different songs in Romanized text and translation, together with an analysis of the prosody, poetry, vocabulary, and themes of the songs. (J.K.S. in *Bulletin of Far Eastern Bibliography* 1(4), Oct 1936).

1225. Jakob, Georg. *Das Chinesische Schattentheater*. Farnsborough: Gregg, 1969. 131p. il. Originally published in 1933. NE.

1226. _____. "Chinesische Shattenschnitte" *Cicerone* 15: 1036-1041, 1923. NE.

1227. _____. *Geschichte des Schattentheaters*. Berlin: 1907. See p.16-20. NE.

1228. Jacobs, A. Gertrude. *The Chinese-American Song and Game Book*. New York: Barnes, 1944. 96p. il., mus. A collection of children's games and songs, the text being authentic; the music supplied ad lib by helpful Americans.

1229. Jacquot, Jean, ed. *Les Théâtres d'Asie*. Paris: Editions du Centre National de la Recherche Scientifique, 1961. viii+308p. il. An anthology of articles on all major Asian theatre genres. Articles on Chinese theater discussed separately under individual authors. Review by George Lobsiger in *Asiatische Studien* 17(1-2):57-58, 1964.

1230. Jaegher, Raymond de. "Chinese Drama: The Popular Art for the General Public" *West and East* 8(8):2-5, Aug 1963. Brief, non-technical.

1231. Jan Yun-hua. "The Traces of Ancient Indian Music in China" *Journal of the Music Academy of Madras* 28: 92-99, 1957. NE.

1232. Janda, M. "Tanec Ve Staré Činé" [Dancing in Ancient China] *Nový Orient* 4:90-91, 1949. NE.

1233. Jang Čou [Chou Yang?]. "Přetváret a Rozvijet Operni Národni Uměni" *Hudebni Rozhledy* 7:237-240, 1954. NE.

1234. Jao Tsong-yi, ed. and Paul Demiéville, trans. *Airs de Touen-houang (Touen-houang k'iu), Textes à chanter des VIIIe-Xe siècles.* Paris: Centre National de la Recherche Scientifique, 1971. NE.

1235. Jeanneret, A. "Le Théâtre d'ombres en Orient" *Asiatische Studien* (Bern) 23(3-4):155-166. il. Comparative survey of shadow-play genres in China, Japan, Southeast Asia, and Turkey.

1236. Jen Teh-Yao. "The Children's Own Theatre" *China Reconstructs* 1:33-37, 1952. NE.

1237. Jenkins, B. "Notions of the Ancient Chinese Respecting Music: A Complete Translation of the Yok-Ki or Memorial of Music According to the Imperial Edition" *Journal of the Royal Asiatic Society, North China Branch* ns 5:30-57, 1868. Reprinted in *Promusica* 7(2):4-20, Dec 1928. A serviceable but not sufficiently annotated translation of this important document.

1238. Jiránek, Jaroslav. "Lidová Čina v Hudbě" [People's China in Musik] *Hudebni Rozhledy* 7:358-366, 1954. NE.

1239. _____. *Volkschina in der Musik.* Dresden: Kunst, 1955. 42p. Translation by B. Liehm. NE.

1240. John, J.W.H. "Chinese Music" *Chinese Recorder* 22 (7):311-313, July 1891. NE.

1241. John-Laugnitz, A. "Neue Beiträge zur Chinesischen Musikästhetik" *Allgemeine Musikzeitung* 32:546-548, 1905. Misleading.

1242. Johnson, Dale Ralph. "One Aspect of Form in the Arias of Yüan Opera" in *Two Studies in Chinese Literature* (Ann Arbor: University of Michigan, Center for Chinese Studies, 1968). (Michigan Papers in Chinese Studies, No. 3).

1243. _____. *The Prosody of Yüan-ch'ü.* Ph.D., University of Michigan, 1968. 2 vols., 418p. NE.

1244. _____. "The Prosody of Yüan Drama" *T'oung Pao* 56 (1-3):96-146, 1970. A detailed technical study, drawn from the author's doctoral thesis.

1245. Johnson, Florence Booco. *A Comparative Study of the Basic Musical Talents of Three Racial Groups: Chinese, Japanese and Part Hawaiian.* M.A. thesis, University of Hawaii, 1933. 95p. NE. "Six tests were administered to 300 subjects aged 14-20;

scores on the tests supported the view that Hawaiians show significant superiority in musical capacity when compared with the Japanese and Chinese." (N.F. Young, in *The Chinese in Hawaii*).

1246. Johnson, Irmgard. "The Reform of Peking Opera in Taiwan" *The China Quarterly* 57:140-145, Jan-March 1974. Johnson argues that the commonly held view that Peking opera is preserved in a traditional state in Taiwan is misleading, since several factors in its political, social, and artistic environment have significantly influenced its development.

1247. Johnson, Kinchen. *Folksongs and Children-Songs from Peiping*. Taipei: Orient Cultural Service, 1971. (Asian Folklore and Social Life Monographs, Vols. 16-17). 2 vols. ii+iv+v+428p. NE.

1248. Johnson, Thor. "Musical Tokyo, Taipei, and Hong Kong" *Music Journal* 16(6):10-11, Sept 1958. il. Report of tour; information on Western music activities.

1249. Johnston, Reginald F. *The Chinese Drama*. Shanghai: Kelly and Walsh, 1921. [vii]+36p., 6 plates. A large folio art book; the 6 color plates are from paintings by C.F. Winzer.

1250. _____. *Confucianism and Modern China*. London: Gollancz, 1934. 272p. See p.101-116 for discussion of music chapter from the *Li Chi*.

1251. Joint Performance Committee of the Proletarian Revolutionary Cultural and Athletic Workers of the Army, Navy and Airforce Units Stationed in Peking. "We Sing of Chairman Mao with Infinite Love" *China Reconstructs* 16(11):19-24, Nov 1967. il. On revolutionary song-and-dance performances.

1252. Jones, F.P. "Chinese Hymnology" *Chinese Christian Advocate*, p.4-5, Jan 1940. NE.

1253. Jones, Idwal. "Cathay on the Coast" *American Mercury* 8:453-460, 1926. On San Francisco's Chinatown, with passing mention of funeral music and theatre. [RR]

1254. Julien, Stanislaus. "Procédé des Chinois pour fabriquer les tam-tams et les cymbales" *Annales de Chimie* 54:329-331, 1833; followed by "Observations de M. Darcet sur la note précédente," p. 331-335. Summary in *Journal of the Asiatic Society of Bengal* 3:595-596.

1255. Jun, Uchimayama. "Doctrine: China; Theatre After 1949"
      Drama Review 15(2):252-257, Spring 1971. NE.

1256. Jungheinrich, Hans Klaus.   "Peking-Oper. Die rote
      Morgensonne, die Eis und Schnee Schmilzt"   *HiFi
      Stereophonie* 5:469-472, 1973. NE.

1257. _____. "Die Schönheit der Farbe Rot" *Die Oper Welt*
      1:45, 1973. NE.

                  * * * * * * * * * *

1258. Kabalevsky, Dimitri.   "Muzyka Svobodnogo Kitaja"
      [The Music of Free China] *Sovetskaya Muzyka* 5:
      105-113, 1952. NE.

1259. Kaellqvist, A.   "Bilder fraan Kina" *Nutida Musik*
      (Stockholm) 18(4):21-22, 1974-1975. NE.

1260. Kagan, Alan L. "Music and the Hundred Flowers Move-
      ment" *Musical Quarterly* 49(4):417-430, Oct 1963.
      Excellent survey of this aesthetico-political ex-
      cursion of Mao's thought and its repercussions.

1261. Kalaš, Julius.   "Ze Země Divů" [From Wonderland]
      Hudebni Rozhledy 11:1011-1012, 1958.   On Chinese
      folk music and instruments.

1262. Kaltenmark, Max.   "Les Danses Sacrées en Chine" in
      Sources Orientales 6: Les Danses Sacrées (Paris:
      Editions du Seuil, 1963), p.411-450. A good sur-
      vey largely devoted to discussion of dance,   as
      reported in the Chinese classics and annals.

1263. Kalvodová, Dana.   *Kchung Šang-ženův Vějiř s brosk-
      vovými Květy: Kapitoly ke studiu mingského dra-
      matu.* Thesis, Universita Karlova, Prague, 1968.

1264. _____. "On the Chinese Ch'uan-ch'i Drama" *Acta Uni-
      versitatis Carolinae: Philosophica et Historica*
      5:52-71, 1969. NE.

1265. _____. "The 'Baroque Spirit' of the Chinese Tradi-
      tional Stage" *Literature East and West* 14(4):511
      -518, 1970. NE.

1266. _____.   "Wang K'uei in Hell" *Dodder* 2:46-48, Jan
      1970.   Traces several versions of this popular
      story in Yüan, Ming, and contemporary drama.

1267. Kalvodová, Dana and Sis, Vanis. *Chinese Theatre*. London: Spring Books, 1957. 44 color plates of Peking Opera with impressionistic text, foldout appendices of properties, costumes, and musical instruments. Also in German as *Schules des Birngartens. Das chinesische Singspiel*.

1268. Kalvodová, Dana and V. Kubica. "O Činské Zpěvohře" [On Chinese Opera] *Nový Orient* 11(8):116-119, 1956. NE.

1269. _____. "Clowns in the Szechuan Theatre" *Bull, School of Oriental and African Studies* 28(2):356-362, 1965. il. NE.

1270. _____. "Lidové Divadlo v Číně" in *Vedeká Konferencia Orientalistov, 5th, Smolnice, 1961. Orientalistický Sborník* (Bratislava: Vydavatel'stvo Slovenskej Akadémie Vied, 1963), p.169-174. NE.

1271. _____. "The Origin and Structure of the Szechwan Theatre" *Archiv Orientalni* 34(4):505-523, 1966. A substantial, scholarly study; one of the few reliable sources of information on a local dramatic genre.

1272. _____. "The Type of Sheng Hero on the Stage in the Szechwan Province" *New Orient* 4:136-139, Oct 1965. il.

1273. Kaminskaia, N.V. and S.A. Strel'tsov, eds. *Kitaiskie Narodne Tantsy: Sbornik* [Chinese Folk Dances: Symposium]. Moscow: Iskusstvo, 1957. 74p. il. NE.

1274. Kao Chang-yin. "A Brilliant Example of Making Foreign Things Serve China: On the Revolutionary Symphonic Music 'Shachiapang'" *Chinese Literature* 11:96f., 1968. NE.

1275. Kao Liang. "'The Red Lantern' Which Cannot Be Put Out" *Chinese Literature* 3:19-23, 1967. On a modern Peking opera.

1276. Kao Tung-chia. *Le P'i-P'a-Ki, ou L'histoire du luth*. Paris: Imprimerie Royale, 1841. xx+275p. Translated by Bazin Ainé. This is a famous Chinese drama, not a scholarly study.

1277. Kao Yung-an. "China's Classical Theater" *Free China Review* 17(9):19-27, Sept 1967. il. Brief popular survey.

1278. Kaplan, Fredric. "China's Directed Drama" *Far Eastern Economic Review* 44:634-636, June 25, 1964. NE.

1279. Karlgren, Bernhard, trans. *The Book of Odes*. Stockholm: Museum of Far Eastern Antiquities, 1950. 270p. Authoritative translation, with Chinese characters and transliteration, but not in polished literary style. A major source book for early Chou and possible late Shang folkways. Detailed glosses have been published in the *Bulletin of the Museum of Far Eastern Antiquities*.

1280. _____. "On the Date of the Piao-Bells" *Bulletin of the Museum of Far Eastern Antiquities* 6:137-139, 1934.

1281. Kate, H. Ten. "The Musical Bow in Formosa" *American Anthropologist* 5:581, 1903. Brief description of three instruments in a Japanese exhibit from the Tsou, Vonum, and Puyama tribes named, respectively, *posoru*, *radyok*, and *ratŏk*.

1282. Kaufmann, Walter. "The Mathematical Determination of the Twelve *Lü* As Performed by Prince Liu An in his *Huai-nan Tzu* (Second Century B.C.)" in *Essays in Ethnomusicology: A Birthday Offering for Lee Hye-Ku* (Seoul: Korean Musicological Society, 1969), p.371-382. A mathematical and numerological study of this significant system for *lü* generation. Kuttner, in "The 749 Temperament ..." (below), points out that the system was most probably originated by Chu Tsai-yü in the 16th century A.D. Reviewed by Rulan Chao Pian in *Journal of the American Oriental Society* 88(3):636-640, July-Sept 1968.

1283. _____. *Musical Notations of the Orient: Notational Systems of East, South, and Central Asia*. Bloomington: Indiana University Press, 1967. xiv+498p. il., mus., index, bibliog. The first volume of a major work of scholarly explication of the main systems of notation in China, India, Tibet, and Japan. Numerous illustrations, transcriptions. The most reliable and substantial work in this field, it is organized in four sections: 1) Chinese *Lü* and Related Notations; 2) The Chinese Kung-Ch'e-P'u and Related Notations; Indian Notations and North Indian Drumming; 3) Zither Tablatures; and 4) The Notations of the Buddhist Chant (Tibet).

1284. _____. *Musical References in the Chinese Classics*. Detroit: Information Coordinators, 1976 (Monographs in Musicology, No. 5). 265p., il., mus. Collation of music-related passages from the five *ching* and the 4 *shu*, with essays on various musical topics as illustrated by usage in the Classics.

1285. _____. "Parallel Trends of Musical Liturgies and Notations in Eastern and Western Asia" *Orbis Musicae* 2(3-4):97-119, 1973-1974. NE.

1286. _____. "The Problem Concerning a Chinese Ming Bronze" *Ethnomusicology* 12(2):251-254, May 1968. il. Unusual bronze of scholar playing a small 4-string zither; four attendants stand by holding bowls. Problematic identification of instrument, context.

1287. Kelley, Edgar Stillman. "Observations on the Music of the Chinese" *American Art Journal* 59(1):22-24, April 16, 1892. il., mus. NE.

1288. Kelsey, Vera. "Gods of the Theatre" *Theatre Arts* 16:240-248, March 1932. NE.

1289. _____. "The New Theatre of China" *Theatre Arts Monthly*, June 1928.

1290. Keng Jen-hsia. "New Heroes on the Peking Opera Stage" *China Reconstructs* 13(8):2-5, Aug 1964. il. 37 new operas presented at Festival of Peking Opera on Contemporary Themes.

1291. Kenny, E.C. "Chinese Gongs" *Man* 27(113):165-168, Sept 1927. On bronze drums of the Karen tribe in Burma: Type 1, higher than wide, of indigenous manufacture. Type 2, wider than high, of Chinese manufacture. Type 2 has subtypes "male" (4 frogs on surface, little engraved decoration) and "female" (no frogs, much engraving).

1292. Kenzō, Hayashi. "Restoration of an Eighth Century Panpipe in the Shōsōin Repository, Nara, Japan" in Fritz A. Kuttner and Fredric Lieberman, eds. *Perspectives on Asian Music: Essays in Honor of Dr. Laurence E.R. Picken* (New York: Society for Asian Music, 1975), p.15-27. il. Detective work succeeds in re-uniting parts of a T'ang panpipe; detailed study of its scale, construction, and discussion of other T'ang instruments.

1293. Kersey, Mary E. "New Music for New China" *Musical America* 41(15):13, 30, Oct 10, 1941. il. Extolls virtues of Westernized mass-singing movement.

1294. Keszkowski, H. "Z Podrozy Chinskiej" *Ruch Muzyczny* 8(1):11-12, 1964. il. NE.

1295. Khê, Trần Văn. "Confucius, musicien et théoricien de la Musique" *France-Asie* 20(3):313-324, Spring 1966. NE.

1296. _____. "Le Théâtre musical de tradition chinoise" in *Zeitgenössisches Musiktheater. Hamburg 1964. Internationaler Kongress*, edited by Ernst Thomas (Hamburg, 1966), pp.121-123.

1297. _____. "Les Échelles régulières du cycle des quintes et leurs déformations occasionnelles" in *La Résonance dans les Echelles Musicales* (Paris: Editions du Centre National de la Recherche Scientifique, 1963), p.161-171. mus. With 20 musical examples on accompanying disc. Explanation of *lü* formation according to Ssu-ma Ch'ien and Lu Puwei. Discussion of modal characteristics of derivative pentatonic music in Vietnam. Theorizes constant pitch 1, 4, 5, 8, and varying 3, 6 due to "l'attraction des degrés faibles par les degrés forts, au facteur géographique, ou à l'intention du musicien de donner une expression quelconque à un dessin mélodique."

1298. _____. "Music Theatre in the Chinese Tradition" *Sangeet Natak* 2:37-42, April 1966. NE.

1299. _____. "Musical Tradition in Asia" *Eastern Horizon* 2(2):11-15, Feb 1962. Problems of preserving traditions in the modern world.

1300. _____. "Presenting the Eastern Tradition Under Conditions of Mass Distribution" in *Music—East and West, Report* (Tokyo: 1961), p.173-177. NE.

1301. _____. "Problems of Sino-Japanese Musical Tradition Today" in *Music—East and West, Report* (Tokyo: 1961), p.54-59. NE.

1302. _____. "Responsibilité des organisations pour la culture et l'éducation dans la préservation des traditions musicales des pays extrême-orientaux" in *Artistic Values in Traditional Music: Proceedings of a Conference Held in Berlin from the 14th to the 16th July 1965*, edited by Peter Crossley-Holland (Berlin: International Institute for Comparative Music Studies and Documentation, 1966), p.23-33.

1303. Ki Tche-jen. "La Musique Chinoise" *Diapason* (Belgium) 25, April-May 1932. NE.

1304. Kim Hak-chu. "Nuo-li and Tsa-hsi, with Emphasis on Those of China" *Journal of Asiatic Studies* (Seoul) 6(2):125-126, 1963. NE.

1305. Kindermann, Heinz, ed. *Fernöstliches Theater*. Stuttgart: Kröner, 1966. vii+526p. (Kröners Taschenausgabe, Bd. 353). NE.

1306. King, Carl Darlington. *The Conservation of Melodic Pitch Patterns by Elementary School Children As Determined by Ancient Chinese Music.* Ph.D. (Music), Ohio State University, 1972. 265p. NE.

1307. King, George. "Hymns and Music in Chinese" *Chinese Recorder* 20(3):133-134, March 1889. Short letter replying to Baldwin's query (see above), with a Chinese tune adopted for hymn singing, with four-part accompaniment.

1308. Kingsmill, Thomas W. "The Music of China" *Journal of the Royal Asiatic Society, North China Branch* 41:26-56, 1910. il. Discussion of history and historical sources, refuting Amiot, and suggesting that Western Asia gave China music theory and instruments.

1309. Kinkeldey, Otto. "Chinese Music" in *Encyclopedia Britannica*, Vol. 5. Introduction based on secondary sources. Has been replaced by Picken's more reliable article in recent editions (since 1966).

1310. Kishibe, Shigeo. "China, People's Republic of. II. Court Tradition (ya-yüeh)" in *Grove's Dictionary of Music and Musicians, 6th ed.* [In press]. Primarily an historical survey, this article is subdivided: 1) Introduction; 2) *Ya-yüeh* as Confucian Music; and 3) Banquet Music.

1311. _____. "Chinese Music" *Encyclopedia International* 1969 ed. IV,379-380.

1312. _____. "A Chinese Painting of the T'ang Court Women's Orchestra" in *The Commonwealth of Music,* edited by Gustav Reese and Rose Brandel (New York: Free Press of Glencoe, 1965), p.104-117. il. Detailed study establishes relative reliability as musicological evidence of a painting used by Sachs in the *Rise of Music.* Sheds light on the whole problem of pictorial evidence in the reconstruction of musical systems.

1313. _____. "La Danse du Confucianisme" in Jacques Porte, editor, *Encyclopédie des Musiques Sacrées* (Paris: Labergerie, 1968), I,265-267. il., trans. by Paul Galloni d'Istria. Brief historical survey, with mention of Korean survivals.

1314. _____. "Emigration of Musicians ..." in *Annals of the Institute of History, Faculty of General Culture, Tokyo University I, 1953.* NE.

1315. _____. *A Historical Study of the Music in the T'ang Dynasty*. Tokyo: University of Tokyo Press, 1960-1961. 2 vols. Part I, "Music Organization in the Court," in Japanese with good English summary (II,1-46). The first installment of a monumental project on T'ang music by the leading scholar in this field. An authoritative study of the performing groups, musicians, their status, duties, etc., in the Imperial Court.

1316. _____. "Musique religieuse en Chine" in *Encyclopédie des Musiques Sacrées, I*, edited by Jacques Porte (Paris: Labergerie, 1968), p.272-274. il., bibliog. Translated by Paul Galloni d'Istria. Short notes on each religion: Shamanism, Confucianism, Taoism, Buddhism, Lamaism.

1317. _____. "The Origin of the K'ung-hou" *Journal of the Society for Research in Asiatic Music (Tōyō Ongaku Kenykū)*, 29(2-3):1-51, 1954. il., maps. Distinguishes 3 types of harp (angular harp, arched harp, zither harp), all of which have been known in China, and traces their routes of migration from West Asia.

1318. _____. "The Origin of the P'i-P'a" *Transactions of the Asiatic Society of Japan* 2s, 19:259-304, 1940. il. Distinguishes three types of short and long-necked lutes, traces their introduction into China, and their subsequent development.

1319. _____. "Rites du Taô" in *Encyclopédie des Musiques Sacrées, I*, edited by Jacques Porte (Paris: Labergerie, 1968), p.268-271. il. Translated by Paul Galloni d'Istria. Brief survey mentioning history, ceremony, and instruments. A sample of music is included on the accompanying disc.

1320. _____. "Twenty-Four Female Musicians Carved on the Stone Coffin of Wang Chien, in the Ch'ien-Shu Dynasty" *Transactions of the International Congress of Orientalists in Japan* 1:9-21, 1956. See p.9-10 for short English summary of Japanese article.

1321. Kitaiskaya Filarmoniya. "Otkrytoe Pismo Rabotnikov Kitaiskoi Filarmonii—Sovetskim Muzykantam" [An Open Letter to Soviet Musicians from the Workers of the Chinese Philharmonia] *Sovetskaya Muzyka* 2: 99-100, 1941. NE.

*   Klabund [pseudonym]. See Alfred Henschke.

1322. Klaproth, Julius Henrich. "Notice de l'encyclopédie littéraire de Ma Touan Lin, intitulée Wen Hian Thoung K'hao. Section XV, de la musique" *Journal Asiatique* 2s, 10:97-101, Aug 1832. Reprinted in *Revue Musicale* 12:316-318, 1832. Translation of part of the preface to the music section of this famous encyclopedia.

1323. _____. "Über die Musik der Chinesen (Brüchstuck eines Brief aus Copenhagen)" *Asiatisches Magazin* 1:64-68, 1802. mus. NE.

1324. Klein, Howard. "After Ping-Pong, Rock 'n' Egg Roll?" *New York Times* Sec. 2, 27:1, Sept 26, 1971. NE.

1325. Kler, Joseph. "Chants de Nomades au Pays des Ortos" *Oriens* 12(1-2):190-197, 1959. Includes information on tunes, instruments, and text.

1326. Kluenter, Beatrice. "Chinese Music" *Christmas: An American Annual of Christmas Literature and Art* 15:52-60, 1945. mus. NE.

1327. Knopff, Max. "Musikinstrumente, Rundfunk- und Fernsehgeräte in der Volksrepublik China" *Instrumentenbau Zeitschrift* 14:32, 1959. NE.

1328. Knosp, Gaston. "Les Chants d'amour dans la musique orientale" *Bulletin Français de la Société Internationale de Musique* 4(7):768-791, July 15, 1908. il., mus. Comparative survey of love songs from Arabia to Japan, stressing South China and Indo-China.

1329. _____. "Le Eulh-Ya et la musique chinoise" *Guide Musical* 54:571-576- 591-595, 1908. il., mus. NE.

1330. _____. "La Musique dans l'éducation chinoise" *Mercure de France* ns 83:757-761, 1910.

1331. _____. "Notes sur la tablature chinoise" *Revue Musicale de Lyon* 6:785-791, 1931. mus. NE.

1332. Ko Hsing. "The 'Flowers' of Chinghai" *China Reconstructs* 11(2):20-21, Feb 1962. Brief description and texts of folk songs from this region.

1333. Ko I-ching. "Tali Folksongs" *Bulletin of Chinese Studies* 7:239-244, Sept 1947. mus. NE.

1334. Koegler, Horst and Edgard Schall. "Zweimal chinesische Oper" *Musikleben* 8(9):319-321, Sept 1955. il. Reviews of performances by Chinese troupes in Paris and Berlin.

1335. Kohl, Louis von. "Die Grundlagen des altchinesisches Staates und die Bedeutung der Riten und der Musik" *Bässeler-Archiv* 17(2):53-98, 1934. NE.

1336. _____. "Tonende Amtsembleme. Zur Entwicklungsgeschichte der chinesischen Musik" *Sinica* 7:5-11, 1932. NE.

1337. Kornfeld, Fritz. "Chinas Katholosche Kirchenmusik im aufbruch einer neuen Zeit" in 2 *Internationalen Kongress für Katholische Kirchenmusik Wien, 4-10 Oct. 1954. Bericht* (Wien: Herold, 1955), p.265-268. NE.

1338. _____. *Die Tonale Struktur Chinesischer Musik.* Mödling bei Wien: St. Gabrieler Verlag, 1955. 143p. il., mus. (St. Gabrieler Studien 26). Study of mode, stressing anhemitonic-pentatonic nature of Chinese music. Numerous transcriptions. Theorizes that mode is determined by relationship of a 3-pitch nucleus to lowest pitch of tune. "... the Chinese fiddler's view of nature of the Peking-Opera styles, *erh-huang, fan erh-huang, hsi-p'i*, and *fan hsi-p'i* was [in this book] for the first time made plain: that they are fingerings, and that each corresponds to a key. What Fr. Kornfeld stated about the structure of pentatonic modes was not a theory, but a fact. In any case, the musical differences between the Peking-Opera styles are not modal." (Laurence Picken, in *Ethnomusicology* 18(1):158, Jan 1974). Review by Hans Eckardt in *Sinologica* 5(1):63-64, 1956.

1339. Krause, Ernst. "Chinas neue Oper" *Aufbau* 11:1025-1028, 1951. Survey of politically induced reforms.

1340. Krauss, ---. "Musique Chinoise" *Bulletin du Comité d'Extrême-Orient, 1904.* NE.

1341. Krauss, H. "Altchinesische Militärmusik und Militärsignale" *Deutsche Militär-Musiker-Zeitung* 29:647, 1907. NE.

1342. Kravchenko, T. "Poezda v Kitai" [A Journey to China] *Sovetskaya Muzyka* 1:107-110, Jan 1950. il., mus. NE.

1343. Krehbiel, Henry Edward. "Chinese Music" *Century Illustrated Monthly* ns 19:449-457, 1891. mus. German translation, "Chinesische Musik" *Globus* 62 (2):25-31, 1892. mus. Brief discussion based on Van Aalst and Amiot. Five tunes harmonized.

1344. Krohn, Ilmari. "Über die Chinesischen Melodien von P. du Halde" *Zeitschrift der Internationalen Musikgesellschaft* 3(4):174-176, 1902. Last of a series of short notes ancillary to Dechevrens article. Krohn query 3(1):40-41; Dechevrens answer 3(3):125-126. Corrects errors in the transcriptions in Dechevrens article.

1345. Krueger, H.E. "Christian Music and Painting in China" *China Journal* 30(2):79-82, Feb 1939. il. General report on Protestant and Catholic missionary work in the first part of this century. Four color plates, one black and white.

1346. Ku I-ts'iao. "Twenty-Five Poems Set to Old Music" *Chinese Culture* 5(4):40-59, June 1964. NE.

1347. Kuan Su-shuang. "How I Played Taino" *Chinese Literature* 10:72-76, 1964. il. On a new Peking opera by the leading actress.

1348. Kuang Hsin. "Mao Tse-tung's Thought Guides Us in the Great Revolution of Peking Opera—A Discussion on the Experience of Scriptwriting and Rehearsing by the Opera Group of *Taking the Bandit's Stronghold* of the Peking Opera Theatre of Shanghai" in *On the Revolution of Peking Opera,* ed. Chiang Ching (Peking, 1968), p.15-26.

1349. Kucharskij, Vasilij Fedos'eveič. "Muzyka Svobodnogo Kitaja" [Music in the Chinese People's Republic] *Sovetskaya Muzyka* 4:167-176; 8:170-180; 10:155-167, April, Aug, Oct 1959. NE.

1350. Kuh Koh-nie. *A Musicological Study of the Important Tonal Systems of the T'ang Dynasty (A.D. 618-907).* Ed.D. dissertation, New York University, 1942. 271p.

1351. Kühnert, F. "Bestehen Beziehungen zwischen chinesischer und hungarischer Musik" *Keleti Szemele* 3:1-13, 1902. mus. NE.

1352. _____. "Chinesische Musik" *Presse,* April 19, 1893. NE.

1353. _____. "Zur Kenntnis der chinesischen Musik" *Wiener Zeitschrift für die Kunde des Morgenlandes* 14:126-148, 1900. NE.

1354. Kummel, Otto. *Ostasiatisches Gerät.* Berlin: Bruno Cassirer, 1925. See "Musikinstrumente," p.137-140, il. NE.

1355. Kuo Chang-yang. *Chinese Art Song: A Melodic Analysis*. Taipei: Hwa Kang Press, College of Chinese Culture, 1972. xvi+232p., mus. Photo-offset publication of author's M.A. thesis, University of Hawaii, 1972. Examines 20th-century acculturated art songs; after detailed analysis, Kuo concludes that "although superficially the Chinese art song sounds like Western music, there are really many Chinese musical characteristics maintained." (p. 200).

1356. Kuo Fu-yu et al. "We Love the New Piano Music with Peking Opera Singing" *China Reconstructs* 17(10): 23-25, Oct 1968. il. Celebrations of "The Red Lantern" by six workers, peasants, and soldiers.

1357. Kuo Han-cheng. "New Developments in the Traditional Chinese Theatre" *Chinese Literature* 1:127-139, 1960. Report on the modernization of traditional operas. Author is head of the Repertory Research Department of the Chinese Drama Research Institute.

1358. _____. "On the Adaptation of China's Classical Drama" *Chinese Literature* 12:100-108, Dec 1962. NE.

1359. Kuo Mo-jo. "And the Jade-Like Firmament Was Cleared at Last" *Chinese Literature* 5:118-122, 1966. On the opera "The Monkey Subdues the Demon." NE.

1360. Kuo Nai-an. "The Militant Task of Critic of Music Theory: To Promote the Proletariat and Eradicate the Bourgeoisie" *Selections from China Mainland Magazines* 463:9-13, April 5, 1965. From *Jen-min Yin-yüeh*, Aug-Sept 1964. NE.

1361. Kuo Nai-nan. "Developing China's Heritage of Folk Music" *People's China* 17:18, 23-26, Sept 1, 1953. il.

1362. _____. "Their Voice Still Lives: Nieh Erh (1912-1935), Hsien Hsing-hai (1905-1945)" *People's China* 23:32-36, 1955. On two of the most popular composers of Westernized music in modern China.

1363. Kuo Shih-wu. "A Ceramic Lute of the Sung Dynasty" *China Journal* 11(5):218-221, Nov 1929. il. Translated by John C. Ferguson. Good description of a unique ceramic *ch'in* in the Imperial Palace Collection.

1364. Kurosawa, Takatomo. *The Musical Bow of the Vunun Tribe in Formosa and Suggestion As to the Origin of the Pentatonic Scale*. Tokyo: Japan Music Institute [*ca*. 1952]. 11p., mus. Vague study based on field research, with transcriptions of 13 tunes. Poor English hampers comprehension.

1365. Kurzbach, Paul. "Meine Eindrücke vom Musikleben in den Volksrepublik China" *Musik und Gesellschaft* 6:105-107, July 1956.

1366. Kuttner, Fritz Alexander [b.1903]. "Acoustical Skills and Techniques in Ancient China." Unpublished manuscript.

1367. _____. "Ch'ien Lo-chih" in *MGG*, Supplement, Cols. 1448-1449.

1368. _____. "China: The Hidden Relations Between Language and Music" *Musical America* 70(2):5, 40, 72, Jan 15, 1950. il. In German as "Die Verborgenen Beziehungen Zwischen Sprache und Musik, Dargestellt am Beispiel Chinas" *Musica* 5(1):13-16, 1951. il. Good explanation of tonal language system and its influence on melody and possibly on instrument construction.

1369. _____. "Ching Fang" in *MGG*, Supplement, Cols. 1456-1457.

1370. _____. "Chu Tsai-yü" in *MGG*, Supplement, Cols. 1481-1483.

1371. _____. "Jean Joseph Marie Amiot" in *MGG*, Supplement, Cols. 182-183.

1372. _____. "The Music of China" *Stereo Review* 31(4):62-69, Oct 1973. il. Survey of the contemporary scene in the People's Republic in the context of Chinese tradition.

1373. _____. "The Music of China: A Short Historical Synopsis Incorporating the Results of Recent Musicological Investigations" *Ethnomusicology* 8(2): 121-127, May 1964. Succinct article stressing findings of archeomusicology and tracing the main lines of historical development. This point of view deserves a more thorough treatment.

1374. _____. "The Musical Significance of Archaic Chinese Jades of the Pi Disk Type" *Artibus Asiae* 16:25-50, Sept 1953. il. Presents controversial hypothesis that *pi*-disks were carefully tuned by sophisticated acoustic techniques, and are closely related to the known forms of sounding jade.

1375. _____. "A Musicological Interpretation of the Twelve Lüs in China's Traditional Tone System" *Ethnomusicology* 9(1):22-38, Jan 1965. Tables. Stimulating discussion of sinomusicological evidence for meaning and derivation of the traditional names given to the 12 pitch tubes. Again, Kuttner stresses the great acoustic sophistication that he feels was present in archaic China.

1376. _____. "La Musique des Sacrifices Confucéens" in *Encyclopédie de Musiques Sacrées*, edited by Jacques Porte (Paris: Editions Labergerie, 1968), I,250-264. il., mus. Translated by Paul Galloni d'Istria. Surveys current knowledge of Confucian ceremonial music in China, with information on sources, history, instruments, and some samples of the text. Does not consider related genres in Korea or Japan.

1377. _____. "Prince Chu Tsai-yü's Life and Work; A Re-Evaluation of his Contribution to Equal Temperament Theory" *Ethnomusicology* 19(2):163-206, May 1975. il., tables. A detailed, thorough study of contributions to equal temperament theory by Chu and Stevin, correcting and clarifying Robinson's discussion (in Needham, below). Includes a biography of Chu, description of his principal works and their original ideas, explanation of his calculation methods, detailed abstract of his major treatise, and discussion of his own comments on the originality of his discoveries. Highly recommended.

1378. _____. "Ein 'Pythagoräisches' Tonsystem in China, mehrere Jahrhunderte vor seinem Auftreten im mitteländischen Kulturkreis." Unpublished manuscript.

1379. _____. "A 'Pythagorean' Tone System in China, Antedating the Early Greek Achievements by Several Centuries" in *Bericht über den 7 Internationalen Musikwissenschaftliche Kongress Köln 1958*, p.174 -176.

1380. _____. "Report on Two Research Grants, Received for the Completion and Research on a Two-Volume Manuscript: The Music of China—A Historical and Sociological Essay" in *1952 Yearbook of the American Philosophical Society*, p.291-292. NE.

1381. _____. "The Science of Music in Ancient China" *High Fidelity* 5(6):32-34, 81-82, Aug 1955. il. Good popular introduction to mathematical and acoustical theory in Chou and Shang dynasties. Discusses tuning methods in bell-casting, lithofacture.

1382. _____. "The 749-Temperament of Huai Nan Tzu" in *Perspectives on Asian Music: Essays in Honor of Dr. Laurence E.R. Picken*, Fritz A. Kuttner and Fredric Lieberman, eds. (New York: Society for Asian Music, 1975), p.88-112. il., charts. A search for the origins of this unusual device for approximating equal temperament reveals that Prince Chu Tsai-yü falsely attributed it to Huai Nan Tzu, and that Prince Chu most probably devised it himself from clues in post-Han sources.

1383. _____. "Transmission of Acoustical-Mathematical Knowledge from West Asia to East China Before 1000 B.C." in *Proceedings of the Fourth International Congress for Iranian Art and Archaeology, April-May 1960, New York and Washington, D.C.* (Kobe: Gluck, in press).

1384. _____. "Zur Entwicklung des Musikbegriffes in Chinas Frühgeschichte" in *Festschrift für Walter Wiora* (Kassel: Bärenreiter, 1967), p.536-544. Aspects of music culture and musical concepts, derived from careful examination of oracle bone characters and other early written sources. English translation by Leroy I. Richmond and Fredric Lieberman, "The Development of the Concept of Music in China's Early History" *Asian Music* 1(2): 12-21, Fall 1969.

1385. Kuttner, Fritz A. and Fredric Lieberman, eds. *Perspectives on Asian Music: Essays in Honor of Dr. Laurence E.R. Picken*. New York: Society for Asian Music, 1975 [Special double issue VI (1-2) of *Asian Music*]. Includes articles on Chinese music by: Chuang Pen-li, Martin Gimm, Kenzō Hayashi, Fritz A. Kuttner, Fredric Lieberman, David M.Y. Liang, A.C. Scott, and Barbara B. Smith. See individual authors for annotations.

1386. Kwong, Edward Y.K. "A Brief History of the Chinese Opera" *Free China Review* 8:6-10, April 1958. il.

* * * * * * * * * *

1387. Laade, Wolfgang. *Die Situation von Musikleben und Musikforschung in den Ländern Afrikas und Asiens und die neuen Aufgaben der Musikethnologie*. Tutzing: Hans Schneider, 1969. 227p. See "China," p.144-157.

1388. Labat, Jean-Baptiste. "Étude sur la musique chinoise" in his *Oeuvres Littéraires-Musicales* (Paris: Bauer, 1879-1883), II,153-169. NE.

1389. Lach, Robert. "Musik in China" *Auftakt* 2(2):35-38,
1922. NE.

1390. Lachmann, Robert. *Musik Des Orients*. Breslau: Jed-
ermann's Bücherei, 1929. Reprint Oosterhout,
Netherlands: Antrhopological Publications, 1966.
136p. il., mus., bibliog. An early, much-used
handbook presenting an overview of the Oriental
music cultures as a large music area, with relatively little detail on individual cultures or
genres.

1391. La Fage, J. Adrien de. *Histoire Générale de la Musique et la Danse*. Paris: Comptoir des Imprimeurs
Unis, 1844. See I,1-400 on "Musique des Chinois."

1392. Laloy, Ernest Louis Alfred (1874-1944). "Chinese
Music" *Musical Times*, March-April 1907. NE.

1393. _____. "Confucius Musicien" *Annales Franco-Chinoises*
(Lyon) 1(2):25-26, 1927. A brief note on Confucius as performer and listener, based on the *Analects* and Han Ying.

1394. _____. "Hoaî-nân Tzè et la musique" *T'oung Pao* 15:
501-530, 1914. Discussion of the musical passages
in the writings of this major classical philosopher.

1395. _____. *La Musique Chinoise*. Paris: Laurens, 1910.
128p. il., mus. A good popular survey with a max-
imum of philosophy and anecdotes drawn from the
Chinese classics and a minimum of technical detail. Most transcriptions are reprinted from Van
Aalst. Spanish translation by Melanie Forest, *La
Musica China*. Buenos Aires: Editorial Schapire.
126p. (Colección Alba, 14). Tr. NE, copy in library of the Pan American Union, Washington, D.C.
Review by A. Mancini in *Bulletin de l'Association
Amicale Franco-Chinoise* 2(3):300-301, July 1910.

1396. _____. "La Musique et les philosophes chinois" *Revue
Musicale* 6(4):132-139, Feb 1, 1925. First part
of a study not continued. Deals with music in
Confucian philosophy.

1397. _____. *Mirror of China.* New York: Knopf, 1936. x+
308p. Impressions of a trip to China made in the
early '30s. Translated from the French *Miroir
de la Chine* (Deschée De Brouwer, 1933) by Catherine Alison Philips. Musical observations *passim*; see especially "A Concert" (p.50-54) mostly
on *ch'in*, "At Mei Lan-fang's" (p.153-156); includes a performance by Liu T'ien-hua, "A Family
Party," with private opera performance (p.156-
161), "The Theatre" (p.162-166).

1398. _____. "T'a Tao" *Revue Musicale de la Société Internationale de la Musique* 10(5):51-53, May 1914.
Short essay on the aesthetic morphology of Chinese dance contrasted with that of the West. Sympathetic, understanding, and idealistic.

1399. Lam, Shui-took. *Der Ursprung der chinesischen Tanz-
masken im Exorzismus.* Ph.D. dissertation, Köln,
1969. vi+130p. NE.

1400. Lamplugh, G.W. "In a Chinese Theatre" *Macmillan's*
57:36-40, 1888. NE.

1401. Landry, R.J. "Red Chinese Put Their Show on the
Road, Wows Zurich But It Ain't Opera" *Variety*
200:2, Sept 14, 1955.

1402. Langdon, William B. *A Descriptive Catalogue of the
Chinese Collection Now Exhibiting at St. George's
Place Hyde Park Corner* ... London: Printed for
the Proprietor, 1843. See p.92-94 for musical
instruments, Nos. 591-617, with brief descriptions.

*   Lao She. See Shu She-yü.

1403. Lapham, Claude. "China Needs American Bands" *Metronome* 52(7):13, 39, July 1936.

1404. _____. "More Jobs in the Orient" *Metronome* 52(11):
17, 56, Nov 1936.

1405. Laszky, B. "Die Anfänge der Musik bei den Chinesen,
Japanern und Indern" *Süddeutsche Wochenschrift* 1
(4):--. NE.

*   Lau Shaw. See Shu She-yü.

1406. Laudermilk, J.D. "Concerning Chinese Music" *California Arts and Architecture* 56:24f., Oct 1939.
NE.

1407. Laufer, Berthold. "Chinese Bells, Drums and Mirrors"
Burlington Magazine 57:183-187, 1930. NE.

132

1408. _____. "Chinese Pigeon Whistles" *Scientific American* ns, 98:394, 1908. il. NE.

1409. _____. *Jade, A Study in Chinese Archaeology and Religion.* Chicago: Field Museum of Natural History, 1912. (Pub. No. 154, Anthropological Series, Vol. X.)

1410. _____. *Oriental Theatricals.* Chicago: Field Museum of Natural History, 1923. 59p. il. Guidebook to an exhibit of masks and puppets. Discusses "Chinese Religious Drama," "Imperial Play," "Lion Dance," "Shadowplay." No musical information.

1411. Law, Frederic S. "Is There a Yellow Peril in Music?" *New Music Review* 9, 1910.

1412. Lay, George Tradescant. *The Chinese As They Are: Their Moral, Social, and Literary Character.* London: Ball, 1841. xii+324p. il. See p.75-93, "Music of the Chinese." Essentially similar to the following article, slightly simplified, though with occasional added material. There is also a less useful chapter on Drama.

1413. _____. "Remarks on the Musical Instruments of the Chinese, With an Outline of Their Harmonic System" *Chinese Repository* 8:38-54, May 1839. il. An interesting early report. Though Lay displays many typical colonial attitudes, his curiosity overpowers his biases, and some valuable observations shine through. One of the earliest scholars to attempt performance on Chinese instruments.

1414. Lebesque, Morvan. "Die Pekinger Oper: Eine Pariser Sensation" *Melos* 22(12):365-366, Dec 1965.

1415. Lederer-Prina, F. "Die Musik bei den Chinesen, Musikgeschichtliche Studie" *Die Musik-Mappe* 1(19): 75-76, 1906. NE.

1416. Lee Dai-Kong. "Musical Instruments of Old and Modern Cathay" *Étude* 53(2):73-74, Feb 1935. il. Descriptions and photos of typical instruments.

1417. Lee, James Zee Min. *Chinese Potpourri.* Hong Kong: Oriental Publishers, 1950. See "Chinese Music," p.240-253. il. Poor.

1418. Lee, Jon. "Some Curious Chinese Customs and Beliefs in California" *California Folklore Quarterly*, p. 191-204, July 1943. Brief notes on Chinese opera, social status of actors. [RR]

1419. Lee Pao-ch'en. "Biography of Prof. Liang Tsai-ping" in *On Chinese Music*, edited by Liang Tsai-ping. Short review of Prof. Liang's numerous musical activities.

1420. _____. "China: Music" in *Encyclopedia Americana*, VI,553-555.

1421. _____. "A Few Striking Features of Chinese Music" in *A Symposium on Chinese Culture*, edited by Cheng Chi-pao (Taipei: China Language Institute in America and American Association of Teachers of Chinese Language and Culture, 1964), p.41-44. Very elementary review of some basic theoretical concepts (*lü-lü*, etc.). A condensation of his "Music of the Chinese People."

1422. _____. "Music in New China" *Étude* 63(8):444, 474, Aug 1945. il. Rise of patriotic songs after Japanese occupation. Acceptance of Western music. Anecdotal, interesting.

1423. _____. "Music of the Chinese People" *China and America* 1(3):6-12, May 1948. Basic introduction to traditional theory, history, instruments, notation.

1424. _____. "Musical Advance in China" *Étude* 63(9):487, 535, 538, Sept 1945. il. Part 2 of "Music in New China."

1425. _____. *Songs of Fighting China*. New York: Chinese News Service, 1939. NE.

1426. Lee, Sherman E. "The Shêng Player: A T'ang Wine Pitcher" *Far Eastern Ceramics Bulletin* 6(3):6-11, Sept 1954. il.

1427. Lee Siow Mong. "Some Popular Chinese Musical Instruments" *Pelita* 3(4):21-24, 1965. il. NE.

1428. Lee, Tommy. "Chinese Drama Asserts Itself" *Free China Review* 16(3):19-24, March 1966. il. Opera in Taiwan aided by Tan Yen-hua, an actress who fled from the Mainland.

1429. _____. "Musical Meteor in Skirts" *Free China Review* 16(5):29-32, May 1966. il. Success of young (25) conductor, Helen Quach.

1430. Lee Tsung-ying. "Eastern Diary" *Eastern Horizon* 6(8):2-9, Aug 1967. il. On the modern Peking opera "Taking the Bandit's Stronghold." Four pages of color photos.

1431. Lee-you Ya-oui. *Le Théâtre Classique en Chine et en France d'après l'Orphelin de la Chine et l'Orphelin de la Famille Tchao.* Paris: Presses Modernes, 1937. vii+186p. Ph.D. dissertation, University of Paris. NE.

1432. Legge, James. *The Chinese Classics.* London: Trübner, 1861-1872. 5 vols. Legge's translations are still considered excellent, though their language is a bit stilted. More recent authors have produced better versions of individual classic books, but Legge's collection remains the only convenient one.

1433. Lemière, J. Em. "The Sing-Song Girl: From a Throne of Glory to a Seat of Ignominy" *China Journal of Science and Arts* 1(2):126-134, 1923. Sociological study. NE.

1434. Lenherr, Joseph. "Advancing Indigenous Church Music" *African Music* 4(2):33-39, 1968. bibliog. On newly composed church music in Rhodesia and Taiwan.

1435. _____. "The Musical Instruments of the Taiwan Aborigines" *Bulletin of the Institute of Ethnology, Academia Sinica* 23:109-128, Spring 1967. il., 4 plates. Ethnographic survey compiling data from many sources and adding material from firsthand field research.

1436. Lenz, Frank B. "He Taught China to Sing" *Christian Herald,* p.30-31, 51-52, Oct 1942. About Liu Liang-mo's mass-singing movement.

1437. Leonida, Madelaine Kao. "Chinese Ethnic Dance for Modern Mankind" *Journal of Health, Physical Education, Recreation* (Washington, D.C.) 42(6): 49-50, June 1971. NE.

1438. Lepel, Felix von. *Die Musik in Alten China: Eine Kulturgeschichtliche Studie.* [n.c., n.p.]: The Author, 1954. 16p. A short section from a larger work, *Theater und Musik im Alten China,* of which the manuscript was lost in the war.

1439. Leung Chun-kin. "Notes on Cantonese Opera in North America" *CHINOPERL Papers* 7:9-21, 1977. il. Descriptive notes on a Toronto club, with social and historical background.

1440. Leung George Kin. "The Chinese Actress" *Asia* 27(12): 1028-1034, 1040, 1042, Dec 1927. Some popular female Peking opera stars described and compared with female impersonators. Leung prefers real females.

1441. _____. "The Chinese Actress" *Pacific Affairs* 4:394
-407, 1931. NE.

1442. _____. "The Chinese Theatre" *Chinese Mercury* 1:26-
27, Spring 1938. NE.

1443. _____. "The Chinese Theatre: A Brief Consideration"
in his *Special Plays and Scenes...* (see below);
also in *Mei Lan-fang: Chinese Drama*, Ernest K.
Moy, ed. (see below), [7-8].

1444. _____. "The Ching or Painted Face Characters of the
Chinese Stage" *China Journal* 13:55-61, 1930. NE.

1445. _____. "Comedians of the Chinese Stage" *Pacific Affairs* 3:437-447, 1930. NE.

1446. _____. "Cross-Currents in the Chinese Theatre" *Pacific Affairs* 8:433-438, Dec 1935. NE.

1447. _____. "Dramas of the Three Kingdoms Period" *China
Journal of Science and Arts* 6(6):281-293, 1927.
On various operas using stories from the *Three
Kingdoms Romance*.

1448. _____. "The Dramatic Role of Kuang Kung as Portrayed
by Mr. Lin Shu-shen of Kung Wutai" *China Journal*
5:4-8, 1926. NE.

1449. _____. "The Enjoyment of Chinese Drama" *China Journal* 6(1):7-12, Jan 1927. Brief, non-technical.

1450. _____. "The Female Impersonator of the Chinese Stage"
China Journal 5:164-174, 1926. NE.

1451. _____. "The Five Incomparables of Peking" *China
Journal* 9(3):111-116, Sept 1928. il. Brief no-
tices on outstanding actors Mei Lan-fang, Yang
Hsiao-lou, Yu Shu-yen, Kung Yun-fu, Chen Te-lin.

1452. _____. "The Historical Drama 'Wen Chi's Return to
Han,' As Produced by Mr. Ch'eng Yen-chiu" *China
Journal* 9(6):270-275, Dec 1928. il.

1453. _____. "Hsin Ch'ao (The New Tide). New Trends in the
Traditional Chinese Drama" *Pacific Affairs*, p.
175-183, 1929. NE.

1454. _____. "Lin Shu-shen in the Dramatic Role of Kuang
Kung" *China Journal of Science and Arts* 5, 1926.
NE.

1455. _____. "Mei Lan-fang" *China Journal* 12(1):5-9, Jan
1930. il.

1456. _____, ed. *Mei Lan-fang: Foremost Actor of China.*
Shanghai: Commercial Press, 1929. xii+132p.,
many photos and plates. Foreword by J. Leighton
Stuart, Preface by George Kin Leung, Chapters by
Chi Ju-shan and Huang Chiu-yao. Introduction to
the Chinese theatre, life and career of Mei Lan-
fang.

1457. _____. "Mei Lan-fang in One of His Plays. Charming
Hsi-Jen" *China Arts and Handicrafts* 1(4):14, 1932.
NE.

1458. _____. "Mei Lan-fang (The Man and His Art)" *Journal
of the Royal Asiatic Society, North China Branch*
58:57-69, 1927. il. NE.

1459. _____. "Melon-Seed Yang" *Asia* 34(12):760-766, Dec
1934. il. Short story about a Peking opera actor.

1460. _____. "The Modern Chinese Theater" *Asia* 36(2):103-
106, Feb 1936. il. On the spoken drama.

1461. _____. "The Sheng or Male Characters of the Chinese
Stage" *China Journal* 12(6):319-325, June 1930. il.

1462. _____. *Special Plays and Scenes to be Presented by
Mei Lan-fang on His American Tour.* Peking: The
Author, 1929. Includes an article, "The Chinese
Theatre: A Brief Consideration," biographical
notes on Mei Lan-fang extracted from Leung's book
on Mei, and synopses of 11 plays and 12 scenes.
The material in this book was reprinted verbatim
in the souvenir program for the American tour,
edited by E.K. Moy (see below). The title is
given on the book's cover as *Repertoire for the
American Tour of Mei Lan-fang.*

1463. Levis, John Hazedel. "Chinese Music" *Asia* 37(12):
863-866, Dec 1937. Short introduction to the mood
of Chinese music and its melodic art.

1464. _____. *Foundations of Chinese Musical Art.* Peiping:
Vetch, 1936. Reprinted, New York: Paragon, 1964.
xiii+233p. il., mus., tables, bibliog. One of
the first scholarly studies to approach Chinese
music from the viewpoint of Western analytic musicology. Deals with the art of melodics associated with classic lyric poetry, and in general
with language-melody relationships. Occasional
errors, idiosyncracies, and sinophilic overstate-
ments. Use with care. Reviewed by: *Times Literary Supplement* p.41, Jan 16, 1937; B.Z.N. Ing in
T'ien-Hsia Monthly 4:317-318, March 1937; J.K.
Shyrock in *Journal of the American Oriental So-*

ciety 57:201-202, June 1937; Jaap Kunst in *T'oung Pao* 33:184-190, 1937; Fredric Lieberman in *Journal of Asian Studies* 29(4):912-913, Aug 1970.

1465. _____. *Fundamentals of Chinese Melody, Rhythm and Form As Seen Through the Music Poems of Ancient China.* Peking: 1933. Preface by Liu Fu. NE.

1466. _____. "The Music of China" *Musical Courier* 104(3): 7, Jan 16, 1932. mus. Good description of heterophony and melodic structure.

1467. _____. "The Musical Art of Ancient China" *T'ien-Hsia Monthly* 1(4):404-422, Nov 1935. mus. Brief exposition of language-melody theory.

1468. _____. "Phonology and Calligraphy in Chinese Art" *T'ien-Hsia Monthly* 5:437-450, Dec 1937. il. NE.

1469. _____. *Vocal and Instrumental Recitals with Explanatory Talks on the Music of China.* New York: Arthur Judson, 1932. 4p. il. Concert program. NE.

1470. Lew, Timothy Tingfang. "The Union Hymnal" *The Chinese Yearbook*, p.1486-1489, 1936-1937. NE.

1471. Lewis, B.D.K. "Chinese Music: The Pentatonic Scale" *Orient* 2(5):23-25, 1951. NE.

1472. Leyda, Si-lan Chen. "Peking Venture: Out of the Goose Pond and into the Common Pot, or Better a Little Lake Than a Big Swan" *Dance Magazine* 46 (5):34-39, May 1972. Photos.

1473. Li Ch'i. "Firmly Carry the Revolution of Peking Opera to the End" *Selections from China Mainland Magazines* 435:28-33, Sept 22, 1964. From *Hungch'i* 15, 1964. NE.

1474. Li Hsi-fan. "An Artistic Gem Born in the Class Struggle" *China Reconstructs* 16(9):39-43, Sept 1967. il. On the ballet "The White-Haired Girl."

1475. Li Hsia-yang. "Bringing Opera to the Village" *China Reconstructs* 10(2):17-19, Feb 1961. il. On a tour by a Kiangsu *hsi-chu* troupe.

1476. Li Hua-wei. "The Unprecedented Rousing Show of Liang and Chu Film in Taiwan" *West and East* 8(7):6-7, July 1963. On the Shaw Brothers' film of "Liang Shan-po, Chu Ying-tai," that set box-office records and of which the music blanketed the air waves.

1477. Li Huang-chih. "Revolutionary Songs in China" *Chinese Literature* 9:97-105, 1965. mus. On songs by Nieh Erh, Hsien Hsing-hai, and others, with music and text for several songs.

1478. Li Hui-chung. "The Achievements of 'Third Sister Liu'" *Chinese Literature* 2:111-120, 1961. Favorable review of a new opera.

1479. Li Hwei. "A Comparative Study of the Jew's Harp Among the Aborigines of Formosa and East Asia" *Bulletin of the Institute of Ethnology, Academia Sinica* 1:85f., March 1956. In Chinese with English summary. NE.

1480. Li Ling. "Ma Ko and His Music" *Chinese Literature* (12):97-99, 1977. Brief summary of his career, on occasion of first anniversary of his death [b.1918; d.1976].

1481. Li Lun. "Socialist Times, Socialist Heroes, Socialist Drama" *China Reconstructs* 14(8):27-30, Aug 1965. il. NE.

1482. Li Shu-chun. "To Create a Heroine" in "Between Actor and Audience" *China Reconstructs* 13(6):8-10, June 1964. il. An actress views modern *k'un-ch'ü* opera.

1483. Li Tche-houa. "Le Dramaturge Chinois Kouan Han-k'ing" in *Les Théâtres d'Asie*, edited by Jean Jacquot (Paris: 1961), p.79-88. Historical and technical background, followed by a short biographical notice of this major Yüan dramatist. Includes summaries of three plays.

1484. _____. "Le Théâtre des Yuan, et présentation d'une pièce du théâtre des Yuan" in *Aspects de la Chine*, II (Paris: 1959). NE.

1485. Li Tsai. *West and East* (Taiwan), April 6, 1959-June 12, 1961. Series on Peking Opera. NE.

1486. Li Yao-tsung. "Pakistan National Dance Ensemble in Peking" *Chinese Literature* 7:97-102, 1973. il.

1487. Li Yuan-ching. "Chinese Musical Instruments" *China Reconstructs* 3(2):35-39, March-April 1954. il. Reprinted as "Traditional Chinese Instruments" in *China in Transition* (Peking: China Reconstructs, 1957), p.372-376. Good photos, popular introduction.

1488. _____ [Li Juan'cin]. "Kitajske Muzykal'nye Instru-
menty" [Chinese Musical Instruments] *Sovetskaya
Muzyka* 10:128-134, Oct 1954. NE.

1489. _____. "Traditional Instruments for New Music" *China
Reconstructs* 9(1):28-30, Jan 1960.   il. (rear
cover). Survey of "improved" instruments.

1490. Liang, D.S. "The Joint Recital of Chinese Classical
Music by Three American Students" *West and East*
9(7):5-6, July 1966. il.   Report of recital by
students of Liang Tsai-ping.

1491. Liang, David Ming-Yüeh.   *The Art of Yin-Jou Techniques for the Seven-Stringed Zither.* Ph.D. dissertation (Music), University of California, Los
Angeles, 1973. xiii+320p. il., mus., bibliog. A
detailed comparative diachronic study of the vi-
brato and ornament finger techniques *yin* and *jou*
in *ch'in* music. Varieties of techniques are demonstrated with graphic notation, and the functional
usage of *yin* and *jou* is investigated in the context of ten representative compositions.

1492. _____. "China, People's Republic of. V. Instruments.
1. Ch'in. 2. Cheng. 3. Hu-ch'in" in *Grove's Dictionary of Music and Musicians,* 6th Ed.   [In
press]. NE.

1493. _____.   *The Chinese Ch'in: Its History and Music.*
Taipei: Chinese National Music Association, 1969.
vi+323p. il., mus.   Published photo-lithographed
version of the author's M.A. thesis,   U.C.L.A.,
1969.   "The purpose of this thesis is to present
a semi-detailed, systematic study of the history,
philosophy, and theory of the ch'in   instrument
and ch'in music" (p.1). Many valuable contributions to *ch'in* study, including transcriptions of
tiao-i, and a detailed analysis with melographs
of "Yu-lan."

1494. _____.   "Neo Taoist Implications in a Melody for
the Chinese Seven-Stringed Zither" *World of Music* 2:19-28, 1975. il., mus. Also in French and
German.

1495. _____.   "Shantung Traditional Music" in *Essays
on Asian Music and Theatre* (New York: Performing Arts Program of the Asia Society, 1971). Introductory descriptive survey of this regional
genre of chamber music,   drawing mainly on personal experience.   Though designed as informal

background notes for the tour of a Shantung music ensemble, this brief essay nevertheless includes much valuable information otherwise unobtainable.

1496. _____. "A Study of Tiao-i, 'The Meaning of the Mode'" in *Perspectives on Asian Music: Essays in Honor of Dr. Laurence E.R. Picken*, Fritz A. Kuttner and Fredric Lieberman, eds. (New York: Society for Asian Music, 1975), p.173-188. mus. A chapter from the author's M.A. thesis, *The Chinese Ch'in: Its History and Music*, including transcription and analysis of modal preludes from several early Ming *ch'in* handbooks.

1497. Liang Hui-chao. "An Acrobat Slips" in "Between Actor and Audience" *China Reconstructs* 13(6):8-10, June 1964. il. Moral anecdote by a Peking opera actor.

1498. Liang Kuan. *Gestalten und Szenen der Peking-Oper*. Wiesbaden: Insel-Verlag, 1959. (Insel-Bücherei 692). Preface by Gerhard Pommeranz-Liedtke. Impressionistic paintings.

1499. Liang Pai-tchin. "Le Théâtre dialogué chinois en contact avec l'Occident" in *Les Théâtres d'Asie*, edited by Jean Jacquot (Paris: 1961), p.127-130.

1500. Liang Sung-ling. "Music Chronicle" *T'ien-Hsia Monthly* 11:174-177, Oct-Nov 1940. NE.

1501. Liang Tsai-ping. "Brief Introduction to Chinese Music" *West and East* 2:16-19, March 1957.

1502. _____. "Chinese Classical Music" in his *On Chinese Music*. A short (3p.) address to East-West Music Encounter, Tokyo.

1503. _____. "Chinese Drum Music" *West and East* 6(1):5-8, Jan 1961. Survey of genres prominently featuring drums.

1504. _____. *Chinese Music*. Taipei: Chinese Classical Music Society, 1955. 10+80+22p. il., mus. After a short introduction comes a reprint of Van Aalst and a reprint of Van Gulik's "Brief Note on the Cheng." Van Aalst is only partially given.

1505. _____. *Chinese Music*. Taipei: Chinese Classical Music Association, 1964. A revised edition of the 1955 volume, giving Van Aalst in full, deleting Van Gulik, adding an essay "On Chinese Music" by Liang, and reprinting two of his articles from *West and East*: "Chinese Drum Music" and "The Future of Chinese Music." Final section "Music Instruments in Pictures" includes several unique illustrations of modern instruments.

1506. _____. "Chinese Music in Asia" in *The Musics of Asia*, José Maceda, ed. (Manila: National Music Council, 1971), p.191-195. Brief remarks introductory to taped examples of Chinese and Chinese-derived music played in Japan, Korea, Vietnam, Thailand, and Taiwan.

1507. _____. *Chinese Musical Instruments and Pictures*. Taipei: Chinese Classical Music Association,1970. 154p. il. A collection of pictures, with brief notes on each instrument.

1508. _____. "Chinoise (Musique)" in *Larousse de la Musique*, edited by Duforcq (Paris: Larousse, 1957). I,188-190. il. Brief article includes review of legendary origins, theory, and instruments.

1509. _____. "The Future of Chinese Music" *West and East* 8(6):7-9, June 1963. Argues for the inclusion of Chinese music studies in the music curriculum of Taiwan colleges.

1510. _____. *On Chinese Music*. Taipei: Chinese Classical Music Association, 1962. 40p. il. Booklet containing long essay "On Chinese Music," which describes main categories and genres in classical, popular, and folk music. Also included are the short essays: "Chinese Classical Music," "Chinese Drum Music," "Biography of Prof. Liang Tsai-ping" by Lee Pao-ch'en, a letter from Lou Harrison, and several good plates.

1511. Liao Fu-shu. "Gemeinsamer Kampf—Gemeinsame Feiertage" *Musik und Gesellschaft* 9(9):539-540, Sept 1959. il. Political blurb of eternal friendship by Chinese delegation to 1954 Leipzig Congress.

1512. Libal, J. "Podminky Vzniku a Vývoje Hnuti za Novou Činskou Hudbu" *Nový Orient* 10:30-32, 1955. NE.

1513. Lieberman, Fredric. *The Chinese Long Zither Ch'in: A Study Based on the Mei-an Ch'in-p'u*. Ph.D. dissertation (music), University of California, Los Angeles, 1977. xxv+850p. il., mus., bibliog., discog., glossary. Includes transcription and translation of a contemporary *ch'in* handbook and studies of various aspects of the *ch'in* tradition.

1514. _____. *Contemporary Japanese Composition, Its Relationship to Concepts of Traditional Oriental Music*. M.A. thesis (music), University of Hawaii, 1965. vii+161p. mus. Study attempts to isolate characteristic elements of Oriental aesthetic morphology and compare their function in traditional context with that in the music of 3 leading contemporary Japanese composers. Includes a survey of Chinese music history emphasizing music in early documents and Confucian philosophy.

1515. _____. "Jean-Joseph Amiot" in *Grove's Dictionary of Music and Musicians*. 6th ed. In press.

1516. _____. "Preface" to *Music of Cheng* by Liang Tsai-ping (Taiwan: Chinese Music Association, 1967), p.1-3. Reprinted 1969, 1971. Basic explanatory notes on performance practice and the system of staff notation used in this set of graded scores for *cheng* students.

1517. _____. "Sound Instruments of Chinese Peddlers" in *Festschrift for Liang Tsai-ping*, David M.Y. Liang, ed. In press. Written in 1967, this is a compilation and classification of reports and source materials.

1518. _____. "Texted Tunes in the Mei-an Ch'in-p'u" in *Perspectives on Asian Music: Essays in Honor of Dr. Laurence E.R. Picken*, Fritz A. Kuttner and Fredric Lieberman, eds. (New York: Society for Asian Music, 1975), p.113-146. il., mus., charts. Study of cultural background, musical structure, and text-melody relationships of three brief *ch'in* compositions in a popular modern handbook, with transcriptions and original scores.

* _____. See also: Fritz A. Kuttner and Fredric Lieberman, editors (above).

* _____, translator. See Hector Berlioz.

143

1519. Lietard, Alfred.   *Au Yun-nan: Les Lo-lo P'o, une Tribes des Aborigènes de la Chine Méridionale.* Munster I.W.: Aschendorff, 1913. vii +272p. (Anthropos Bibliothek I,5). See p.109-110, 111-124, NE.

1520. Lieu, D.K. "Chinese Music" in *Peking Leader Special Anniversary Supplement: China in 1918* (Peking: 1919), p.103-110. NE.

1521. _____. "The Origin and Growth of Chinese Music" *The Far Eastern Republic* 1(2):21-25, Nov 1919. (From *Peking Leader Special Anniversary Supplement*).

1522. Lim Chew-pah.   *The Two Main Singing Styles in Cantonese Opera: /bɔ̄ŋ dʑi/ and /jǐ wɔ̄ŋ /.* M.A. thesis (music), University of Washington, 1973. ix+234p. mus., bibliog. Analysis of the main aria types in Cantonese opera, with some introductory background material. Analyses focus on metric-rhythmic structures and text-setting.

1523. Lin' E. "Narodnoe Pesennoe Iskusstvo v Novom Kitae" [The Art of Folk Song in New China]   *Sovetskaya Muzyka* 10:126, 128, Oct 1954. NE.

1524. Lin Hsia. "Yang Sheng, Master Puppeteer" *China Reconstructs* 12(6):20-23, June 1963. il. About the glove-puppet theatre, with color photos.

1525. Lin Shuen-fu. *A Structural Study of Chiang K'uei's Songs.* Ph.D. dissertation (classical language and literature), Princeton University, 1972.   188p. NE.

1526. Lin Ta-kuang.   "Broadcasting for the People" *China Reconstructs* 4(8):2-5, 1955. NE.

1527. Lin Yutang. "Singing Patriots of China" *Asia* 41(2): 70-72, Feb 1941. il.   On Liu Liang-mo and the mass singing movement.

1528. _____. *The Wisdom of Confucius.*   New York: Random House, 1938. xvii+290p. See p.251-272, "On Music," a good translation of most of the "Yüeh Chi" chapter from the *Li Chi*.

1529. Ling Ching-yen. "The Music of Wei Han-ching and the Ta Ch'eng Institute of the Sung Dynasty" *Yenching Journal of Chinese Studies* 28:105-132, 303-304, Dec 1940. In Chinese, with English abstract.

1530. Ling, Mary. "Musical Instruments of the Ami Tribe" *Bulletin of the Institute of Ethnology, Academia Sinica* 11:185-220, Spring 1961. il., 6 plates. A well-illustrated ethnographic survey. Article in Chinese; all illustrations have English captions; adequate English abridgement, p.217-220.

1531. List, Eugene. "Discovering a Musical Far East" *Music Journal* 17:14f., March 1959. NE.

1532. Litter, H. "Musik in China" *Neue Musik* 1933. NE.

1533. Little, Archibald. "The Chinese Drama" *Nineteenth Century* 51:1017-1022, June 1902. NE.

1534. Liu, Charles. "On the Jew's Harps from Hainan Island" *Journal of the Science Society of China* 20: 12-24, 1938. il. NE.

1535. Liu Cheng-yi. "My Day As 'Cheerer'" *China Reconstructs* 15(4):39-40, April 1966. il. Farm girl joins professional cheerers who sing patriotic work songs to field laborers.

1536. Liu Chün-jo. "New Oral Recitals [*Hsin Ch'ü-i*] in Peking" *CHINOPERL News* 5:168-183, 1975. Report from Prof. Liu's 1973 trip, including text, Romanization and translation of examples of eight narrative genres, and brief notes on formal features.

1537. _____. "Report on Field Research in Taiwan and Hong Kong—1969-1970" *CHINOPERL News* 4:110-122, 1974. Notes in the form of a diary, primarily relating to recording Buddhist rituals.

1538. _____. *A Study of the Tsa-chü of the 13th Century in China*. Ph.D. dissertation, University of Wisconsin, 1952. Includes translations of 3 plays: "Injustice to Tou O," "Rain on the Wu-t'ung Tree," "Li K'uei Carries Thorns."

1539. Liu Chungshee Hsien. "Sur un Instrument musical à anches libres en usage chez les Miao dans la Chine du Sud-Ouest" *Ethnographie* ns 28:27-39, 1934. il. Detailed description of the *lu-sheng* (6-tube mouth organ) among the Miao, with survey of geographic distribution of derivative forms and an account of the dance typically correlated with its music. No music or information on tuning or scale.

1540. Liu Fu. "Chu Tsai-yu, the Inventor of the Chromatic
      Scale of Equal Temperament" *China Institute Bul-*
      letin 4(8):78-79, May 1940. English abstract by
      Hsien Chin Hu of a Chinese article in the *Studies*
      Presented to Dr. Tsai Yuan-pei on His 65th Birth-
      day by fellows and assistants at the National Re-
      search Institute of History and Philology. Peiping:
      Academia Sinica. I (1933); II (1935). Holds that
      Chu's ideas antedated Western ones, and may have
      directly influenced Mersenne, via Jesuit reports.

1541. _____. *Étude experimentale sur les tons du Chinois.*
      Paris: 1925. NE.

1542. _____. *Five Tones to Three-Hundred and Sixty Tones.*
      [n.p.]: 1930. NE.

1543. _____.   "Musique chinoise: le développement de
      l'échelle musicale chinoise de 5 à 360 tons"
      Bulletin de l'Université l'Aurore 3s, 9(36):332-
      366, Oct 1948. tables. Translated by R.P. Tcheou.
      It has excellent detailed presentation of cyclic
      scale theories with mathematical viewpoint. Ta-
      bles in cents for Ching Fang (60) and Ch'ien Lo-
      chih (360) systems. Concludes that 23 tones suf-
      fice for complete cyclic system.   Minor errors
      due to computation inaccuracies, but okay to two
      decimal places.

1544. Liu Hou-sheng.   "Co-Workers Against the Party and
      Socialism: A General Discussion of *Li Hui-nung,*
      Hai Jui Relieved of His Office, and *Hsieh Yao-*
      huan" Selections from China Mainland Magazines
      528:25-35, June 13, 1966.   From *Hsi-ch'ü Pao,*
      April 10, 1966. NE.

1545. Liu, James J.Y. *Elizabethan and Yuan.* London: China
      Society, 1955. "A brief essay comparing the dra-
      matic conventions of England's Elizabethan drama
      with those of China's *Tsa-chü* of the Yuan era."
      (Hucker).

1546. _____. *The Art of Chinese Poetry.* Chicago: Univer-
      sity of Chicago Press, 1962. xii+164p. The best
      study of form and technique in Chinese poetry.
      Because musical and poetic forms are closely re-
      lated in China, this book is of primary impor-
      tance for musicological studies, though it does
      not deal with music per se.

1547. _____. "Li Shang-yin's Poem 'The Ornamented Zither'
(*Chin-Sê*)" *Journal of the American Oriental Society* 85(2):129-138, April-June 1965. A translation and interpretation of a difficult symbolic
poem from the late T'ang dynasty, with an ornamented *sê* central to the imagery.

1548. Liu Jung-en, trans. *Six Yüan Plays*. Baltimore: Penguin Books, 1972. 285p. Excellent translations
of "Chao Shih Ku-erh" [The Orphan of Chao],"Ch'ien
-nü Li Hun" [The Soul of Ch'ien-nü Leaves Her
Body], "Tou-O Yüan" [The Injustice Done to Tou
Ngo], "Chang Sheng Chu Hai" [Chang Boils the
Sea], "Han Kung Ch'iu" [Autumn in Han Palance],
and "Lien-huan Chi" [A Strategem of Interlocking
Rings]. There is an extensive introduction on
history and background of the genre and the plays
selected, and brief textual annotations.

1549. Liu Liang-mo and Evelyn Modoi. *China Sings*. New
York: Carl Fischer, 1955. 28p. Texts with characters, Romanization, translation, Western harmonic arrangements of several Chinese popular and
folk songs.

1550. Liu, Marjory Bong-ray. "From Kunch'ü to Revolutionary Opera: A Study in Continuity and Change in
Chinese Society" in *Special Reports No. 7*, Center
for Asian Studies, Arizona State University, 1975,
p.17-30. NE.

1551. _____. "The Influence of Tonal Speech on K'unch'ü
Opera Style" *Selected Reports* [UCLA] 2(1):63-86,
1974. mus. "This article ... proceeds by analyz-
ing speech tones, articulation in speech and
song, and K'unch'ü song form, and it verifies the
fusion of linguistic and musical components
through melogram transcriptions of audiotape recordings of speech, heightened speech, and song,
..." [from author's abstract].

1552. _____. "Music Education and Community Life in Taiwan, China" *Musart* 20(5), 1968. NE.

1553. _____. "Syncretism: An Aesthetic Approach to Chinese Arts" *Journal of Western Conference, Association for Asian Studies* 2, 1976. NE.

1554. _____. *Tradition and Change in Kunqü Opera*. Ph.D.
dissertation (music), U.C.L.A., 1976. 270p. NE.
This study is primarily an investigation of Kungü,
the classical operatic style of the Ming dynasty
in China, through its structural base, the Qüpai,
or tone-tune model. It is an attempt to ascer-

tain the determinants and characteristics of
Kunqu style, in order to discover those musical
and extramusical values of the tradition which
were continued in some form from previous artistic genres, and that were either changed or dis-
carded in later operatic styles. [Author]

1555. Liu Mau-tsai. "Kulturelle Beziehungen zwischen den
Ost-Türken (T'u-küe) und China" *Central Asiatic
Journal* 3(3):190-205, 1957. Includes discussion
of some musical interchange.

1556. _____. "Puppenspiel und Schattentheater unter der
Sung-Dynasty. Ihre Entstehung und ihre Formen"
Oriens Extremus 14(2):129-142, Dec 1967. Detailed
historical study of these important relatives of
the operatic drama.

1557. Liu, Rosie. "Chi Ju-shan, Great Authority on Chinese
Opera, Dies at 86" *China Today* 5(3):48, March
1962.   Obituary notice with brief biographical
sketch.

1558. Liu, Sydney C.   "The Dance of the Chinese Harvest
Song (Yang-ko)" *Orient* 2(6):49-50, 1952.

1559. Liu Ta-chun. *Kitaiskaya Muzyka* [Chinese Music]. Har-
bin: Tipolitigrafiya T-va., 1924. 26p. il. NE.

1560. Liu T'ieh-yün [1857-1909]. *The Travels of Lao Ts'an.*
Ithaca: Cornell University Press, 1952.   Paperback edition 1966. xxvi+277p. Translated and annotated by Harold Shadick. A novel that includes
an important (because rare) description of a
drum-song performance (Chap. 2);   there is also
an extensive musical fantasy (Chap. 10).   The
translation is excellent and well annotated.

1561. Liu T'ien-hua. *The Musical Compositions of the Late
Liu T'ien-hua.* Peiping: 1933. 114, 136p. music.
Reprint with preface by Liang Tsai-ping, Taipei:
1964. Collection of modern compositions for *nan-
hu* and *p'i-p'a* by the most respected master of
traditional-style composition. Both Chinese and
Western notations are given.

1562. _____. *Selections from the Repertoire of Operatic
Songs and Terpsichorean Melodies of Mei Lan-fang.*
Peiping: National Library, 1930.   106p. music.

1563. Liu Wu-chi. "Notes on the Sex of a Yüan Dramatist"
Tsing Hua Journal of Chinese Studies ns I(2):
246-252, April 1957. NE.

1564. Liu Wu-chi. "The Original Orphan of China" *Comparative Literature* 5(3):193-212, Summer 1953. Examines the source of a popular 18th-century dramatic theme used by Voltaire and others.

1565. Liu Yi-fang. "Old Plays: A Treasury Reopened" *China Reconstructs* 6(2):6-9, Feb 1957. il. On revival of several previously neglected banned operas, with discussion of their political and social impact.

1566. Lloyd, Benjamin E. *Lights and Shades in San Francisco*. San Francisco: A.L. Bancroft & Co., 1876. il. Unusually detailed ethnographic notes of Chinese. Music figures in funerals (p.226-229), social gatherings (p.238), and the theatre (p.264-266). [RR]

1567. Lo Chiang. "New Piano Music" *Chinese Literature* 6: 110-113, 1975. On post-Cultural Revolution repertoire arranged for piano by Liu Shih-kun and others.

1568. Lo Chuan-fang. "Changing China and the Eternal Arts" *Asia* 45:584-585, Dec 1945. NE.

1569. Lo Liang-chü. "Hauptwerke Chinesischer Musik" in *Chinesische Musik*, edited by Richard Wilhelm (Frankfurt A.M.: China Institut, 1927), p.57-63. Also in *Sinica* 2:145-150, 1927. Chronological table gives composer and title of about 100 famous compositions.

1570. Loeb, David. *Chinese and Japanese Musical Instruments and Their Notation*. New York: Harold Branch Publishing, 1972. [ii]+60p. il., mus., glossary. Survey by a composer interested in getting firsthand access to these musics.

1571. Loewe, Michael. "The Office of Music, c. 114 to 7 B.C." *Bull, School of Oriental and African Studies* (London) 36(2):340-351, 1973. Historical study of the Han *Yüeh Fu*, its functions, organization, and the reasons behind its eventual dissolution.

1572. Loh Wei-chung. "Chinese Classical Music" in *The Musicraft Album*. [n.p.]: 1939. Record notes? NE.

1573. London, Miriam and Ivan D. London. "Three Stories From the Chinese Countryside: The Song" *China News Analysis* 960:6-8, 17 May 1974. Narrative by a peasant who escaped to Hong Kong in 1973, involving the role of a propaganda song in a village meeting.

149

1574. Loveglio, Eluthère. "La Musique Chinoise" *Musica* 42:10-14, Sept 1957. il., mus. NE. [NYPL].

1575. _____. "La Musique Chinoise" *Monde Musical* 47:141-143, 205-206, 1936. il., mus. NE.

1576. Lowe, H.Y. *Stories from the Chinese Drama.* Peking: The Peking Chronicle Press, 1942. xii+414+xxxviii p. 202 stories, with index to plays.

1577. Lowe, Pardee. *Father and Glorious Descendant.* Boston: Little Brown, 1943. Occasional notes on music in this autobiographical account of growing up in San Francisco's Chinatown (e.g., music of singsong girls, p.45). [RR]

1578. Lu Chi. "Muzyka v Kitaiskih Kinofilmah" [Music in Chinese Films] *Sovetskaya Muzyka* 11:170f., 1959. NE.

1579. _____. "Muzykal'naia Kultura Novovo Kitaia" [Musical Culture of New China] *Sovetskaya Muzyka* 4: 126f., April 1954. NE.

1580. _____. "O Kitaiskoi Norodnoi Muzyke" [About Chinese National Music] *Sovetskaya Muzyka* 11:75f., 1953. NE.

1581. _____. "Sovetskaya Pesn'a v Kitae" [Soviet Song in China] *Sovetskaya Muzyka* 1:90f., 1951. NE.

1582. Lu Hsun. "The Art of the Number-Two Clown" in *Selected Works of Lu Hsun,* Vol. 3. (Peking: Foreign Languages Press, 1959), p.277-278. Written in 1933, this brief essay uses the description of a role-type in East Chekiang opera to satirize current political figures.

1583. _____. "Forgetting Meat and Forgetting Water" *Chinese Literature* 9:7-9, 1974. A satirical essay, written in 1934, echoing Mo Ti's "Against Music." Despite interest in reviving ancient Confucian music, people kill each other fighting over water in drought areas. "So in addition to the Shao music which makes meat-eaters forget the taste of meat, we need another type of 'Shao music' to make thirsty men no longer thirst for water." Also published in *Selected Works of Lu Hsun,* Vol. IV. Peking: Foreign Languages Press, 1960, p.124-126. In 1934, the satiric barb was directed primarily at improvident behavior, wastefulness, and lack of cooperation. The essay is republished in 1974 as a contribution to the anti-Confucian campaign. See commentary in article by Chung Wen.

1584. _____. "The Hanging Woman" in *Selected Works of Lu Hsun*, Vol. 1. (Peking: Foreign Languages Press, 1959), p.432-440. An essay from 1936 describing a religious opera of Shaohsing.

1585. _____. "Village Opera" in *Selected Works of Lu Hsun* (Peking: Foreign Languages Press, 1959), p.136-149. Short story compares a crowded, noisy Peking opera performance to a more relaxed and pleasant one in a village setting.

1586. Lu Kung-ta. "A Revolution in Symphonic Music" *China Reconstructs* 16(9):17-24, Sept 1967. il. On "Shachiapang."

1587. Lu, Steve. *Face Painting in Chinese Opera*. Singapore: MPH Publications, 1968. 183p. il.

1588. Lu Ting-yi. "For More and Finer Peking Operas on Contemporary Themes" *Peking Review* 7:7-9, June 12, 1964. NE.

1589. Lu Yun-an. "Muzykal'naya Zhizn' Novovo Kitaya (Obzor Kitaiskovo Muzykal'novo Zhurnala 'Jen-min Yin-yüeh')" [Survey of the Chinese Musical Magazine "People's Music"] *Sovetskaya Muzyka* 10:93f., Oct 1951. NE.

1590. Lübke, Anton. *Der Himmel der Chinesen*. Leipzig: 1931. See p.67f., "Glocken und Trommeln als Zeitkünder in China" and p.126f., "Astronomie und Chinesische Musik." NE.

1591. Lucignani, L. "Il teatro cinese" *Belfagor* (Firenze) 11(2):137-147, March 1956. NE.

1592. Lück, Hartmut. "Blaue Schlange und Rote Frauenkompanie—Bühne und Konzertsaal in China vor und nach der Kulturrevolution" *Neue Musikzeitung* 23 (1):3, 1974. NE.

1593. _____. "Die Bühne leuchtet feuerrot. Pekingoper und Kulturrevolution" *Sozialistische Zeitschrift für Kunst und Gesellschaft* 8-9, 1971. (Tübingen: Verlag Kunst und Gesellschaft, 1971). NE.

1594. _____. "Chinesische Musik aus deutscher Sicht" *Neue Musikzeitschrift* 2:16, 1973. NE.

1595. Luh Chih-wei. *On Chinese Poetry*. Peiping: 1935. 118p. mus. See p.27-55, "Folk Songs Ancient and Modern." NE.

1596. Lui Tsun-yuen. "Ch'in Techniques of the Right Hand (Translation from the Chinese)" *Selected Reports* 1(1):83-88, 1966. Translation, with brief annotations, of relevant material from an 18th-century *ch'in* handbook.

1597. _____. "China, People's Republic of: V. Instruments. 2. P'i-p'a" in *Grove's Dictionary of Music and Musicians*, 6th ed. In press. NE.

1598. _____. "Music and Dance of the Shang Dynasty" *Asian Pacific Quarterly of Cultural and Social Affairs* (Seoul) 3(3):47-50, Winter 1971. Bibliog. NE.

1599. _____. "A Short Guide to Ch'in" *Selected Reports* 1 (2):180-204, 1968. il., mus. Historical and technical survey with translation of finger techniques for right and left hands.

1600. Lum, Maryette Hawley. *Songs of Chinese Children.* Peking: 1936. 2nd ed. New York: Suttonhouse, 1939. 32p. mus. Illustrations by Lin Yu-ts'ang. Piano-voice arrangements, with Chinese characters and translations.

1601. Ly Sing-ko. "Face-Painting in the Chinese Theatre" *Straights Times Annual* p.38-39, 1963. il. NE.

1602. _____. "Lakhon and the Chinese Theatre" *Eastern Horizon* 4(6):25-29, June 1965. il. Intriguing and unique article describes reciprocal influences of Lakhon (Thai drama) and Chinese theatre.

1603. _____. "The Peking Opera" *Asia* (Saigon) 1(3):354-359, Dec 1951. Popular, non-technical.

1604. Lynch, Charles. "Music in Red China" *Bravo* 6(4): 12-13, 19, 1967. NE.

* * * * * * * * * *

1605. M., C. "Notes and Queries" *New China Review* 1:625 -627, 1919. Remarks on a Ming dynasty painting depicting musicians. Identifies some instruments. See Anonymous, "A Ming Dynasty Painting" and related articles by Kishibe and Rowley.

1606. M., L. "The Ma Brothers" *High Fidelity* 17(10):97, Oct 1967. NE.

1607. _____. "Mms. Mao and Liu. Callas and Tebaldi?" *High Fidelity* 17(10):95, Oct 1967. NE.

1608. Ma Hiao-ts'iun. "La Musique Chinoise" in *La Musique des Origines à Nos Jours*, edited by Duforcq (Paris: Larousse, 1946), p.438-446.   il., mus. Review of theory and theater music.   No instruments, except in plates from Amiot.

1609. _____. "La Musique Chinoise" in *Histoire de la Musique*, edited by Roland-Manuel (Paris: Encyclopédie de la Pléiade, Gallimard, 1960), p.283-304. mus., bibliog.

1610. _____. *La Musique Chinoise de Style Européen*. Paris: Jouve, 1941.   Dissertation, University of Paris, 1941. 135p. mus., bibliog.   Good study of styles in contemporary Chinese composition.

1611. _____. "Le Théâtre de Pékin" in *Les Théâtres d'Asie*, edited by Jean Jacquot (Paris: Centre National de la Recherche Scientifique, 1961), p.89-97.

1612. Ma K'o.   "China's Modern Opera" *People's China* 17: 27-31, Sept 1, 1957. il., mus.   Popular survey, good coverage.

1613. _____. "Chinese Folk Song" *People's China* 5:10-14, March 1, 1957. mus. Popular survey.

1614. _____. "A Fighting Song Is Born" *China Reconstructs* 12(5):24-29, May 1963. il., mus. On the composer Hsien Hsing-hai.

1615. _____.   "From 'Yangko' Opera to 'The White-Haired Girl'" *Peking Review* 21:20-23, May 25, 1962. NE.

1616. _____.   "Go Deep Into Life and Raise the Quality of Musical Compositions" *Selections from China Mainland Magazines* 364:23-28, May 13, 1963. NE.

1617. _____.   "Hsien Hsing-hai the Composer" *Chinese Literature* 12:110-116, 1965. il. Anecdotal biographical sketch.

1618. _____.   "Istoki Kitaiskoi Klassicheskoi Opery" [Sources of Chinese Classical Opera] *Sovetskaya Muzyka* 6:186f., June 1959. NE.

1619. _____.   "Songs Play Their Part in Revolution" *China Reconstructs* 14(6):31-35, June 1965. il., mus.

1620. Ma Shao-po. "Mei Lan-fang and Chou Hsin-fang" *Chinese Literature* 3:142-148, 1953. il. Eulogies on their 50th year of stage appearances.

1621. _____. "Pearls Cleansed of Sand" *China Reconstructs* 10(3):12-15, March 1961. il. (cover). On revisions of traditional operas.

1622. Ma Sitson [Ma Su Cung, Ma Ssu-tsung]. "Hudba Lidovych Democracii. Nova Cinska Hudba" [Music of the People's Democracy. New Chinese Music] *Hudebni Rozhledy* 5(1):28-29, 1952. NE.

1623. _____. [Ma Sy-cun]. "Symfoniceskaja Muzyka Novogo Kitaja" [Symphonic Music of New China] *Sovetskaya Muzyka* 3:169-171, 1960. NE.

1624. _____. "Terror at the Hands of the Red Guard" *Life* 62(22):22-29, 63-66, June 2, 1967. il. On his escape to the West, China's leading violinist tells of musical life under the Cultural Revolution and the persecutions he and his colleagues endured.

1625. _____. "We Are Slaves Who Have Been Betrayed" *Life* 63(14):64-73, July 1967. il. (portrait). Autobiographical account of musical activities and developments in the People's Republic.

1626. Ma Yen-hsiang. "'Painted Faces' of the Chinese Theatre" *China Reconstructs* 3(6):25-27, Nov-Dec 1954. Short text with color photos.

1627. Macartney, The Earl of. *An Embassy to China; Being the Journal Kept by Lord Macartney During His Embassy to the Emperor Ch'ien-lung, 1792-1794,* edited by J.L. Cranmer-Byng. London: Longmans, 1962. Passages relating to music are excerpted in Frank Harrison, *Time, Place and Music* (q.v.).

1628. MacDowell, Edward Alexander. "Music of the Chinese" in his *Critical and Historical Essays: Lectures Delivered at Columbia University* (Boston, New York: A.P. Schmidt [*ca.* 1912]), p.49-68. Short survey based on Amiot, with many gross misconceptions and errors of fact, by a composer who should have known better.

1629. MacGillivray, D. "Hymnology in the Chinese Church. III. A List of Hymn Books" *China Mission Year Book 1912* (Shanghai: Christian Literature Society for China, 1912), p.253-259. Selectively annotated bibliography of 62 hymn books produced in China in the 19th century.

1630. Mackenzie, M.C.   "Solfa Notation. Tunes Involving Changes from One Key to Another" *Chinese Record-er* 40(11):642-643, Nov 1909.   Letter advising caution when modulating.

1631. Mackerras, Colin Patrick. *Amateur Theatre in China 1946-1966.* Canberra: Australian National University Press, 1973. 50p.   (Contemporary China Papers, No. 5).   Based largely on the Chinese regional press, this fascinating article explores ideological and social factors in the surge of amateur performances in the People's Republic.

1632. _____.   "China, People's Republic of. III. Musical Drama and Narratives. 1. Regional Opera. 2. Peking Opera" in *Grove's Dictionary of Music and Musicians*, 6th Ed. In press. Excellent survey of dramatic forms stressing contemporary genres.

1633. _____.   "China, People's Republic of. V.   Instruments. 5.[Other Instruments]" in *Grove's Dictionary of Music and Musicians*, 6th Ed. In press. NE.

1634. _____. "Chinese Opera After the Cultural Revolution (1970-72)" *China Quarterly* 55:478-510, July-Sept 1973.   Excellent study based on opera libretti and articles in the Mainland press; includes comparison of pre- and post-Cultural Revolution versions of *The Red Lantern, On the Docks,* and *Ode to Dragon River,* and discussions of performance contexts and amateur theatre.

1635. _____. *The Chinese Theatre in Modern Times: From 1840 to the Present Day.* London: Thames and Hudson, 1975. 256p. il., bibliog., chronological table, index.   Excellent study of historical and social aspects of the Peking Opera, regional opera forms, and modern opera in the People's Republic.   U.S. publication by the University of Massachusetts Press. Review in *Musical Times* 117: 491f., June 1976.

1636. _____. "Chinese Theatre in the Seventies" *The Elizabethan Trust News* 10:6-7, March 1974. NE.

1637. _____. "The Decline of Theatre in China" *Masque* (Sydney, Australia) 15:20-25, Aug 1970. il. An expert brief survey of opera ideology and practice in the People's Republic, with much attention to the Cultural Revolution and its aftermath.   Danish translation, "Operaen i Kina efter Revolutionen" *Teatrets Teori og Teknikk* 15:58-63, 1971.

1638. _____. "The Growth of the Chinese Regional Drama in the Ming and the Ch'ing" *Journal of Oriental Studies* 9(1):58-91, Jan 1971. A detailed account of the styles of local opera (*ti-fang hsi*), many of which contributed to the Peking Opera style.

1639. _____. "Opera and the Campaign to Criticize Lin Piao and Confucius" *Papers on Far Eastern History* (Australian National University), 11:169-198, March 1975. Analysis of the structure and political background of *Azalea Mountain* and *Going Up Peach Peak Three Times*.

1640. _____. "Recent Trends in Chinese Opera" *Twentieth Century* 21(4):345-351, Winter 1967. On the rich variety of local operas exploited (but thereby kept alive as a performing art) by the Communist propaganda teams.

1641. _____. *The Rise of the Peking Opera 1770-1870; Social Aspects of the Theatre in Manchu China.* Oxford: Oxford University Press, 1972. xiv+316p. il., bibliog., glossary, index. A significant contribution to the history of Chinese theatre. Using primary sources extensively, data are assembled on actors and troupes, leading to a clear outline of historic and geographic development of local genres and their eventual synthesis into Peking Opera. Biographies of leading actors are given, and considerations of social functions, status, economics are discussed. Appendices survey the bibliographical sources and the dramatic repertoire. Very little discussion of the music itself. Reviewed by: Hsu Dao-lin in *Journal of the American Oriental Society* 95(1):118-119,1975.

1642. _____. "The Theatre in Yang-chou in the Late Eighteenth Century" *Papers on Far Eastern History* 1: 1-30, March 1970. NE.

1643. _____. "Theatre and the Taipings" *Modern China* 2 (4):474-501, Oct 1976. A historical and sociological study of the situation of opera in the mid-19th century, arguing that: "The effect of the Taiping wars was harmful overall to Chinese theatre. The converse, however, does not necessarily follow and would be, in my opinion, false; that is to say, the drama would have helped, rather than hindered, the Taipings."

1644. MacMinn, George R. *The Theater of the Golden Era in
       California*. Caldwell, Id.: Caxton Printers, 1941.
       Good chapter on San Francisco's Chinese theatre
       in the 19th century—"Celestial Entertainments,"
       p.493-508. Describes "Punch and Judy show," re-
       prints review of a Chinese play in 1860, narrates
       stories of plays. Most material from San Fran-
       cisco newspapers of 1800s. Only cursory atten-
       tion to music. [RR]

1645. Mai Hsin. "'Ch'i Lai!' and Its Composer" *China Di-
       gest* 4(6):17-18, July 27, 1948.   Portrait, mus.
       On Nieh Erh and his music.

1646. Mailla, Joseph Anne Marie de Moyriac de, translator.
       Histoire Générale de la Chine.   Paris: Pierres,
       1777-1785. 13 vols. il.   See XIII,772-781, "Mu-
       sique Chinoise." NE.

1647. Maillaud, Jeanne.   "The Peking Opera" *Opera* 6(9):
       573-575, Sept 1955. il.   Enthusiastic review of
       troupe visit to Europe.

1648. Malm, William P. "Chinese Music in the Edo and Meiji
       Periods in Japan" in *Perspectives on Asian Music:
       Essays in Honor of Dr. Laurence E.R. Picken*,
       Fritz A. Kuttner and Fredric Lieberman, eds. (New
       York: Society for Asian Music, 1975), p.147-172.
       il., mus., bibliog. Based primarily on surviving
       scores and instruction books, this fascinating
       study surveys the adaptation of Ming and Ch'ing
       music in Japan (*minshingaku*); discusses the in-
       struments, notation, and performance practice of
       minshingaku, as well as presents some of its bet-
       ter known songs in Western notation, along with
       certain adaptations of the music in other gen-
       res. In this way it will also show the manner in
       which a Chinese music oriented toward intellec-
       tual, or the displaced native stuck in the Naga-
       saki Chinatown, became more Japanese and plebian
       with the aid of serious teachers, naughty geisha,
       and intrepid minstrels [adapted from author's ab-
       stract].

1649. _____. "Japanese Research in Chinese Music" *Journal
       of the American Oriental Society* 79(2):124, April
       -June 1959. Brief note on leading scholars, with
       short bibliography.

1650. _____. *Music Cultures of the Pacific, the Near East and Asia*. Englewood Cliffs, N.J.: Prentice-Hall, 1967. xiv+169p. il., mus. "East Asia: China," p.107-129, is a generally reliable, though too brief, historical survey stressing theory and instruments; also discusses Peking Opera and contemporary trends. A second, revised and enlarged edition was published in 1977 which has improved coverage.

1651. Malmqvist, N.G.D. "A Confucian Philosopher's Working Song" *Acta Bibliothecae Regiae Stockholiniensis* 15:1973. NE. Annotated translation of the ballad "Cheng hsiang" from the *Hsün Tzu*.

1652. _____. "A Note on the *Cherng Shiang* Ballad in the *Shyun Tzyy*" *Bull, School of Oriental and African Studies* (London) 36(2):352-358, 1973. Study of metrics, and translation of Chinese sources that seek an explanation of the name of this early ballad, mainly by reference to musical instruments.

1653. Manley, Grace. "The Road Calls of Chair Coolies" *Journal of the West China Border Research Society* 13:13-41, 1941.

1654. Mano, D.K. "Culture in Middletown" *National Review* 26:1414, Dec 6, 1974. il. NE.

1655. Mao Chi-tseng. "Reform of Traditional Musical Instruments" *Chinese Literature* 8:110-116, 1965. il. Technological advances produce the "quick-change dulcimer," the "keyed kuan-tzu," the "enlarged set of gongs." Article gives a good idea of contemporary musicological-acoustic efforts in Mainland China.

1656. _____. "Traditional Chinese Orchestras" *Chinese Literature* 6:102-108, 1964. il. Brief survey with some valuable information on National Minority musical ensembles.

1657. Mao Hua. "New Features in Sinkiang Music" *Chinese Literature* 2:110-116, 1966. il. Survey of Uighur music, political orientation.

1658. Mao Tse-tung. *Five Documents on Literature and Art*. Peking: Foreign Languages Press, 1967. 12p. Pamphlet includes a 1944 letter encouraging production of Peking Opera on modern themes.

1659. _____. *Talks at the Yenan Forum on Literature and Art*. Peking: Foreign Languages Press, 1965. 4th ed. Forms the ideological base of all Communist reform movements in opera, music, and other arts.

1660. Mao Tun. "On Mao Tse-tung's Teachings on Literature and Art" *People's China* (11):5-8, 30-32, June 1, 1952. Essay commemorating 10th anniversary of *Talks at the Yenan Forum*.

1661. Marcel, Jean. "Notes sur la musique chinoise" *Courrier Musical* 9:587-588, 1906. NE.

1662. Marceron. "Le Théâtre en Chine et au Japon" *Études Japonaises* 6:42. NE.

1663. March, Benjamin. "A Chinese Puppetman" *Puppetry* 1:36-42, 1930. NE.

1664. _____. *Chinese Shadow-Figure Plays and Their Making*. Detroit: Puppetry Imprints, 1938 (Handbook XI). il. "An abundantly illustrated introduction, in popular style. With English renderings of three representative librettos." (Hucker).

★ Marett, Alan. See Rembrandt Wolpert et al.

1665. Mariani, Fosco. "L'esotico inverso: Cina e Giappone guardano l'Europa" in *La Musica occidentale e la civiltà musicali extraeuropee: alti della tavola rotunda organizzata in occasione de XXXIV Maggio Musicale Fiorentino*, Eugenio Garin et al., eds. (Florence: Centro Di, 1971), p.94-129. il. NE.

1666. Mark, Lindy Li and Fang Kuei Li. "Speech Tone and Melody in Wu-Ming Folk Songs" in *Essays Offered to G.H. Luce by His Colleagues and Friends in Honour of His Seventy-Fifth Birthday*, edited by Ba Shin, Jean Boisselier, and A.B. Griswold (Ascona, Switzerland: Artibus Asiae, 1966), I,167-186. mus. (Artibus Asiae Supplementum 23). Analysis based on field recordings from this district in Kwangsi, concluding that there are tendencies for each speech tone to be sung in specific pitch ranges, and for speech contours to "find parallel expression in slurred pitches," but that "the correlation between speech tone and pitch is more conventional than absolute."

1667. Marks, Robert W. "The Music and Musical Instruments of Ancient China" *Musical Quarterly* 18(4):593-607, Oct 1932. il. A general survey based largely on the Classics and published Western sources, drawing indiscriminately on legend and picturesque anecdote.

1668. Marshall, W.G. *Through America; Or, Nine Months in the United States*. London: Sampson Low, Marson, Searle & Rivington, 1882. il. Describes performance at Royal China Theatre in San Francisco, p.297-301. [RR]

1669. Marsi Paribatra, S.A.S. "La Cancion popular en la China Antiqua" *Revista de Dialectología y Tradiciones Populares* (Madrid), 15(1):43-49, 1959. NE.

1670. Martens, Frederick H. "Music in Chinese Fairytale and Legend" *Musical Quarterly* 8(4):528-554, 1922. il. An interesting collection of musical references in Chinese popular literature, but not annotated sufficiently.

1671. Martin, Helmut. *Li Li-weng über das Theater. Eine chinesische Dramaturgie d. 17. Jhs*. Heidelberg: 1966. iv+395p. il. (Ph.D. dissertation, Heidelberg, 1966). NE.

1672. _____. "Neue Peking-Oper als Politlehrstück" *China Aktuell* 1(11):37-38, Dec 1972. NE.

1673. Martinie, Jean and Nancy. "La Musique chinoise ancienne" *Musikforschung* ns 285:633-641, 1938. NE.

1674. Mas, Sinibaldo de. *La Chine et les Puissances Chrétiennes*. Paris: Hachette, 1861 [?]. 2 vols. See I,92-130 on Chinese theater. NE.

1675. Mason, Bruce. "The Chinese Classical Theatre" *Landfall* 11:72-75, March 1957. NE.

1676. Mason, Eric. "China Report (LPO Tour)" *Music and Musicians* 21(10):18f., June 1973. NE.

1677. _____. "Music in Modern China" *Contemporary Review* (London) 223(1295):295-299, Dec 1973. NE.

1678. Masters, Frederic J. "The Chinese Drama" *Chautauquan* 21:434-442, 1895. Detailed, knowledgeable. Based mostly on the San Francisco Chinese theatre. Much attention to economics, sociology of acting profession. Relatively little on music. Excellent photographs. [RR]

1679. Mateer, Mrs. J.B. "List of Musical Terms" in *A Vocabulary and Handbook of the Chinese Language* by Justus Doolittle (Foochow: Rozario, Marcal, 1872), II,307-308. NE.

1680. Mathieu, G. "Le Système musical" *T'oung Pao* 15:339-381, 1914. 16:489-514, Oct 1915. 18:31-48, March 1917. 19:41-49, March 1918-1919. 20:40-50, Jan 1920-1921. 355-360, Dec 1920-1921. il., mus., tables. NE.

1681. Matignon, Jean Jacques. "Instruments de musique des Chinois" *La Nature* 23(2):309-311, Oct 11, 1895. il. NE.

1682. _____. "Les Instruments de musique des Chinois" in his *Superstition, Crime, et Misère en Chine* (Lyon: Storck, 1899), p.369-379. NE. [NYPL]

1683. Maurer, Walter. "Die Ziehharmonika" *Jahrbuch Osterreich Volksliedwerkes* 17:49-57, 1968. il. NE.

1684. May, Alfred J. "Chinese Nursery Rhymes" *China Review* 25(6):--. NE.

1685. Mayhew, Athol. "Some Personal Recollections of Chinese Music" *Metronome* 27(8):23, 38, 1911. NE.

1686. McCloud, Alexander. *Pigtails and Gold Dust*. Caldwell, Id.: Caxton Printers, 1947. Chapter 23, p.307-318, is on the Chinese theatre in California in the 19th century. Slapdash scholarship. Not recommended. [RR]

1687. McDowell, Henry Burden. "The Chinese Theater" *Century Magazine* 24(1):27-44, Nov 1884. il. Probably the best all-around eyewitness account of the Chinese theatre in America in the 19th century. Careful scholarship with many historical notes. Based on observations in San Francisco theatres. Illustrations exceptionally good. Relatively little on music per se. [RR]

1688. McLachlan, Ian. "Introductory Notes to a Chinese Opera" *Eastern Horizon* 3:43-45, Jan 1964. Notes on the translation of "The Orphan Chao," which was a popular bit of Chinoiserie in 18th-century France and England.

1689. Medhurst, Walter Henry. *Ancient China: The Shoo King*. Shanghai: Mission Press, 1846. xvi+413p. il., mus. See p.33-37, 76-80. Legge and Karlgren are more reliable translations.

1690. Mei, Ginsiang. *The Influence of Music on Chinese Culture*. M.A. thesis (music), Wayne State University, 1952. 77p. mus. An incompetent rehash of poorly chosen secondary sources.

1691. Mei, Lan-fang. "The Filming of a Tradition" *Eastern Horizon* 4(7):13-22, July 1965; 4(8):43-49, Aug 1965. Translated by Chen Li. Mei's experiences filming Peking opera.

1692. _____. "My Life on the Stage" *Chinese Literature* 11: 3-35, 1961. Also in *Eastern Horizon* 1(15):11-29, Dec 1961. il. Good photos.

1693. _____. "My New Opera" *Chinese Literature* 10:133-139, 1959. il. Describes his innovations in the new opera "Mu Kuei-ying Takes Command."

1694. _____. "On Peking Opera" *People's China* 12:12-16, 1955. Also in *Music Mirror* 1(3):28-33, March 1958.

1695. _____. "Old Art with a New Future" *China Reconstructs* 1(5):21-24, Sept-Oct 1952. il., portrait. On reforming the opera by eliminating bad plays. Reprinted as "Bright Future for Peking Opera" in *China In Transition* (Peking: China Reconstructs, 1957), p.346-350.

1696. _____. "Picturing Characters of the Stage" *China Reconstructs* 10(10):38-39, Oct 1961. il. On artists' interpretations of opera scenes.

1697. _____. "Il Teatro Cinese" *Quaderni de Civilta Cinese* 5:335-338, July 1956. NE.

1698. _____. "The Traditional Theatre Today" *China Reconstructs* 8(10):18-21, Oct 1959. il. Survey of genres and new operas.

*   _____. See also Association des Amitiés Franco-Chinoises, ed.

1699. Mei, Y.P. *Motse, the Neglected Rival of Confucius.* London: Probsthain, 1934. See p.140-142 on Confucian-Mohist music controversy.

1700. _____, trans. *The Ethical and Political Works of Motse.* London: Probsthain, 1929. 275p. See p.120 -134, 175-181. Motse condemned Confucian theories about music because of the great expenditures for orchestras, instruments, singing girls, and so on, incurred by the Emperors, while the common people went hungry.

1701. Meng Chih. *Remarks on Chinese Music and Musical In-struments*. New York: China Institute in America, 1932. 14p. il., mus. A short introduction to basic principles. Interesting chart of notations. Line drawings of instruments.

1702. Mertens, Pierre-Xavier, S.J.   "Le Théâtre Chrétien dans nos collèges Chinois. Un drame Chinois sur les martyrs Chinois, 'Les Martyrs de Tcho-kin-ho'" *Bulletin Catholique de Pékin* 18:579-583, 1931. NE.

1703. _____. "Le Théâtre d'oeuvre. Est-il utilisable en Chine comme moyen d'apostolat.   Le Drame de la Passion" *Bulletin Catholique de Pékin* 7:463-468, 1921. NE.

1704. _____. "Le Théâtre en Chine comme moyen d'apostolat. Le Drame de la Passion" *Les Missions Catholiques* 54:125-127, 1922. NE.

1705. Meserve, Walter J. and Ruth I. Meserve.   "China's Persecuted Playwrights: The Theatre in Communist China's Current Cultural Revolution" *Journal of Asian and African Studies* 5(3):209-214, July 1970. NE.

1706. _____, eds. *Modern Drama from Communist China*. New York: New York University Press, 1970.   368p. Scripts of model operas.

1707. Metzger, Emil. "Musik und Gesang bei den Chinesen" *Globus* 46:376-380, 1884. NE.

1708. Meyer, Kathi. *Bedeutung und Wesen der Musik*. Strass-burg: Heitz, 1932. vii+267p. See p.3-19 and *pas-sim*. NE.

1709. Mickey, Portia. "The Ha P'a Miao of Kweichow" *Jour-nal of the West China Border Research Society* 15: 57-78. See p.68-69. NE.

1710. Mihailov, G.   "Vechera Muzyki Novovo Kitaia" [Eve-nings of Music of New China] *Sovetskaya Muzyka* 9: 76f., Sept 1952. NE.

1711. Milburn, Frank, Jr. "Tucker Finds Rewarding Role as Musical Envoy to Far East" *Musical America* 77(9): 16-17, Aug 1957. Report of Richard Tucker's tour of Asia.

1712. Mills, H.P.   "China Show Biz Balked by NG Pay" *Var-iety* 173:207f., Jan 5, 1949. NE.

1713. _____. "Commies Spell Doom to Shanghai Entertain-
      ment" *Downbeat* 16:2, Dec 2, 1949. NE.

1714. _____. "Musicians Get 'U.S. Scale' on Holidays in
      Shanghai" *Downbeat* 16:3, Jan 28, 1949. NE.

1715. _____. "Shanghai's Famed Night Life Ended by Commies"
      Variety 176:1f., Nov 9, 1949. NE.

1716. Mimart, Auguste. "Chine et Chinois. Musique et thé-
      âtre de l'Empereur" *L'Arte Musicale* 2:331-333,
      1861-1862. NE.

1717. Min Ming. "Impressions of the Albanian Folk Song
      and Dance Ensemble" *Chinese Literature* 9:108-111,
      1974. il.

1718. Miner, Luella. "China" in *The American History and
      Encyclopedia of Music. Foreign Music*, edited by
      Hubbard (Toledo: Squire, 1908), p.17-26. "No other
      nation has exalted and practised any art for long
      ages and made such poor attainment in it as have
      the Chinese in the art of music." With this be-
      ginning the author goes on to give a synthesis
      of a few hostile sources. Needless to say, a
      somewhat unreliable essay.

1719. Mitchell, John D., ed. *The Red Pear Garden: Three
      Great Dramas of Revolutionary China*. Boston: Go-
      dine, 1974. Translations of "The White Snake,"
      "The Wild Boar Forest," and "Taking Tiger Moun-
      tain by Strategy." Helpful introductory chapters
      on history of revolutionary opera by Richard
      Strassberg, and on "The Staging of Peking Opera"
      by John D. Mitchell and Donald Chang. Review by
      F. Merkling in *Opera News* 38:41, May 1974.

1720. Mitchell, John D., Donald Chang, and Robert Yeu.
      "Two Faces of China" *Opera News* 38(24):24-27,
      April 20-27, 1974. il., mus. NE.

1721. Mok, Robert T. "China: A Short History of Music"
      Hinrichsen's Musical Yearbook 4-5:307-311, 1947-
      1948. Largely a recount of Western-trained musi-
      cians in contemporary China.

1722. _____. "Heterophony in Chinese Folk Music" *Journal
      of the International Folk Music Council* 18:14-23,
      1966. mus., bibliog.

1723. Mollard, Sidney G., Jr. "Confucius and Music" *East-
      West Center Review* 3(3):31-38, Feb 1967.

1724. Moor, Arthur Prichard. "Oriental Music" in *International Cyclopedia of Music and Musicians*, edited by Oscar Thompson (New York: Dodd, Mead, 1946), 4th ed., p.1322-1332. Poor.

1725. Moresby, Isabelle. "Chinese Music" *Canon* 15(3-5):61, Christmas 1961.

1726. [Morgan, Harry Titterton]. *Chinese Music*. Los Angeles: Quon-Quon Co., 1944. Rev. ed. 16p. il., mus. (Chinese Classics in Miniature Series). Pamphlet with line drawings of 13 Chinese instruments. 3 musical examples showing pentatonic scale. Origin legend.

1727. Morris, M.D. "Out of Peking: Chinese Opera Preserves the Many-Splendored Traditions of Forty Centuries" *Opera News* 33(21):8-13, March 22, 1969. il.

1728. Morrison, Hedda.   "Chinese Harmony" *Geographical Magazine* 21:151-154, Aug 1948. NE.

1729. _____. "A Chinese Theatre Club in Sarawak" *Geographical Magazine* 29(5):243-249, 1956. NE.

1730. Moser, Hans Joachim. "Chinesische Musik" in his *Musik Lexicon* (Hamburg: Sikorski, 1955), I,198-199.

1731. Moule, Arthur Christopher [1873-?]. "Chinese Music" *Musical Times* 48:163-166, 231-233, 1907. il., mus. NE.

1732. _____. "A List of the Musical and Other Sound Producing Instruments of the Chinese" *Journal of the Royal Asiatic Society, North China Branch* 39:1-160, 1908. il., mus. Valuable study classifying Chinese instruments according to structure, with additional notes on scales, music in the theatre, some Chinese attempts at instrument classification.   The best available source on Chinese instruments, but in need of an enlarged, revised edition.

1733. _____. "A Western Organ in Medieval China—I. The Chinese Texts" *Journal of the Royal Asiatic Society*, p.193-206, 726-727, 1926; 899-900, 1928. See also Galpin, same title.   Translation of the source material, with original text, on an organ presented to Kublai Khan from the West.

1734. Moule, G.E. "Notes on the Ting-chi, or Half Yearly Sacrifice to Confucius" *Journal of the Royal Asiatic Society, North China Branch* 33:120-156, 1899-1900. Frequent references to music and musical instruments in the rites, and translations of 6 hymn texts. Much excellent musical information.

1735. Mow, Joseph B. "Chinese Coolie Chants" *Ethnomusicology* 5(1):76, Jan 1961. mus. Brief note, with two transcribed chants.

1736. Mowry, Hua-yuan Li. *Yang-pan Hsi—New Theater in China*. Berkeley: Center for Chinese Studies, University of California, 1973. (Studies in Chinese Communist Terminology, No. 15). viii+117p. Careful study of the development, theory, and practice of revolutionary modern opera, with synopses of seven works.

1737. Moy, C. "Communist China's Use of the Yang-Ko" *Papers on China* 6:112-148, 1952.

1738. Moy, Ernest K., ed. *Mei Lan-fang: Chinese Drama*. New York: China Institute in America, [1930]. 40p. Souvenir program for Mei's American tour. Includes articles by Hu Shih "Mei Lan-fang and the Chinese Drama," George Kin Leung "The Chinese Theatre, a Brief Consideration of the Outstanding Peculiarities of the Old Chinese Drama," and unsigned articles on varied aspects of the drama. Also included are the synopses of each play and scene, reprinted from George Kin Leung's book *Special Plays and Scenes* ...

1739. Mulford, Prentice. "Glimpses of John Chinaman" *Lippincott's Magazine* 11:219-225, Feb 1873. Brief mentions of music. [RR]

1740. Müller, Herbert. "Beiträge zur Ethnographie der Lolo" *Bässeler-Archiv* 3:38-68, 1912. il. See p. 56-58. NE.

1741. Munk, Erica, ed. *Theatre in Asia*. (Special issue of *The Drama Review* 15(3), Spring 1971). New York: New York University, 1971. il. A collection of 35 articles, documents and plays from numerous Asian opera-drama genres: "folk, ritual, classic and proletarian theatres, aesthetics, politics, social change, cinema, music, dance, the impact of the West." Materials relating to China are given separate entries.

1742. Munn, W. "Chinese Hymnology" *Chinese Recorder*, p.701-709, Dec 1911. NE.

1743. _____. "Chinese Music" *Church Missionary Review* 63:
532-536, 1912. NE.

1744. _____. "Hymnology in the Chinese Church. I." in
China Mission Year Book, 1912 (Shanghai: Christian Literature Society for China, 1912), p.244-
249. Problems of translating texts into accept-
able Chinese idioms. Comments on some available
hymn books.

1745. Munro, Thomas. *Oriental Aesthetics*. Cleveland: Western Reserve University, 1965. x+138p. See Chapter 6, p.21-29, "Some Comparisons Between Chinese
and Western Theories of Music, Fiction, and Drama."

1746. _____. "Oriental Traditions in Aesthetics" *Journal
of Aesthetics and Art Criticism* 24:3-6, Fall 1965.
NE.

1747. Munsterberg, Oskar. *Chinesische Kunstgeschichte*.
Esslinger a.N.: Paul Neff Verlag, 1924. See II,
426-434, "Musikinstrumente."

1748. Mututantri, Barbara. "The New Face of Peking Opera"
Eastern Horizon 9(1):37-43, 1970. The state of
the art after Chiang Ching's revisions. Mainly
refers to "On the Docks."

* * * * * * * * * *

1749. Nacken, J. "Chinese Street Cries in Hong Kong" *Journal of the Royal Asiatic Society, Hong Kong
Branch* 8:119-127, 1968. il. NE.

1750. Nakajima, C. "On the Musical Idea of Ya Ch'in" *Shi-
nagaku Kenkyū* 13:4, 54-71, Sept 1955. In Japanese, with brief English summary.

1751. Nakaseko, Kazu. "Symbolism in Ancient Chinese Music
Theory" *Journal of Music Theory* 1(2):147-180, Nov
1957. Tables, bibliog. Abridgment of the author's
M.A. thesis. A detailed and scholarly exposition
of the major systems of Chinese music theory and
the attendant complexes of numerological-cosmo-
logical symbolism elaborated to excess by Han sco-
liasts and unfortunately overstressed by unso-
phisticated Western writers. An important monograph.

1752. Narodny, Ivan. "Music of China Was 'Futurist' 2000 Years Ago" *Musical America* 18(11):11, 28, July 19, 1913. NE.

1753. Needham, Noël Joseph Terence Montgomery [1900-] and Kenneth Robinson. "Sound (Acoustics)" in *Science and Civilization in China*, by Joseph Needham (Cambridge: Cambridge University Press, 1962), Vol. IV, Pt. I, Sec. 26. Chap. H, p.126-228. il., mus., tables, bibliog., index. Authoritative survey of the development of Chinese music theory and acoustic science. Based on Robinson's Oxford B.A. thesis on Chu Tsai-yü, and Robinson's other papers, compiled and edited by Needham. Many fascinating theories not found elsewhere. Required reading.

1754. Neefe, Konrad. "Die Kriegsmusik der Chinesen in vorchristlichen Zeitalter" *Allgemeine Musikzeitung* 17:235-236, 245-246, 1890. NE.

1755. Netter, Émile. "Chinese Music and Musician" *China Digest* 1(8):16-19, April 10, 1947. On Ma Sitson.

1756. Ng Poon Chew. "The Chinese in Los Angeles" *Land of Sunshine* 1:102-103, Oct 1894. Brief description of Chinese theatre. [RR]

1757. Ngawang Zangpo. "We Go to Peking" *China Reconstructs* 14(3):32-33, March 1965. il. Impressions by a member of a Tibetan dance group at the Peking National Minorities Amateur Song and Dance Festival.

1758. Nian Yi. "Volkslieder der Tong-Nationalität" *Beiträge zur Musikwissenschaft* 3-4(8):302-309, 1966. mus. Translated by Gerd Schönfelder.

1759. Nikolaev, O. and F. Yarikov. "Narodni Kompozitor Sien Sin-Khai" [The Popular Composer Hsien Hsinghai] *Sovetskaya Muzyka* 10:100-102, 1950. il. NE.

1760. Nio Joe-lan. "Chinese Songs and Plays in Batavia" *China Journal* 23(4):198-200, Oct 1935. il. On a Chinese music and opera club in Java which studies gambang and produces opera in Mandarin.

1761. Nordhoff, Charles. *California: For Health, Pleasure and Residence*. New York: Harper & Bros., 1873. Description of Chinese theatre in San Francisco, p.86-88. [RR]

1762. Norlind, Tobias. "Beiträge zur chinesischen Instru-
mentengeschichte" *Svensk Tidskrift för Musik-
forskning* 15:48-83, 1933. il. Good in-depth study
of some major instrumental types.

1763. Normande, Suzanne. "La Tournée chinoise. II—à
l'opéra de Pékin" *Revue des Deux Mondes*, p.72-84,
Jan 1, 1966. NE.

1764. Norris, F.L. "Music in the Chinese Church" *Chinese
Recorder* 40(4):179-184, April 1909. Suggests
unison singing with octave accompaniment; proposes use of Gregorian chant instead of Chinese
tunes.

1765. _____. "Music in the Chinese Church" *Church Missionary Review* 63, 1912. NE.

1766. Numile, L.G. "Notes sur la musique chinoise" *Revue
Bleue* 68:410-412, 1930. Brief secondhand introduction.

1767. Nye, Robert E. *The Music of India, China, Japan,
and Oceania: A Source Book.* D. Music, University
of Arizona, 1969. NE.

* * * * * * * * * *

1768. Oakes, Vanya. "The Music of War-Torn China" *Étude*
56(1):11-12, Jan 1938. il., mus.

1769. Obraztsov, Sergei Vladimirovich. *The Chinese Puppet
Theatre.* London: Faber and Faber, 1961. 55p. 37
plates. A chapter from *Teatr Kitaiskogo Naroda*,
translated by J.T. MacDermott.

1770. _____. *Das Chinesische Theater.* Velber: Friedrich
Verlag, 1965. (Series: Theater Heute, Vol. 21).
Translation from Russian.

1771. _____. *Teatr Kitaiskogo Naroda* [The Theater of the
Chinese People]. Moscow: Isskusstvo, 1957. 375p.
il. German translation by Wolfgang Pintzka: *The-
ter in China*, Berlin: Henschelverlag, 1963. 236p.
Short version, *Das Chinesische Theater*, Velber
bei Hanover: Friedrich Verlag, 1965. 84p. Pro-
fusely illustrated; covers numerous theater forms.
German version omits color plates and some black
and white photos.

1772. O'Connor, John J. "TV: Ballet from China" *New York Times* 70:3, March 13, 1972. NE.

1773. Ogawa, Tamaki. "The Song of Ch'ih-le, Chinese Translations of Turkic Folksongs and Their Influence on Chinese Poetry" *Acta Asiatica* 1:43-55, 1960. NE.

1774. "On the Docks" Theatrical Unit of Shanghai Peking Opera Troupe. "Reflect the Militant Life of the Working Class in the Socialist Era: Some Understanding from Creating the Revolutionary Modern Peking Opera 'On the Docks'" *Selections from China Mainland Magazines* 729-730:63-73, May 30-June 5, 1972. From *Hung-ch'i* 5, May 1, 1972.

1775. Onnen, F. "Opera van Peking" *Mens en Melody* 10:224-226, July 1955. NE.

1776. Oost, Joseph van. "A propos d'une chanson populaire chinoise" *Bulletin de la Société d'Études Coloniales* 31:168-174, 1924. NE.

1777. _____. "Chansons populaires chinoises de la région sud des Ortos: Introduction, notation, traduction et Notes" *Anthropos* 7:161-193, 373-388, 765-782, 893-919, 1912. il., mus. 32 songs transcribed, with translation and copious annotation. No Chinese characters or musical analysis.

1778. _____. "Les musiciens professionnels au Nord de la Chine" *La Revue Belge* 7, 1930. NE.

1779. _____. "Notes sur le T'oemet" *Variétés Sinologiques* 53, 1922. III. iii+190p. mus. See p.79-182, "Chansons et Musique Populaires." NE.

1780. _____. *Vingt Cantiques sur Texte Chinois avec Accompagnement d'Orgue, à l'Usage des Séminaires, Collèges, et Congrégations.* Zikawei: T'ou-Sewe, 1925. NE.

1781. Ore, Harry. "Hong Kong, China" *Southwestern Musician* 16(8):7, April 1950. Brief note on Western music in Hong Kong.

1782. Osgood, Cornelius. *Village Life in Old China: A Community Study of Kao Yao, Yunnan.* New York: Ronald Press, 1963. xii+401p. il. An anthropologist's report of field work done just prior to W.W. II. Though the claim is made that music is not found in Kao Yao—purely social music-making does not seem to flourish there—many instances of functional music are recorded (weddings, p.281-282;

funerals, p.294, 297; shaman, p.301-317; festivals, p.333-335) and a fairly good catalog of musical instruments is given (p.240-245).

1783. Otsuka, Jun. "Music in Manchukuo" *Manchuria* 4(15): 24-26, July 20, 1938. Survey of Western-music activities.

1784. Oueng Ting. *Chansons Populaires Chinoises*. Peiping: Imprimerie de la Politique de Pékin, 1935. NE.

1785. Ouyang Yu-chien. "The Dance in China" *People's China* 14:19-20, 22-23, 25-27, July 16, 1957. il. Popular historical survey.

1786. _____. "The Modern Chinese Theatre and the Dramatic Tradition" *Chinese Literature* 11:102-103, 1959. NE.

1787. _____. "The Traditions of Chinese Dancing" *Chinese Literature* 4:182-187, 1957. il. Good short introduction to the various genres of classical dance.

* * * * * * * * * *

1788. P., H. "Did Weber Compose Chinese Music?" *China Review* 2:--, 1874. NE.

1789. Page, Frederick. "Music in China" *Musical Times* 104 (1443):331-332, May 1963. Report of trip to Peking—musical activities and Western music.

1790. _____. "A Musician's Journal" *Landfall* 15(57):44-46, March 1961. Reprinted in *Arts and Sciences in China* 1(1):9-16, Jan-March 1963. Diary of musical activities in Canton, Peking, and Shanghai.

1791. Palazzo, Elena. *Musica e Strumenti de Terre Lontane*. Rome: Signorelli, 1933. 95p. il., mus. NE.

1792. Pang, Margaret Young. *Marn-ling and the Chinese Musical Instruments*. Honolulu: Aloha Publishing Co., [n.d.]. 42p. il. With 45 r.p.m. record. Children's book.

1793. _____. *Marn-ling Sees the Chinese Lion Dance*. Honolulu: The Author, 1961. 32p. il., mus. With 45 r.p.m. record. Children's book.

1794. Parker, E.H. *Ancient China Simplified*. London: Chapman and Hall, 1908. See p.206-269, "Music."

1795. _____. "Music (China)" *China Review* 25:54. NE.

1796. Parmentier, H. "Anciens tambours de bronze" *Bulletin de l'Ecole Française de l'Extrême-Orient* 18: 1-30, 1918. il. NE.

1797. Parry, D. "The Chinese Theatre" *Eastern World* 8(1): 41-42, 1954. NE.

1798. Pasenchuk, V. "Novyi Kitaiski Zhurnal" [New Chinese Journal] *Sovetskaya Muzyka* 6:182f., June 1958. NE.

1799. _____. "Problemy Muzykal'novo Nasledia Kitaia" [Problems of China's Musical Heritage] *Sovetskaya Muzyka* 10:145f., 1957. NE.

1800. _____. "Rastvet National'nogo Isskusstva" *Sovetskaya Muzyka* 26:125-129, Oct 1962. il. NE.

1801. Pei Taj. "Singing Birds of China" *Music Mirror* 1(5): 14-15, May 1958. Short popular article on songbirds as household pets.

1802. Pelliot, Paul. "Le K'ong-heou et le qobuz" in *Mélanges Naitô* (Kyoto: 1926). Theorizing relationship between the Chinese angular harp and a Persian form, based on etymological and other evidence, not generally accepted.

1803. Pemberton, Murdock. "A Chinese Theatrical Triumph" *Creative Art*, p.31-35, Jan 1931. il. Brief note on Mei Lan-fang's American tour. Good full-page plates.

1804. Peng Chen. "Peking Opera To Serve Socialism: Talk at the Festival of Peking Opera on Contemporary Themes" *Peking Review* 7:6-11, Aug 7, 1964.

1805. _____. "Talk at the Festival of Peking Opera on Contemporary Themes" *Selections From China Mainland Magazines* 433:7-14, Sept 8, 1964. From *Hung-ch'i* 14, 1964. NE.

1806. Perny, Paul. *Dictionnaire Français-Latin-Chinois*. Paris: Didot, 1869. See II:143-154, "Musique des Chinois" (Append. No. 14).

1807. Petrov, N.A. "Kitaisky Narodnoi Teatr Na Puti k Realizmu" [Chinese Theater on the Path to Realism] *Sovetskaya Etnografiya* 3:171-177, 1949. NE.

1808. Petzoldt, Rochard. "Musik des Fernen Ostens" *Allge-meine Musikzeitung* 63:134-135, Feb 1936. NE.

1809. Pfrogner, H. *Die Zwölfordnung d. Töne.* Zurich: Amal-thea-Verlag, 1953. NE. On 12-tone music, cited in *Riemann Musik Lexicon* article on the *lü*.

1810. Phelps, D.L. "The Plan of Music in the Platonic and Confucian System of Moral Education" *Journal of the Royal Asiatic Society, North China Branch* 59: 128-145, 1928. Comparison of the view of music in the *Analects* and the *Republic*.

1811. Phillips, Grace D. "Music of China, Old and New" *Music Journal* 16:36-37, March 1958. il. Non-technical; much misinformation.

1812. Phillips, H.A. "China's Vanishing Shadow Show" *Asia* 34:412-415, 1934. NE.

1813. Pian Rulan Chao. "Aria Structural Patterns in the Peking Opera" in *Chinese and Japanese Music-Dramas*, J.I. Crump and William P. Malm, editors (Ann Arbor: 1975), p.65-97. The *pan* aria types are defined, and their linking into typical se-quences described, attempting to uncover the main organizational pattern and strategy in the musical, textual, and dramatic structure of Pe-king opera scenes.

1814. _____. "China" in *Harvard Dictionary of Music*, Willi Apel, ed., 2nd ed. (Cambridge: Harvard University Press, 1969), p. 151-157. A concise overview concentrating on history and theory.

1815. _____. "China, People's Republic of. I. General" in *Grove's Dictionary of Music and Musicians*. 6th ed. In press. Good survey, serving to introduce and tie together the specialized articles follow-ing by Shigeo Kishibe, Colin P. Mackerras, Kate Stevens, Bell N. Yung, David Ming-yüeh Liang, Lui Tsun-yüen, and A.C. Scott. Divided into sections: 1) Introduction, 2) Sources, 3) History, 4) Folk, Popular, and Religious Music.

1816. _____. "Chyn" in *Harvard Dictionary of Music*, Willi Apel, ed., 2nd ed. (Cambridge: Harvard University Press, 1969), p.170-171. Concise description of the long zither *ch'in* and its music.

1817. _____. "The Function of Rhythm in the Peking Opera" in *The Musics of Asia*, José Maceda, ed. (Manila: National Music Council, 1971), p.114-131. music. Surveys rhythmic elements of aria types, percussion patterns, and declamatory speech; a fascinating glimpse of Peking opera music practice, based on firsthand experience.

1818. _____. "Jeng," "Pien," "Pyiba" in *Harvard Dictionary of Music*, Willi Apel, ed., 2nd ed. (Cambridge: Harvard University Press, 1969), pp.444, 677, 709. Brief entries.

1819. _____. "Report on Field Work in Taiwan in the Summer of 1964" *CHINOPERL News* 4:123-128, 1974. Narrative report, primarily on recording and studying Peking opera.

1820. _____. "Report on Research in the Year 1965-66" *CHINOPERL News* 4:129-132, 1974. Narrative of research in Los Angeles on Peking opera, and travel in the Far East and Europe.

1821. _____. "Rewriting of an Act of the Yüan Drama, Lii Kwei Fuh Jing, in the Style of the Peking Opera: A Fieldworker's Experiment" *CHINOPERL News* 2:19-39, Dec 1970. mus. A "selected, translated, summarized and annotated" report of a discussion between Dr. Pian and Yang Hsi-mei as to how one would go about choosing aria types and setting text appropriately. An interesting attempt at simulating the compositional process.

1822. _____. *Sonq Dynasty Musical Sources and Their Interpretation*. Cambridge: Harvard University Press, 1967. xvi+252p. il., mus., bibliog. (Ph.D. dissertation, Radcliffe, 1960. 306p.). Thorough study with much valuable information on bibliographic sources for music and musicological literature of the Sung dynasty. Discussion of notation, mode, transcriptions and analysis of all extant compositions. Strong in sinology; less so in music theory. See review essay by Laurence Picken in *Journal of the American Oriental Society* 89(3):600-621, July-Sept 1969. Reviewed by: Fritz Kuttner in *Ethnomusicology* 13(3):553-557, Sept 1969; Fredric Lieberman in *Notes* 26(1):23-24, Sept 1969; Peter Crossley-Holland in *Musical Times* 109:634, 1968; Eta Harich-Schneider in *Sinologica* 11(1-2):93-100; Colin Mackerras in *Monumenta Serica* 27:447-450, 1968.

1823. _____. "Text Setting with the *Shipyi* Animated Aria"
      in *Words and Music: The Scholar's View; A Medley
      of Problems and Solutions Compiled in Honor of A.
      Tillman Merritt by Sundry Hands*, Laurence Berman,
      ed. (Cambridge: Department of Music, Harvard Uni-
      versity, 1972), p.237-270. mus. A carefully de-
      tailed study of the formal structure of Peking
      opera arias of the *hsi-pi liu-shui-pan* category
      (*Shipyi Lioushoei-baan* in GR). Motivic structure,
      tone-setting, rhythmic patterns, melodic formu-
      lae are considered in analyzing a sample aria
      transcribed from "The Trial of Su San."

1824. _____. "Videotaping Peking Opera" *CHINOPERL News*
      4:133-137, 1974. Brief report on a project to
      videotape performances of Peking opera in New
      York's Chinese community.

1825. Pick, Vivien. "Der Einfluss der Kulturrevolution
      auf die Peking-Oper" *China Report* 1:20-25, 1971.
      NE.

1826. Picken, Laurence E.R. "Chiang K'uei's Nine Songs
      for Yüeh" *Musical Quarterly* 43:201-219, 1957.
      Excellent and provocative paper containing back-
      ground material, translations, transcriptions,
      structural and modal analyses of 10 songs pre-
      served from the Sung dynasty. Suggests presence
      of *maqam* technique. Microtonal alterations com-
      pared to contemporary *gagaku*.

1827. _____. "Chinese Music" in *Encyclopedia Britannica*
      [1966 ed.] V,639-641. il., mus., bibliog. Out-
      standing brief survey.

1828. _____. "Chinese Music: Present Day Music" in *Grove's
      Dictionary of Music and Musicians*. 5th ed. II,
      245-247. Short review of Chinese and Western music
      and musicians in contemporary China.

1829. _____. "Early Chinese Friction-Chordophones" *Galpin
      Society Journal* 18:82-89, March 1965. A valuable
      paper translating and analyzing, for the first
      time, the earliest Chinese sources on the fric-
      tion-zither *ya-cheng* and on prototypes of the
      spike-fiddle *hu-ch'in*.

1830. _____. "Music and Musical Sources of the Sonq Dyna-
      sty" *Journal of the American Oriental Society* 89
      (3):600-621, July-Sept 1969. An extensive review
      essay of Rulan Chao Pian's *Song Dynasty Musical
      Sources and Their Interpretation*. Most attention
      is paid to modal theory, and there is a careful
      exposition of *ch'in* technique and terminology.

1831. _____. "The Music of Far-Eastern Asia—I. China" in
        New Oxford History of Music. 3rd ed. I,83-134.
        il., mus., bibliog. Expert survey stresses anal-
        ysis of extant music, with a little detailed in-
        formation on archeological finds, technology,
        etc. Avoids reliance on legend and anecdotal his-
        tory. Partly reprinted in *Readings in Ethnomusi-
        cology*, David P. McAllester, ed. (New York: John-
        son Reprint Corp., 1971), p.336-352.

1832. _____. "The Music of Far-Eastern Asia—II. Other
        Countries" in *New Oxford History of Music*. 3rd
        ed. I,135-194. "Other countries" is something of
        a misnomer, as this survey includes regions and
        national minorities which are usually considered
        part of China—Sinkiang, Miao, Lolo, etc. Picken
        keeps one foot in China when discussing surround-
        ing countries, and sums up cultural interrela-
        tions in a short final section—an important at-
        tempt at perspective for the entire Far- and
        South-Eastern Asian area.

1833. _____. "The Musical Implications of Line-Sharing in
        the *Book of Songs (Shih Ching)*" *Journal of the
        American Oriental Society* 89(2):408-410, April-
        June 1969.   Reports briefly on a study of Chu
        Hsi's collection of 12 melodies and suggests
        that text-melody relationships can throw much
        light on ancient processes of musical composi-
        tion.

1834. _____. "Musical Terms in a Chinese Dictionary of
        the First Century" *Journal of the International
        Folk Music Council* 14:40-43, 1962. Discussion of
        some musical terms culled from the *Shuo Wen Chieh
        Tzu* of Hsu Shen (ca.+100).   Case study of the
        types of musical inference to be drawn from anal-
        ysis of musical vocabulary.

1835. _____. "Oriental Music" in *Encyclopedia Britannica*
        1966 ed. XVI,1092-1093. Good short introduction,
        stressing major stylistic features.

1836. _____. "The Origin of the Short Lute" *Galpin Soci-
        ety Journal* 8:32-42, March 1955.   Collates and
        translates earliest Chinese evidence of *p'i-p'a*.
        Suggests original form circular, short straight
        neck. Ovoid, bent neck does not appear until 5th
        century.

1837. _____. "Secular Chinese Songs of the Twelfth Century" *Studia Musicologica* 8:125-171, 1966. il.,
mus.   Detailed study of the secular songs published by Chiang K'uei.   Unravels many problems
of the Sung dynasty notation, drawing on Chinese
research of recent years. Much discussion of poetic form, prosody, and their effect in determining rhythm in musical settings.   Transcriptions
and translations of the songs, with analyses.

1838. _____. "Some Central Asian Tunes from the Gagaku
Repertoire" in *Festschrift für Walter Wiora* (Kassel: Bärenreiter, 1967), p.546-551. mus.   Analysis shows striking similarities between Central-
Asian tunes and some speeded-up lines in *gagaku*
(treating the slower parts as nuclear themes).

1839. _____. "Some Chinese Terms for Musical Repeats, Sections, and Forms, Common to T'ang, *Yüan*, and *Tōgaku* Scores" *Bulletin of the School of Oriental
and African Studies* 34(1):113-118, 1971. Comparisons of Japanese and Chinese sources suggests
that "the language of the part-books to some ex-
tent reflects the technical vocabulary current
among Chinese musicians from T'ang to Sung and
Yüan times."

1840. _____. "T'ang Music and Musical Instruments" *T'oung
Pao* 55(1):74-122, 1969. An extensive review essay
on Martin Gimm's *Das Yüeh-fu tsa-lu des Tuan An-
chieh*, discussing the main problems of T'ang musicology.

1841. _____. "Three-Note Instruments in the Chinese People's Republic" *Journal of the International Folk
Music Council* 12:28-30, Jan 1960.   Archeological
and ethnological evidence suggests possibility
of 3-note ritual music in Shang China.   Russian
translation in Victor Vinogradov, ed. [Music of
the Peoples of Asia and Africa] (Moskva: Sovets-
kij Kompositor, 1969) as "Trekhvuchnye Instru-
menty v Kitaiskoi Norodni Respublike" (p.310-
316).

1842. _____. "Tunes Apt for T'ang Lyrics from the *Shō*
Part-Books of *Tōgaku*" in *Essays in Ethnomusicology: A Birthday Offering for Lee Hye-ku* (Seoul:
Korean Musicological Society, 1969), p.401-420.
mus.   Argues that *shō* part-books preserve T'ang
and Sung tunes, though slowed down 16 times; internal evidence of tune structure and external
corroboration from early documents are adduced.

1843. _____. "A Twelfth-Century Secular Chinese Song in Zither Tablature" *Asia Major* 16(1-2):102-120, 1971. Study, with annotated transcription, of the *ch'in* tablature "Ku Yüan" by Ch'iang K'uei.

1844. _____. "Twelve Ritual Melodies of the T'ang Dynasty" in *Studia Memoriae Belae Bartok Sacra*, p.147-173. A comprehensive analysis of the melodies published by Chu Hsi, which probably derive from a source in the K'ai-Yüan period. The tunes are those of the *Shih Ching* odes 161, 162, 163, 170, 172, 1, 2, 3, 12, 13, 15. All are transcribed into staff notation, and variorum information is given keyed to other surviving texts of the melodies. Philological information from Karlgren.

*   _____. See also Rembrandt Wolpert et al.

1845. Pickowitz, Paul G. "The Modern Revolutionary Peking Opera 'Taking Tiger Mountain by Strategy': An American's View" *Eastern Horizon* 10(4):31-34, 1971. NE.

1846. Piguet, J.C.   "L'Opéra de Pékin" *Paru* 93:113-116, 1955. NE.

1847. Pilone, R. *Teatro in Cina.* Bologna: Capelli, 1966. 110p. NE.

1848. Pimpaneau, J.   "Culture populaire, culture des lettres en Chine" *La Musique dans la Vie* 2:107-120, 1969. NE.

1849. Pin Chih.   "Peasant Poets and Their Songs" *Chinese Literature* 10:101-107, 1965. Only texts are discussed.

1850. Ping Sheng.   "The Color, Drama, and Taste of the Liang-Chu Film" *West and East* 8(7):11-12, July 1963.

1851. Pischner, Hans.   "Musik im neuen China" *Musik und Gesellschaft* 4:175-179, 217-219, 294-295, 322-323, 363-366, 404-407, 1954.   Report on musical life in China of the People's Republic by leader of East German Folk Music Troupe touring in China. Some good materials on composers.

1852. _____. *Musik in China*. Berlin: Henschelverlag, 1955. 152p. il. Growing out of his tour in Red China, this book is a non-technical survey with much space devoted to contemporary music.

1853. Plath, J. Heinrich. *Die Religion und der Cultus der Alten Chinesen*. München: 1862. See Pt. 2, p.70f., "Von der Musik und den Tanzen bei den Opfern der Kaiser." NE.

1854. Plavec, J. "Pohled na Činskou Hudbu" [A Look at Chinese Music] *Nový Orient* 7:131-132, 1952. NE. Development of Chinese music since W.W. I.

1855. Playfair, G.M.H. "Notes on the Language of the Formosan Savages" *China Review* 7:342-345, 1878. NE.

1856. Portnoy, Julius. "Similarities of Musical Concepts in Ancient and Medieval Philosophy" *Journal of Aesthetics and Art Criticism* 7:235-243, 1948-1949. NE.

1857. Poupeye, Camille. *Le Théâtre Chinois*. Paris, Brussels: Editions "Labor," 1933. 194p. il. 41 plates.

1858. Priest, A. "Additions to the Chinese Collection (Theatrical Costumes)" *Bulletin of the Metropolitan Museum of Art* 31:112-114, 1936. NE.

1859. _____. "An Exhibition of Chinese Shadow Players and Scenery" *Bulletin of the Metropolitan Museum of Art* 37:34-35, 1942. NE.

1860. Prieto, Guillermo. *San Francisco in the Seventies. The City as Viewed by a Political Exile*. Translated and edited by Edwin S. Morby. San Francisco: John Henry Nash, 1938. Brief and bewildered notes on Chinatown's music and drama, p.383-384. [RR]

1861. Profeta, Rosario. *Storia e Letteratura Degli Strumenti Musicali*. Florence: Marzocco, 1942. 662p. il., mus. See p.15-20. NE.

1862. Provine, Robert C. "The Treatise on Ceremonial Music (1430) in the Annals of the Korean King Sejong" *Ethnomusicology* 18(1):1-29, Jan 1974. il., mus. A careful study of a document interpreting Confucian ceremonial music, which includes quotations from early Chinese source material, "thereby preserving fifteen Chinese ritual melodies that exist in no other source, Korean or Chinese." Includes transcriptions of the melodies and photocopy of the text.

1863. Průsek, Jaroslav. "Die Chui-tsi-shu, Erzählende Volksgesänge aus Ho-nan" in *Asiatica: Festschrift Friedrich Weller* (Leipzig: Harrassowitz, 1954), p.453-483. 6 plates of Chinese characters. Extensive literary study of this genre of folk narrative song from Honan. English version in his collected essays *Chinese History and Literature* (Dordrecht, Holland: Reidel, 1970), p.170-198.

1864. Purcell, William L. "From Lui Tsun-Yuen, A Record to Cherish" *American Record Guide* 30(9):808-809, May 1964. il. Rave review of Lui's second Lyrichord album.

1865. _____. *An Introduction to Asian Music*. New York: The Asia Society, 1965. ii+11p. Too brief a survey. Not recommended.

1866. _____. "Lyrichord's Superb Chinese Series" *American Record Guide* 32:432, Jan 1966. NE.

1867. Purvis-Smith, C. "Music and the Chinaman" *Pacific Coast Musician* 18(45):17, 22, Nov 2, 1929.

* * * * * * * * * *

1868. Quon, Maple. "Status of Music Education in Hong Kong" in *ISME International Conference Report 1963* (Tokyo: 1963), p.295-297.

* * * * * * * * * *

1869. Rada, Stephen E. "Peking Opera" *Viltis* 26(1):5-6, May 1967. NE.

1870. Radtke, Kurt W. "The Development of Chinese Versification: Studies on the *Shih*, *Tz'u* and *Ch'ü* Genres" *Oriens Extremus* 23(1):1-37, June 1976. NE.

1871. Ramey, M. "Comparative Studies of Musical Instruments" *Computers and the Humanities* 10(2):93-100, 1976. il. Computer-aided study, including some Chinese instruments.

1872. Rault, Lucie. *La Cithare Zhēng*. Ph.D. dissertation, University of Paris (Nanterre), 1973. viii+520p. NE.

1873. Rawlinson, F.   "New Union Hymnal" *China Christian Yearbook*, p.496-497, 1932-1933. NE.

1874. Raymont, Henry.   "A Musician-Defector Denounces Excesses by China's Red Guard" *New York Times*, 1966-1967? Portrait. On Ma Ssu-tsung.

1875. Red Guards of the Middle School of the Central Conservatory of Music. "How the 'Red Guards' Battle Song' Was Born" *China Reconstructs* 17(3):36-39, March 1968. il., mus. Political discussion, score of song.

1876. Reichwein, Adolf.   *China and Europe, Intellectual and Artistic Contacts in the 18th Century.* New York: Knopf, 1925. 174p.   Translated by J.C. Powell.

1877. Reinhard, Kurt.   "Acht Lieder Sinisierter Lolo" *Bässeler-Archiv* ns 4:105-116, 1956. mus., tables. Continuation of "Die Musik der Lolo."

1878. _____. *Chinesische Musik.* Eisenach, Kassel: Roth, 1956. 248p. il., mus., bibliog. Well-organized and thorough presentation of Chinese music as reflected in Western language sources, designed for the general reader. Large bibliography arranged chronologically. Useful musical examples, good illustrations. Reviewed by: Fritz Kuttner in *Ethnomusicology* 2(2):85-86, May 1958; W. Graf in *Anthropos* 52(5-6)978-979, 1957. 1967 reprint reviewed by Jörg Martin in *Musik im Unterricht* 59:23-24, 1968.

1879. _____. "Juwelenstrom (Chinesisches Shattenspiel)" *Musikblätter* 8:195f., 1954. NE.

1880. _____. "Die Musik der Lolo" *Bässeler-Archiv* ns 3: 195-216, 1955. mus., tables. A musicological study of a West-Szechwan and Yünnan tribal group based on recorded examples in the Berlin Phonogrammarchiv.

1881. Reinhardt, Richard. *Out West on the Overland Train; Across the Continent Excursion with Leslie's Magazine in 1877, and the Overland Trip in 1967.* Palo Alto, Cal.: American West Publishing Co. [1967]. il. Observations on Chinese theatre in San Francisco (p.182-184) include descriptions of activities backstage and downstairs. Excellent illustrations. [RR]

1882. Reinhart, Rainer.   "Das Musikleben in Rotchina" *Hochland* 51:291, 293, 1958-1959. NE.

1883. _____. "Die Oper im heutigen China" *Frankfurter Hefte* 15:353-356, 1960. NE.

1884. Reissmann, August. *Allgemeine Geschichte der Musik*. Munich: Bruckmann, 1863-1864. 3 vols. See I,15-26. NE.

1885. Revolutionary Committee of the China Peking Opera Theatre. "Let Heroic Images of the Proletariat Shine on the Peking Opera Stage!" in *On the Revolution of Peking Opera*, Chiang Ching, ed. (Peking: 1968), p.34-43.

1886. Revolutionary Committee of the Peking Opera Company of Shantung. "*Raid on the White Tiger Regiment*— Born and Matured in Struggle" in *On the Revolution of Peking Opera*, Chiang Ching, ed. (Peking: 1968), p.56-65.

1887. Richard, Mary [Mrs. Timothy Richard]. "Airs Founded on Pentatonic Scale" *Chinese Recorder* 22:313-314, 1891. music. NE.

1888. _____. "Chinese Music" *Chinese Recorder* 21(7):305-314, July 1890; 21(8):339-347, Aug 1890; 21(9): 416-419, Sept 1890. Introductory survey; history, theory, instruments, practice. Superficial.

1889. _____. "Chinese Music" *Leisure Hour*, p.91-94, 1897-1898. music. NE.

1890. _____. "Chinese Music" *East of Asia Magazine* 1:301-314, 1902. il., music. Popular survey based on Chinese sources; little detailed information.

1891. _____. *Paper on Chinese Music Read Before the China Branch of the Royal Asiatic Society, Shanghai, November 1898*. Shanghai: American Presbyterian Mission Press, 1907. 43p. il., music. 4th ed. Shanghai: Presbyterian Mission Press, 1930. 40p. il., mus. A sketchy introduction, the text of an hour-long lecture. Original data were taken from standard Chinese classics, but not enough to save this very missionary-minded effort from deserved obscurity.

1892. Riddle, Ronald William. "The Cantonese Opera: A Chapter in Chinese-American History" in *The Life, Influence and Role of the Chinese in the United States, 1776-1960* (San Francisco: Chinese Historical Society of America, 1976), p.40-47.

1893. _____. *Chinatown's Music: A History and Ethnography of Music and Music-Drama in San Francisco's Chinese Community*. Ph.D. dissertation (musicology), University of Illinois, Urbana-Champaign, 1976. ix+326p. A detailed, extensive historical study, followed by a shorter but valuable investigation of the current situation in San Francisco based on field work.

1894. _____. "Music Clubs and Ensembles in San Francisco's Chinese Community" in *Tradition and Change in Eight Urban Musical Cultures*, Bruno Nettl, ed. (Urbana: University of Illinois Press [forthcoming 1978]). Based on observation and interviews, this is an extensive sociological, descriptive survey of formally organized music-making groups categorized as: 1) Cantonese Opera, 2) Peking Opera, and 3) Instrumental Music. Discusses the membership, history, audience, and repertory of each.

1895. _____. "Music in America's Chinatowns in the Nineteenth Century" *Bulletin of the Chinese Historical Society of America* 12(5):1-5, May 1977. Historical introduction.

1896. Ridgeway, William. "Ancestor Worship and the Chinese Drama" *Quarterly Review* 231:296-317, 1919. NE.

1897. Ritter, Herm. "Musik in China" *Neue Musikzeitung*, 1900. NE.

1898. Robins, Rae. "Tones and Heart-Strings of China" *China Monthly* 2(3):16-18, Feb 1941. il. On the activities of Ida Hoyt Chamberlain (see No. 575 above), composer, lecturer, and proto-ethnomusicologist.

1899. Robinson, Douglas. "Chinese Musician, Red Guard Target, Gets Asylum Here" *New York Times*, April 13, 1967. p.1, 4. Portrait. On the much-publicized defection of composer-violinist Ma Ssu-tsung.

1900. Robinson, Kenneth. "Chinesische Musik. Geschichtliche Entwicklung von der Frühzeit (Shang-Dynastie bis zum ende der Han-Zeit)" in *Musik in Geschichte und Gegenwart* II,1195-1205. il., bibliog. An excellent article, thorough and reliable. Large bibliography.

1901. _____. *A Critical Study of Chu Tsai Yü's Account of the System of the Lü or Twelve Musical Tubes in Ancient China.* B. Litt. thesis, Oxford University, 1950-1951. This study forms the basis for the major article listed above under Needham (No. 1753).

1902. _____. "Ichthy-Acoustics" *Annual of the China Society of Singapore* 67, 1953. "A rather light-hearted article with a certain amount of solid matter in it in which I was comparing the primitive method by which the Malays detect the presence of shoals of fish by taking a deep breath and remaining under water listening to the fish, whereas the Chinese with characteristic inventiveness remained sitting in their boats listening to the movement of the shoals through bamboo tubes." (Robinson—personal communication).

1903. _____. "New Thoughts on Ancient Chinese Music" *Annual of the China Society of Singapore,* p.30-33, 1954. Provocative article correcting popular misconceptions and suggesting that: 1) The Ch'in book-burning did not eradicate music; 2) *'Yüeh,'* mistranslated as 'music,' should include: music, dance, religious festive-atmosphere; 3) 'Pythagorean' is a misnomer for Chinese scale, no influence from Greece being probable; 4) 'Quarter tones' is a misnomer for intervals in the untempered Chinese scale; 5) There are no universally valid aesthetic criteria.

*   _____. See also Joseph Needham, No. 1754 above.

1904. Robinson, Roland. "Eastern and Western Dancing" *Hemisphere* 9(1):33-35, Jan 1965. il. NE.

1905. Rodecape, Lois. "Celestial Drama in the Golden Hills: The Chinese Theatre in California, 1849-1869" *California Historical Quarterly* 23:97-116, 1944. Excellent, thoroughly documented. Research mostly from 19th-century newspaper accounts. [RR]

1906. Rodyenko, Peter. "Napoleon in Shanghai" *Theatre Arts Monthly* 17:298-306, April 1933. NE.

1907. Rogers, Sister Mary James. *Elements of Musical Study in the Missionary School and in Some Missions Afar.* M.A. thesis, Catholic University, 1938. 99p. NE.

1908. _____. *Music in the Maryknoll Mission Field, The Problem and Our Efforts to Meet It.* New York: Maryknoll, 1938. 75p. il., mus. NE.

1909. Root, L.H. "Hymnology" *China Mission Year Book*, Pt. 7, Chap. 37, 1916. NE.

1910. Roper, Myra. "Taking the Bandits' Stronghold" *Eastern Horizon* 6(8):10-11, Aug 1967. Favorable review of modern Peking opera.

1911. _____. "A Theatre-Goer in China" *Eastern Horizon* 3(6):46-49, June 1964.

1912. Rousset, Léon. *A Travers la Chine*. Paris: Hachette, 1878. See p.285-288. NE.

1913. Roussier, Pierre Joseph. *Mémoire sur la Musique des Anciens*. Paris: Lacombe, 1770. xxiv+252p. See p.14-16, 24, 121-131, 135-138. One of the earliest books to include Chinese music theory with Green and Egyptian. Roussier later edited the work of Amiot.

1914. Rowley, George A. "A Chinese Scroll of the Ming Dynasty 'Ming Huang and Yang Kuei-fei Listening to Music'" *Artibus Asiae* 31(1):5-31, 1969. 17 plates. Foreword and Addendum by Alexander C. Soper. Reprinted from Worchester Art Museum *Annual* 2, 1936 -1937. A detailed stylistic analysis of this scroll in the Worchester Art Museum; Soper's addendum uses material from Kishibe's "A Chinese Painting of the T'ang Court Women's Orchestra," which deals with the same scroll from a musicological viewpoint.

1915. Roy, Basanta Koomer. "East Meets West and Cultures Fuse in Land of the Dragon" *Musical America* 42 (12):7, 30, July 11, 1925.

1916. Roy, Claude. "Incontro col Teatro Cinese" *Società*, p.981-1010, 1955. NE.

1917. _____. *L'Opéra de Pékin*. Paris: Cercle d'Art, [1955]. 100p. il. Photographs by Pic, commentary by R. Ruhlmann. A picture book, the new Peking troupe. Good shots of "Monkey," "White Snake," and others. See p.35-39, "De la Musique Considerée comme un Décor" and p.93-94, "Les Instruments de Musique." Review by E.H. v. Tscharner in *Asiatische Studien* 10(1-4):154-155, 1956.

1918. _____. "Quelques clefs pour le théâtre chinois" *Théâtre Populaire* 14:3-28, July-Aug 1955. NE. [NYPL].

*   _____. See also Association des Amitiés Franco-Chinoises, ed.

1919. Rud, A.M. "Chinese Music" *Illustrated World* 25:393-394, May 1916. NE.

1920. Rudder, May de. "La Musique au théâtre populaire Chinois" *Guide Musical* 58(309):312, 1912. NE.

1921. Rudman, Vladimir. "Muzyka v Kitaiskom Teatre" [Music in the Chinese Theater] *Sovetskaya Muzyka* 8:37-54, Aug 1937. il., mus. NE.

1922. ____. "Pesni Kitaiskogo Naroda" [Songs of the Chinese People] *Sovetskaya Muzyka* 12:72-83, Dec 1937. il., mus. NE.

1923. Rudolph, Richard C. "Dynastic Booty: An Altered Chinese Bronze" *Harvard Journal of Asiatic Studies* 11:174-180, 1948. il. On a bronze bell of the "chung" type, cast about 1105 A.D.

1924. ____. "Newly Discovered Chinese Painted Tombs" *Archeology* 18(3):171-180, Sept 1965. il. Paintings in some T'ang tombs, including a man holding a *p'i-p'a*, and one whole wall portraying an orchestra, dancer, 2 singers, *pai-hsiao*, *ch'in*, *k'ung-hou*, *ti-tzu*, *p'i-p'a*, *sheng*, vertical flute, small cymbals, clapper. Said to date from 745, Shensi.

1925. ____. "Two Recently Discovered Han Tombs" *Archaeology* (Cambridge) 26(2):106-115, April 1973. Photos. Includes instruments. NE.

1926. Rühl, Theo. "Kirchenmusik in China und Japan. Ihr Verhältnis zur allgemeinen Musikpflege" *Kirchenmusik* 70:11-16, 1950. NE.

1927. Ruhlmann, Robert. "Les jeux et le théâtre au temps des Song" in *L'Art de la Chine des Song* (Paris: Musée Cernuschi, 1956). NE.

* ____. See also Association des Amities Franco-Chinoises, ed.

* * * * * * * * * *

1928. S., R.B. "On the Chinese Musical Scales" *China Mail* 30, Sept 1845. NE.

1929. Sachs, Curt. "Chinesische Musik" in *Musiklexicon* (Mainz: 1958); edited by Riemann. NE.

1930. _____. *The History of Musical Instruments*. New York: Norton, 1940. 505p. il., index.   See p.162-191, "Antiquity: The Far East" and p.207-220, "The Middle Ages: The Far East."   Good study of the major types of Chinese musical instruments, emphasizing origins and cultural interrelations with West Asia.

1931. _____. "Notes on Chinese Music and Dance" *Journal of the American Musicological Society* 3:292-293, 1950.   Brief communication, translating a letter by Dr. W. Lurje, who was an army physician in China, 1939-1941.   Attempts of recruits from the interior to sing together Western-style anthem. First, no trace of the melody; after a week in parallel seconds, then occasional fifths, another week in perfect fifths, soon some octaves, ultimately all octaves.   Never thirds, fourths, or sixths.   Occasionally late starters produced canons. Also short description of Miao marriage ritual dance.   Needless to say, this letter did fit Sachs' *kulturkreis* proclivities   and was much vaunted by him in later publications.

1932. _____. *Rhythm and Tempo*.   New York: Norton, 1953. 391p. mus.   See p.55-67, "The Far East."

1933. _____. *The Rise of Music in the Ancient World East and West*. New York: Norton, 1943. 324p. il., mus. Sec. 3, p.105-153, "East Asia," gives an introductory overview of Chinese music in context of other East Asian musics, devoted largely to basic problems of music theory,   generally satisfactory despite limited scope and occasional errors; based on Western studies.

1934. _____. *The Wellsprings of Music*. The Hague: Nijhoff, 1962. 228p.   Sachs' last book surveys the basic problems of ethnomusicology, particularly in melody, scale, and rhythm.   China and Chinese music *passim*.

1935. _____. *World History of the Dance*. New York: Norton, 1937. 469p. il. See p.218-236, "The Evolution to the Spectacular Dance and the Oriental Civilizations."

1936. Sadie, Stanley, ed.   "China, People's Republic of" in *Grove's Dictionary of Music and Musicians*, 6th ed. In press.   An extensive introductory survey, recommended as a good starting place for students; composed of articles by several scholars: General (R.C. Pian), Court Tradition (S. Kishibe), Musical Drama (C.P. Mackerras),   Narratives (K.

Stevens), Theory (B.N. Yung), Instruments (D.M.
Y. Liang, T.Y. Lui, C.P. Mackerras), China After
1949 (A.C. Scott). See under individual contrib-
utors for details on each section.

1937. Sala, Don Juan. *Instrumentos Músicos Chinos Exis-
tentes en el Museo Arquelógico Nacional*. Madrid:
Fortanet, 1873. NE.

1938. Sala, George Augustus. *America Revisited*. London:
Vizetelly & Co., 1882. 2 vols. Literate, chatty,
tourist's account of music and theatre in San
Francisco's Chinatown II, 474-486. [RR]

1939. Sargeant, Winthrop. "Chinese Music" *Theatre Arts
Monthly* 14:389-397, 1930. NE.

1940. Satoh, Mary Miki. "Women in Chinese Folk Songs"
Eastern Asia 5:59-64, Spring 1941. Folk song
texts translated, emphasizing inferior position
of women.

1941. Savagner, A. *Histoire de la Chine*. Paris: Ardant,
1851. See II, 252, 276 on theatre and music. NE.

1942. Schafer, Edward H. *The Golden Peaches of Samarkand:
A Study of T'ang Exotics*. Berkeley, Los Angeles:
University of California Press, 1963. An excellent study of the period in which China experi-
enced contact with many neighboring cultures in
a truly international, cosmopolitan city environment. "Musicians and Dancers," (p.50-57) is a
thorough discussion of intercultural contact in
music, drawn from both Western and Oriental
sources.

1943. Schaffhauser, G. "Chinesisches Musik im Dienste der
Kirche. Gedanken zur neuen Chinesischen Psalmen-
Vertonung" *Neue Zeitschrift für Missionswissen-
schaft* 4(3):214-219, 1948. NE.

1944. Schafhautel, Carl von. "Über das Gut-komm, eine
Chinesische Viersaitige Laute, und über Chinesische Musik" *Allgemeine Musikalische Zeitung* 11
:593-599, 609-614, 625-630, 641-646, 657-662, 671
-679. il. NE.

1945. Schall, Edgar. "Zweimal chinesische Oper" *Das Musikleben* 9:319-321, 1955. NE.

1946. Scheepers, Will D. "Folk-Dance Instruments, Chinese
Mouth-Organ (Sheng)" *The Folklorist* 6(3):396,
Winter 1960-1961. il. NE.

1947. _____. "Peking Opera" *Dansbalans* (Rotterdam), p.1-2, Autumn 1972. il., mus. NE.

1948. _____. "Shêng, de chinese mondharmonica" *Dansbalans* (Rotterdam), p.6-7, Autumn 1972. il. NE.

1949. Scheffer, Paul. "Playgoing in China and Japan" *Living Age* 329:638-641, 1926. NE.

1950. Schenk, Paul. "Als Musiktheoretiker in Volkschina" *Musik und Gesellschaft* 9(12):713-715, Dec 1959. il. Report of seven-week trip.

1951. Scherchen, Hermann. "Die Musik des Chinesischen Theaters" *Musica Viva* 1:46-48, 1936. English, French, Italian abstracts. NE.

1952. Schindler, Bruno. "On the Dramatic Character of Some of the Old Chinese Festival Songs" in *Studia Sino-Altaica: Festschrift für Erich Haenisch zum 80 Geburtstag* (Wiesbaden: Steiner, 1961), p.179-183. Literary study of the *Shih Ching* ode "Fu-T'ien" (Mao 211).

1953. Schipper, K.M. "The Divine Jester, Some Remarks on the Gods of the Chinese Marionette Theater" *Bulletin of the Institute of Ethnology, Academia Sinica* 21:81-94, Spring 1966. NE.

1954. Schlegel. *Dictionnaire Chinois—Néerlandais*. See III,1016 on music. NE.

1955. Schlepp, Wayne. *San-ch'ü; Its Technique and Imagery*. Madison: University of Wisconsin Press, 1970. x+150p. bibliog., index. Study, with many translations, of the companion song/text genre to Yüan tsa-chü.

1956. Schlesinger, Kathleen. "Notes on Musical Instruments Represented in the Stein Collection" in *Serindia* (Oxford: Clarendon, 1921), edited by Stein, III, 1467-1468. il. NE.

1957. _____. "Researches into the Organs of the Ancients" *Sammelbände der Internationalen Musikgesellschaft* 2:167-202, 1900-1901. Brief notices on the *pai-hsiao* and *sheng*, p.172-173, 186-187.

1958. Schlösser, R. "Klanggerätmünzen im alten China" *Sinica* 3:97-110, 1928. NE.

1959. Schneerson, Grigorij Michajlovič. "Isskusstvo Kitaiskih Druzei" [The Art of Chinese Friends] *Sovetskaya Muzyka* 9:38f., 1957. NE.

1960. _____. "Kantata o Novom Kitae" [Cantata of New Chi-
na] *Sovetskaya Muzyka* 3:40f., March 1951. NE.

1961. _____. "Kitaiski Dirizher, Li Te-lun" [The Chinese
Conductor, Li Te-lun] *Sovetskaya Muzyka,* 1957.
NE.

1962. _____. *Muzykaln'aia Kul'tura Kitaia.* Moscow: Gos.
Muzykal'noe Izd-vo., 1952. 248p. il.   German
translation by Renate Schubert, Foreword by Dmi-
tri Kabalevsky, *Die Musikkultur Chinas.* Leipzig:
Hofmeister, 1955. 212p. il. Survey for the general reader, with no doubt an admixture of People's Propaganda, as fully 112 pages are devoted
to music in People's China.

1963. _____. "Na Kontserte Kitaiskovo Dirizhera" [At the
Concert of a Chinese Conductor] *Sovetskaya Muzyka* 1:44f., Jan 1959. NE.

1964. _____. *O Kitaiskoi Muzyke: Stat'i Kitaiskikh Kom-
positorov I Muzykovedov* [Chinese Music: Articles
by Chinese Composers and Musicians]. Moscow: Gos.
Muzykal'noe Izd-vo., 1958. music. NE.

1965. _____. *Si Sin-khai* [Hsien Hsing-hai]. Moscow: Gos.
Muzykal'noe Izd-vo., 1956. 47p. il. NE.

1966. Schneider, Marius. "La Relation entre la mélodie et
le langage dans la musique chinoise" *Annuario
Musical Español* 5:62-77, 1950.   Examines some
Chinese melodies in light of previous study of
music-language relationships in African tonal
languages. Attempts a tentative statement of general rules for melodics in a tonal language.
Transcriptions with transliterated text, translations.

1967. Schneider, M. and D. Jameux. "Dossier-débat: musique
et politique" *Musique en Jeu* 3:101, May 1971. NE.

1968. Schoen, Victor R.   *"Yüeh-lü Ch'üan-shu" by Prince
Chu Tsai-yü: Translation with Critical Analysis
and Commentary.* Ph.D. (theory), Indiana University. NE.

1969. Schönfelder, Gerd. *Das ban-Prinzip als musikalische
Gestaltungsweise der Stile Erhuang und Zipi   in
der Peking Oper: Ein Beitrag zur Entwicklungsgeschichte der Musik.* Inaug. dissertation, Hum-
boldt University, Berlin, 1967.   NE.

1970. _____.   "Bemerkungen zum vorliegenden Notationsar-
tikel von Yang Yin-liu" *Beiträge zur Musikwissenschaft* 9(1):41-44, 1967. See Yang Yin-Liu, "Zum

Problem der Übertragung ..."

1971. _____. "Chinesische Musik" in Seeger, *Musiklexicon* (Leipzig: 1966). NE.

1972. _____. "Die melodische Gerüstgestalt des Orlhuang und ihre Realisation" in *Bericht über Internationalen Musikwissenschaftlichen Kongress Leipzig 1966*, Carl Dahlhaus et al., eds. (Leipzig: VEB Deutsche Verlag für Musik, 1970), p.561-571. NE.

1973. _____. *Die Musik der Peking-Oper*. Leipzig: Deutscher Verlag für Musik, 1972. 2 vols. 287, 64. il., mus., bibliog., glossary. An extensive exposition of the melodic and rhythmic structures of Peking opera. A second volume contains transcriptions. Bibliography almost exclusively of Chinese sources.

1974. _____. "Die Peking-Oper: 'Die Beschwörung des Ostwinds' (Jie Dong Feng), aus dem Zyklus: *Die Schlacht bei der roten Wand*" *Beiträge zur Musikwissenschaft* 5:183-212. music.

1975. _____. *Das "yue mu ci zi" und seine schlagrhythmische und formstructurelle Gestalt*. Ph.D. dissertation, Karl Marx University, Leipzig, 1969. xviii+176 p. NE.

1976. _____. "Zum chinesischen Ban-Prinzip" *Jahrbuch für Musikalische Volks- und Völkerkunde* 4:98-105, 1968. mus. On one of the basic elements of formal structure in Peking opera music.

1977. _____. "Zum Gebrauch der Schlaginstrumente im traditionellen chinesischen Musik-theater" *Studia Musicologica* 13:137-176, 1971. NE.

1978. Schonberg, Harold C. "I Coolly Face the Enemy Firm as a Mountain" *New York Times*, Sec. 2, 23:2, March 5, 1972. NE.

1979. _____. "The Music: Movie Like" *New York Times* 15:4, Feb 23, 1972. NE.

1980. _____. "Must Ideology Command a Culture?" *New York Times*, Oct 7, 1973.

1981. _____. "Peking Opens Door to Philadelphians" *New York Times*, Sept 13, 1973.

1982. _____. "Philadelphians a 'Big Success' in Their First Concert in China" *New York Times*, Sept 15, 1973.

1983. _____. "Philadelphians Play Committee Music" *New York Times*, Sept 18, 1973.

1984. _____. "Yin Spoke Only Chinese, Ormandy Only English" *New York Times*, Oct 14, 1973.

1985. Schwartz, Tracy E. "The Harps of East Asia" *Folk Harp Journal* (Mount Laguna, Cal.), 5-18, 23-31, June 1974. il. A copiously illustrated survey bringing together much secondary source material and iconographic evidence on the *k'ung hou* and related instruments in China, Japan, Korea, and Soviet East Asia.

1986. Scott, Adolphe Clarence. "The Butterfly Dream: The Record of a Chinese Theatre Workshop in New York" *Drama Survey* 2:158-174, Oct 1962. il. NE.

1987. _____. "China, People's Republic of. VI. China After 1949" in *Grove's Dictionary of Music and Musicians*. 6th ed. In press. Surveys history, Maoist aesthetics. Includes biographical sketches of Nieh Erh. Hsien Hsing-hai, Ma Ssu-tsung, and Yin Cheng-ts'ung. Subdivided into: 1) National Organization and Education; 2) Music and Musicians; 3) Theatre and Dance Music.

1988. _____. "Chinese Theatre Notebook" *Orient* 4(12):29, 32, 1954; 5(1):24-25, 1954; 5(3):23-24, 1954; 5(7):67-69, 1955; 5(8):61-63, 1955; 5(9):70-72, 1955; 5(10):59-60, 1955; 5(11):49-50, 1955. NE.

1989. _____. "The Chinese Theatre Toy Box" *Orient* 2(10):24-25, 1952. NE.

1990. _____. "*Ch'ou Chiao Erh*: The Comic Roles of the Chinese Classical Theatre" in *Akten des 24. Internationalen Orientalisten-Kongresses München, 1957* (Wiesbaden: Steiner, 1959), p.643-646. NE.

1991. _____. *The Classical Theatre of China*. London: Allen and Unwin, 1957. il. Authoritative study emphasizing acting technique; material on history, music, role types, stories. Many technical terms explained.

1992. _____. "Contemporary China—Fact vs. Fancy" *Theatre Arts Monthly* 45(4):54-55, 76-77, 1961. NE.

1993. _____. "Costumes of the Chinese Drama" *Orient* 9:20-21, April 1951; 10:20, May 1951; 11:23-24, June 1951; 12:30, July 1951; 2(1):30, 1951; 2(3):35, 1951; 2(4):15, 1951; 2(5):22, 1951; 2(7):30, 1952; 2(8):28, 1952; 2(9):28, 1952. NE.

1994. _____. "Dance in Contemporary China" *World Theatre* 6(3):211-216, 1957. NE.

1995. _____. "The Foo Hsing Troupe in New York" *Drama Survey* 3:143-144, May 1963. NE.

1996. _____. "A Great Chinese Actor Yü Chen Fei" *Orient* 1(10):21-22, May 1951. NE.

1997. _____. "Hung Teng Chi, 'The Red Lantern': An Example of Contemporary Chinese Dramatic Experimentation" *Modern Drama* (Lawrence, Kan.) 9:404f., 1967. NE.

1998. _____. *Introduction to the Chinese Theatre*. Singapore: Moore, 1958. viii+92p. il. A general, non-technical introduction for the tourist or curious non-specialist.

1999. _____. *Literature and the Arts in 20th Century China*. New York: Anchor Books, 1962. Includes chapters on drama and music.

2000. _____. *Mei Lan-fang, Leader of the Pear Garden*. Hong Kong: Hong Kong University Press, 1959. iv+140p. il. Biographical study of the man and his art.

2001. _____. "Reflections on the Aesthetic Background of the Performing Arts in East Asia" in *Perspectives on Asian Music: Essays in Honor of Dr. Laurence E.R. Picken*, Fritz A. Kuttner and Fredric Lieberman, eds. (New York: Society for Asian Music, 1975), p.207-216. "A discursive essay on the physical basis of East Asian acting and performance as it has been influenced by Zen, Taoism, etc. There is a description of Asian physical training methods and some comparison with Western theatre" [author].

2002. _____. "Reflections on the Chinese Classical Drama" *Orient* 1:25-27, Aug 1950; 2:25-27, Sept 1950; 3:25-28, Oct 1950; 4:24-27, Nov 1950; 5:23-26, Dec 1950; 6:23-27, Jan 1951. NE.

2003. _____. "Students of the Pear Garden" *Journal of Oriental Studies* 3(1):69-74, Jan 1956. On the training of Peking opera actors.

2004. _____ . *The Theatre in Asia.* New York: Macmillan, 1973. x+289p. il. See Chapter 4, "China," p.126-173. Social history and descriptive survey, aimed at the general reader, but thanks to Professor Scott's long, practical experience in Asian theatre, there is considerable firsthand material of interest to the specialist.

2005. _____ . *Traditional Chinese Plays. Vol. 1: Ssu Lang Visits His Mother; The Butterfly Dream.* Madison: University of Wisconsin Press, 1967. xiv+165p. il. These excellent translations are thoroughly annotated. A tape may be purchased separately with excerpts of music and dialogue for which the texts are given in an appendix.

2006. _____ . *Traditional Chinese Plays. Vol. 2: Longing for Worldly Pleasures; Fifteen Strings of Cash.* Madison: University of Wisconsin Press, 1969. 156p. Two *k'un ch'ü* operas in performing translations, with introductory essays.

2007. _____ . *Traditional Chinese Plays. Vol. 3: Picking Up the Jade Bracelet [Shih yü-cho]; A Girl Setting Out for Trial [Nü ch'i-chieh].* Madison: University of Wisconsin Press, 1975. xvi+96p. Two Peking operas which feature the clown role. Scott provides introductory essays on the clown's type and actions. The annotated, performing translations maintain Scott's usual high quality.

2008. Scriabine, Marina. "La Musique et la Chine ancienne" *Revue Française de Sociologie* 3(4):398-406, Oct-Dec 1962. On the ancient system and music aesthetic, largely derived from the classic books and Amiot. Not reliable.

2009. Scudo, P. "De la musique chinoise" *Revue des Deux Mondes* 2s 29:252-256, Sept 1860. Report of a tourist.

2010. Seaman, Gary. "Ethnographic Film from the Field to the Classroom: Film Records of Popular Religion in China" *CHINOPERL Papers* 7:106-135. Bibliog.

2011. Seaman, Julian. "Chinese Sounds" *Musical Courier* 101 (24):8, Dec 13, 1930. music. NE.

2012. _____ . "Music and Instruments of the Chinese" *Jacob's Orchestra Monthly* 15(8):5, 23, Sept 1924. mus. NE.

2013. Seaton, Jerome P. *A Critical Study of Kuan Han-ch'ing: The Man and His Works.* Ph.D. dissertation, Indiana University, 1969. NE.

2014. Seelig, Paul J. "Over Chineesche Muziek" *Weekblad Voor Muziek* 8(15):--, 1902; 9(21):--, 1902. NE.

2015. Semenoff, Marc. "Chine et Cambodge" *Le Courrier* 34: 505, Dec 15, 1933. NE.

2016. Semmedo, Alvaro. *Imperio de la China*. Madrid: P. Coello, 1642. 14+360p. English translation, *The History of That Great and Renowned Monarchy of China*. London: Tyler, Cook, 1655. See p.54-55. NE.

2017. Serova, Svetlana Andreevna. "Istoki Kanoniczeskogo Zesta w Kitaiskom Tieatre" *Narody Azii i Afriki* 5:114-122, 1970. NE.

2018. _____. *Pekinskaia Muzykal'naia Drama*. Moskva: Nauka, 1970. 195p. NE. "A compendious handbook of information on the origin and growth till 1940's of the most widely known form of Chinese traditional theatre, the Peking Opera, of its repertory and conventions of performing art." (Zbikowski 1970:16).

2019. _____. "P'esy v Sovremennykh Kostiûmakh v Kitaiskoi Muzykal'nom Drame" *Narody Azii i Afriki* 3:102-109, 1966. NE.

2020. Serruys, Paul. "Children's Riddles and Ditties from the South of Tatung (Shansi)" *Folklore Studies* 4:213-290, 1945. NE.

2021. Sestakov. V.A., ed. *Musical Aesthetics of Countries of the East: Monuments of Musical-Aesthetic Thought*. Moscow: Muzyka, 1967. 414p. In Russian. Includes treatises on folk music and sacred music. NE.

2022. Seyfried, Ignaz Xaver. "La Musique en Chine" *Revue et Gazette Musicale* 1:190-192, 1884. NE.

2023. Sha Ou. "Ma Sitson and 'Our Motherland Cantata'" *China Digest* 3(12):17-18, May 4, 1948. Portrait, mus. Brief review with list of works to date.

2024. "Shachiapang" Revolutionary Fighting Regiment of the No. 1 Peking Opera Company of Peking. "Mao Tse-tung's Thought Illuminates the Road of Revolution of Peking Opera" in *On the Revolution of Peking Opera*, Chiang Ching, ed. (Peking: 1968), p. 44-55.

2025. Shadick, Harold. "Chinese Drama" *Collier's Encyclopedia*. 1965 ed. VI,344.

2026. Shan Hsiang. "Peking Theatres During the Spring Festival" *Chinese Literature* 4:99-106, 1966. il. On the variety of local operas playing in Peking.

2027. Shapiro, Sidney. "Chinese Local Operetta" *Eastern Horizon* 3(4):21-23, April 1964.

2028. Sharp, J. "Peking Cools to Classics of Music" *Christian Science Monitor* 65:5c. Jan 18, 1974. NE.

2029. Sheffield, D.Z. "Chinese Church Music" *China Review* April 1909. NE.

2030. _____. "Church Music" *Chinese Recorder* 40(4):184-189, April 1909. Surveys church music and concludes China has none yet.

2031. Shen Ke-wu. "A Club with Many Purposes" *China Reconstructs* 7(8):27-29, Aug 1958. il. The cultural club of the Yang Lin farm co-op: music, dance and drama down on the collective farm.

2032. Shen, Lucille. "Music of and for the Soul" *Free China Review* 13:31-37, Aug 1963. NE.

2033. Shen Ting-shu. "Chinese Folk Dances" *Free China Review* 10(10):13-15, 1960. NE.

2034. Shen Tsung-wen. "Recent Finds in a 2300-Year-Old Tomb" *China Pictorial* 2:27-29, 1958. il. Series of bronze bells and parts of a lacquered *se* found in Hsinyang, Honan, formerly Chu.

2035. Sheng Chieh. "Folk Dances of China" *China Reconstructs* 11(2):2-5, Feb 1962. il. Describes *yang-ko* and other dances.

2036. Sheng, David Shuan-en. *A Study of the Indigenous Elements in Chinese Christian Hymnody.* D.M.A. dissertation (church music), University of Southern California, June 1964. x+557p. il., music. Tunes with "indigenous elements" are identified but not analyzed. Musical questions receive short shrift. Textual analysis is better; historical-bibliographical survey of hymnology in China is excellent.

2037. Shih Chan-chun. "Workers' Clubs and Cultural Groups" *China Reconstructs* 1(4):22-27, July-Aug 1952. il. On the organization of music, dance, and drama groups.

2038. Shih Chung-wen. *The Golden Age of Chinese Drama: Yüan Tsa-chü.* Princeton: Princeton University Press, 1976. xvii+312p. The first book-length study in English of *tsa-chü*, this study is solidly made and accessible to the general reader. Musical topics are covered in Chapter 6, p.180-197. Appendices include a list of extant plays, bibliography, bibliography of translations, glossary, and index.

2039. _____. *Injustice to Tou O (Tou O Yüan): A Study and Translation.* Cambridge: Cambridge University Press, 1972. xvi+390p. glossary, bibliog. The importance of this work rests in its translation, which includes the original text, Romanization, literal translation, colloquial translation. Excellent introduction to *tsa-chü* for students already somewhat familiar with the Chinese language.

2040. Shih Hwa-fu. "Old Bards Sing New Themes" *China Reconstructs* 8(2):14-16, Feb 1959. il. Updating several genres of the narrative ballad.

2041. Shih Kuo-hua and Tien Lien-yuan. "An Interrupted Performance" *Chinese Literature* 12:75-80, 1974. il. Short story about a PLA traveling variety troupe helping villagers.

2042. Shih, Peter. "Chinese Tonal System Turned Inside Out" *Musical America* 45(1):23, 28, Jan 1, 1927. NE.

2043. Shih Yen-sheng. "Speaking for the People Is Comrade T'ien Han's Consistent Reactionary Thought" *Selections from China Mainland Magazines* 528:40-46, June 13, 1966. From *Hsi-ch'ü Pao*, April 10, 1966. NE.

2044. Shirokogoroff, Elizabeth N. "Folk Music in China" *China Journal of Science and Arts* 2:116-121, 1924. mus. Valuable brief report with 51 musical examples: 26 street-vendors' tunes from Peking; a group of Manchu and Tungus shaman songs; and several zoomorphic motives.

2045. Shu Chiung [Mrs. Wu Lien-teh]. "Mei Lan-fang in the Role of Yang Kuei-fei" *China Journal* 6:166-169, 1927. NE.

2046. Shu She-yu [Lau Shaw]. *The Drum Singers*. New York: Harcourt, Brace and Co., 1952. 283p. Translated from Chinese by Helena Kuo. Novel about a family of entertainer-musicians during the Second World War. Stresses their problems and low social status, but gives much flavor of the *ta-ku* performer's life-style and the workings of the music business.

2047. Shu Tsang-houei. "Chinese Musical Terminology" Addendum A in *Historical Musicology*, Lincoln Bunce Spiess, ed. (Brooklyn: Institute of Mediaeval Music, 1963), p.234-236. A brief glossary.

2048. Shuai Wen-yen. "Amateur Night at Liuliho" *People's China* (24):10-11, Dec 16, 1952. il. Music, song, and dance at cement works.

2049. Shyrock, John K. "Ch'en Ting's Account of Marriage Customs of the Chiefs of Yunnan and Kueichou" *American Anthropologist* 36:524-547. 1934. Translation of a 17th-century Chinese text, including description of the uses of music in the marriage ceremony, particularly the Miao bronze drums (p.535-539).

2050. Sickman, Laurence C.S. "Chinese Bell from the Age of Confucius" *Gazette des Beaux-Arts* ns 623:377-350. 1943. NE.

2051. Sie, C.K. "Le Théâtre chinois" in *Cong. Or. 20, 1938*, p.238-239. NE.

2052. Simbriger, Heinrich. "Betrachtungen über Yang und Yin" *Antaios* 7(2):126-148, July 1965. NE.

2053. _____. *Gong und Gongspiele*. Leiden: Brill, 1939. xv+180p. il., mus. (Internationales Archiv für Ethnographie. Bd. 36). "A fine secondary source on the uses and types of gongs throughout Southeast Asia. He discusses probable origins of gongs, their manufacture and distribution routes, types, gong instruments, uses of gongs, tunings, and ritual significance. A well-documented study, it affords a general overview of the gong-music area" (R. Trimillos).

2054. Simms, Mary E. "Chinese Music" *Music* 6:485-490, Sept 1894. Non-technical introduction based on Amiot.

2055. Singer, Caroline. "Peking Clangor: Noise No Longer Alien When Resolved into the Melody of Humble Living" *Asia* 24(2):1080-1083, 1092, 1094, Dec 1925. il., mus. Sounds of daily life, street calls, etc.

2056. Singer, Caroline and C. Leroy Baldrige. *Turn to the East*. New York: Minton, Balch, [n.d.]. 72p. See p. 50-51, 67-72. NE.

2057. Sittard, Joseph. "Das Theater und Drama der Chinesen" in his *Studien und Charakteristiken* (Hamburg, Leipzig: Vos, 1889), I,187-196. NE.

2058. Sizes, Gabriel. "La Résonance multiple des gongs et des tam-tams chinois" *Association Française pour l'Avancement des Sciences. Compte Rendu* 41:160-161, 1912. NE.

2059. Smirnova, I. "Svobodnyi Kitai" [Free China] *Sovetskaya Muzyka* 11:43f., Nov 1959. NE.

2060. Smith, Barbara Barnard. "Chinese Music in Hawaii" in *Perspectives on Asian Music: Essays in Honor of Dr. Laurence E.R. Picken.* Fritz A. Kuttner and Fredric Lieberman, eds. (New York: Society for Asian Music, 1975), p.225-230. "A description of Chinese musical culture in Hawaii, its introduction and present status, with some speculations on the reasons for the selectivity of survival and relative vitality of the genres performed" (author).

2061. Smith, W. Meishke. *Croquis Chinois.* Paris: E. Flammerion, [n.d.]. See p.253 on theatre. NE.

2062. Sneed, Adelaide B. *Musical Instruments from Earliest Records to the Year 1 A.D.* M.A. thesis, Boston University. 1954. NE,

2063. Snow, Lois Wheeler. *China on Stage: An American Actress in the People's Republic.* New York: Random House. 1972. xviii+330p. il., glossary, index. A sympathetic survey of revolutionary opera by the wife of Edgar Snow. Includes the full texts of "Taking Tiger Mountain by Strategy," "Shachiapang," "Red Detachment of Women," and "The Red Lantern."

2064. _____. "The Cultural Revolution Is Over, But Mao's Melodies Linger On" *Saturday Review* 50(45):36-40, Nov 1972. il. NE.

2065. Sonnerat, Pierre. *Voyage aux Indes Orientales et à la Chine fait par Ordre du Roi, Depuis 1774 Jusqu'en 1782.* Paris: 1782. NE.

2066. Soothill, William Edward. "Chinese Music and its Relation to Our Native Services" *Chinese Recorder* 21(5):221-228, May 1890; 21(7):336-338, July 1890. mus. Brief comments on Chinese music, with recommendations on use of native tunes and even native instruments in the service. Several examples of hymn settings included as appendices.

2067. Souen K'ai-ti. "L'Origine et le développement du théâtre des marionnettes chinoises" *Bulletin du Centre Franco-Chinois d'Études Sinologiques* 1:85 -105, 1944. In Chinese with French summary.

2068. Soulé, Frank, John Gihon, and James Nisbet. *The Annals of San Francisco.* New York: D. Appleton & Co., 1855. il. Describes music in Chinese gambling halls and theatre, p.383-385. [RR]

2069. Soulié de Morant, Charles Georges [1878-?]. "La Musique en Chine" *Bulletin de l'Association Amicale Franco-Chinoise* 2:13-23, 139-155 238-263, 369-394, 1910: 3:24-43, 156-173, 1911. il., mus. In book form. Paris: Leroux, 1911. 110p. Good popular survey, stressing instruments.

2070. _____. "The Modern Chinese Theatre" *Living Age* 315: 231-235. NE

2071. _____. *Théâtre et Musique Modernes en Chine: Avec une Étude Technique de la Musique Chinoise et Transcriptions pour Piano par André Gailhard.* Paris: Geuthner, 1926. xvi+195p. il., mus. Excellent study of Peking opera with historical, sociological, literary, and musicological information.

2072. Soiuz Rabotnikov Muzykalnoi Kultury Kitaia. "Pismo Iz Kitaya Soyuzo Sovetski Kompozitorov" [Letter from China to the Union of Soviet Composers] *Sovetskaya Muzyka* 11:17-20, 1949. il., mus. NE.

2073. Speiser, Werner. "Eine Komposition des Dschou Wengu" *Sinica* 13:39-45, 1938. Painting of a musical performance.

2074. Šrám. Josef. "Chinese Acrobatics of the Han Period" *Eastern Horizon* 3(5):28-31, May 1964. il. Acrobatic entertainments with musical accompaniment, as depicted on stone reliefs.

*   Ssu-ma Ch'ien. See Chavannes.

2075. Staley, S. James. "Is It True What They Say About China?" *Metronome* 52(12):--, Dec 1936. NE.

2076. Stanley, Arthur. "Putoshan" *Journal of the Royal Asiatic Society, North China Branch* 46:1-18, 1915. Includes a discussion of Buddhist polyphonic chanting.

2077. Stanton, W. "Contributions to the Folklore of China" *China Review* 15:123-125, 1886-1887. NE.

2078. Starr, Laura B. "Chinese Musical Instruments" *Music* 14:499-514. 1898. il. Non-technical introduction to basic types of classical instruments. Based on Van Aalst.

2079. Staunton, Sir George. *An Authentic Account of an Embassy from the King of Great Britain to the Emperor of China.* London: G. Nicol, 1797. Narrative of the Macartney expedition. Passages on music excerpted in Frank Harrison's *Time, Place and Music* (q. v.).

2080. Steele, John. *The I-Li, or Book of Etiquette and Ceremonial.* London: Probsthain, 1917. 2 vols. xxiv+286p.,242p. An early but still serviceable translation of this important classic on rites.

2081. Stein, F. "Zur Vergleichung Chinesischer und Japanischer Musik" *Mitteilungen der Deutsche Gesellschaft für Volk- und Naturkunde des Orient* 1:60-62, 1873. mus. Brief notice with 3 Chinese tunes.

2082. Steinen, Diether von den. "Notes on a Theatrical Museum in Peking" *Monumenta Serica* 3:278-285, 1938. See p.279-280. NE.

2083. Stent, George Carter. "Chinese Lyrics" *Journal of the Royal Asiatic Society, North China Branch* 7: 93-135. 1871-1872. mus. Four songs in Western notation, with character text and English translation.

2084. _____. *The Jade Chaplet in Twenty-Four Beads: A Collection of Songs, Ballads, Etc. (From the Chinese).* London: Trübner, 1874. 166p. NE.

2085. Stern, Ph. "Une Nouvelle Collection Musicale Consacrée Principalement aux Musiques de l'Orient et des Contrées Lointaines" *Journal Asiatique* 213:129-139, 1928. Describes the collection, study, and publication project "Bibliothèque Musicale du Musée de la Parole et du Musée Guimet."

2086. Stevens, Catherine. "China, People's Republic of. III. Musical Drama and Narratives. 3. Popular Narratives" in *Grove's Dictionary of Music and Musicians*. 6th ed. In press. Though concise, this article is noteworthy in being the first treatment of Chinese popular narrative in a Western musical reference work.

2087. _____. "City of Peking Ballad Troupe: 1973" *Asian Music* 5(1):24-27, 1973. The author visited Peking in the summer of 1973, and reports here on ballad-singing activities, as discussed in an interview with a professional troupe.

2088. _____. *Peking Drumsinging* Ph.D. dissertation, Harvard University, 1973. 300p. Based on field-work training with the *ta-ku* singer Chang Tsui-feng, this is the most extensive study of the genre, an important contribution to our understanding of sung narrative poetry.

2089. _____. "Sea Swallow" *CHINOPERL Papers* 6:144-154, 1976. Translation of a recent (early 1970s) *hsiang-sheng* cross-talk.

2090. Stimson, Hugh M. "Song Arrangements in Shianleu Acts of Yüan Tzarjiuh" *Tsing Hua Journal of Chinese Studies* ns 5(1):86-105, July 1965. In tabular form gives ordering of all tunes used in first (Shianleu-key) acts in Yüan drama; discussion of formal patterns of tune usage and sequence which emerge.

2091. Stone, W.H. "Acoustics in China" *Nature* 23:448-449, 1880-1881. NE.

2092. Strang, Gerald. "Sliding Tones in Oriental Music" *Bulletin of the American Musicological Society* 8:29-30, 1945. Abstract of paper. Suggests that sung portamenti or glides in Chinese may be due to language inflections.

2093. Strassberg, Richard E. "The Singing Techniques of K'un-ch'ü and Their Musical Notation" *CHINOPERL Papers* 6:45-81, 1976. Translation of Yü Chen-fei's treatise "Essential Points in Studying Ch'ü" with commentary and musical examples.

2094. Strassl, Alois. "Zur Geschichte der Chinesischen Musik" *Osterreichische Musik-Zeitschrift* 5:261-270. 1950. NE.

2095. Strickland, Lily. "Music in the Old Dragon Empire" *Étude* 52(10):588, 625, Oct 1934. il. Mistakenly attributes invention of the pipe organ (rather than reed organ) to China.

2096. Su Hua. *Ancient Melodies*. London: Hogarth, 1953. NE. Description of several pieces of *ch'in* music on p.200-210; context and transcription of song "Hua Fei Hua" on p.214-216 (Bruce Brooks).

2097. Subira, José. *Historia de la Musica*. Barcelona: Salvat Editores, 1951. 2nd ed. Refer to I, Chap. 2, p.35-56, "La Musica en China, Japon y la India." il., mus.

2098. Sun Chi-kuang. "We Studied Dances in Cuba" *China Reconstructs* 13(9):26-27, Sept 1964. il. Cultural interchange by the Tungfang Song and Dance Ensemble.

2099. Sun Liu-chen. "An Actor and His Responsibility" *China Reconstructs* 9(7):22-24, July 1960. il. About Li Shao-chun and the reforms he made in opera.

2100. Sun Schen. "Die chinesische Musik im Zuge des 'grossen Sprunges nach vorn" *Musik und Gesellschaft* 8 (12):14-16, Dec 1958. NE.

2101. Sung Hung-hua. "A Remarkable Achievement of Theatrical Transplanting" *Selections from China Mainland Magazines* 727-728:105-110, May 1-8, 1972. On the new version of "Red Detachment of Women" as an opera. From *Hung-ch'i* 4, April 1, 1972.

2102. Sung Yu-Ching. "Life and Art" *Chinese Literature* 10: 67-72, 1964. il. On modernized Peking operas.

2103. Sweetland, Reginald. I. "Courtesy Marks Japan Theatre; Hot Steam Towels, Garlic, the Chinese." II. "Chinese Theatre Is Acme of Noise, Confusion, Action and Complication" *Hokubei Asahi* (San Francisco), March 13-14, 1935. NE.

2104. Swift, Mary Grace. "Storming the Fortress of the Peking Opera" *Modern Drama* 12:111-123, Sept 1969.

2105. Syle, Edward. "Music Among the Chinese" *Dwight's Journal of Music* 27(4):28-29, May 11, 1867. Long letter correcting errors of an earlier column which denigrated Chinese musicality (Anon., "The Musical Capabilities of the Chinese," *idem* 27(3):20, April 27, 1867).

2106. _____.   "On the Musical Notation of the Chinese"
      *Journal of the Royal Asiatic Society, North China
      Branch* 1(2):176-179, May 1859.   Four songs in
      kung-chih notation, one transcribed into Western
      notation, with brief explanation.

2107. Szabolcsi, Bence.   "Five-Tone Scales and Civiliza-
      tion" *Acta Musicologica* 15(1-4):24-34, 1943. mus.
      Examines various pentatonic scale systems and
      their relationships to melodic form, concluding
      that they can nowhere be considered as primitive
      stages.

                 * * * * * * * * * *

2108. Tai, David C.L.   "A Brief Report on Music Education
      in the Republic of China" in *ISME International
      Conference Report, 1963* (Tokyo: 1963), p.257-259.

2109. Tai, Pu-fan. "Shaohsing Opera" *People's China* 8:16-
      18, 23, 1955. NE.

2110. Taki, Ryoichi.   "Chinese Musical Instruments; North
      and South China Music" *Canton* 1(4):35-42, Aug-
      Sept 1939. NE.

2111. Tan Man-ni.   "'The Red Lantern', An Example for New
      Peking Opera" *China Reconstructs* 14(12):35-38,
      Dec 1965. il.

2112. Tan Yuan-shou.   "Create Heroic Images by Applying
      Mao Tse-tung's Thought" *Chinese Literature* 11:98
      -102, 1967. By an opera actor; tells of genesis
      of the modern Peking opera *Shachiapang*. Interest-
      ing description of Chiang Ching's revisions.

2113. Tanabe, Hisao. "Die Weltbedeutung der alten chine-
      sischen Musik" *Musikwelt* 4, 1923. (Shanghai). NE

2114. Tanaka, Issei. "Development of Chinese Local Plays
      in the 17th and 18th Centuries" *Acta Asiatica*
      (Tokyo), 23:42-62, 1972. NE.

2115. Tanaka, Kenji.   "A History of Japanese Studies of
      Yüan Drama" *Acta Asiatica* 16:51-69, 1969. NE.

2116. Tannebaum, Gerald. "Another Triumph in Chinese Bal-
      let: 'The White-Haired Girl'" *Eastern Horizon* 5
      (12):13-20, Dec 1966. Includes 8 pages of plates.

2117. _____. "The Living Peking Opera" *Eastern Horizon* 4 (8):5-15, Aug 1965. il. On modernized operas on the Mainland; music mentioned briefly.

2118. _____. "National Minorities Folk Art Festival" *Eastern Horizon* 4(6):16-20, June 1965. il.

2119. _____. "A Never-To-Be-Forgotten Performance" *Eastern Horizon* 4(11):9-12, Nov 1965. il. On "The East Is Red." NE.

2120. _____. "The New Ballet in China" *Eastern Horizon* 4(10):7-19, Oct 1965. il.

2121. Tao Chu. "Some Problems Concerning Dramas on Revolutionary Modern Themes" *Chinese Literature* 6: 104-118, 1966.

2122. Taylor, Deems. *Of Men and Music.* New York: Simon and Schuster, 1937. A collection of essays on music. One, "Celestial Airs," p.259-262, discusses Chinese music heard at a China Institute recital. Coy, uninformed.

2123. Taylor, Eugene F. *The Chinese Musical Tradition Compared with the Western Tradition in the Light of Northrop's Hypothesis.* Dissertation (music - humanities), Florida State University. NE.

2124. Taylor, Frank J. "San Francisco's New Chinese City" *Travel* 52:18-21, 54, March 1929. Alleged effects of opera on Chinese social and economic life.[RR]

2125. Taylor, Lenore. "A Forum with Artists from the Shanghai Ballet" *Eastern Horizon* 7(4):30-36, July -Aug 1968. Discussion, with dancers, of political and artistic elements in production of "The White -Haired Girl" and other new ballets.

2126. Tch'ang, Joseph. *Chineesche Muziekmethode.* 1932. NE.

2127. Tchen Ysia. *La Musique Chinoise en France au XVIII Siècle.* Thèse Lettres, Paris, 1948. A study of Jesuit reports on Chinese music, primarily Amiot's and their effects in France.

2128. Tcheng Mien. *Répertoire Analytique du Théâtre Chinois.* 1929.

2129. _____. *Le Théâtre Chinois Moderne.* Paris: Presses Modernes, 1929. 195p. mus. See p.76-96. NE.

2130. Tcherepnine, Alexandre. [Letter on Chinese Music] *Musical Courier*, Feb 23, 1935. Text of a letter on some of the important musicians in China at that time.

2131. _____. [Letter to Walter Koons] *Musical Courier* 2834, Nov 17, 1934. Text of a letter reporting on the Chinese musical scene dated July 25, 1934.

2132. _____. "Music in Modern China" *Musical Quarterly* 21 (4):391-400, 1935. il., mus. Translated, "Musik im China" *Auftakt* 15:115-117, 1935; and "Musik im Modernen China" *Musik und Gesellschaft* 21. Good review of Western music in China in the 1930s. based on the author's personal experiences as a teacher and sponsor of Western music activity in China.

2133. Tchiao Tch'eng-Tchih. *Le Théâtre Chinois d'Aujour-d'hui*. Paris: Droz, 1938. 180p. 6 plates, index, bibliog. [Bibliothèque de la Société des Historiens du Théâtre, IX]. After a brief historical introduction, chapters follow surveying the dramatic literature, technical aspects of the production, social conditions of the acting profession, methods of instruction, the stage area, the integral production, and aspects of reform and change.

2134. Teh Yung. "The Story of a Ballad Singer" *Chinese Literature* (9):49-53. 1977. A post- "Gang of Four" short story about a Soochow ballad singer and *p'i-p'a* player; the genre must be *p'ing-t'an*.

2135. Teng Chang-kuo. *Chinese Music*. Taipei: China Publishing Co., [1964?]. 12p. il. Text of a speech delivered at Women's Association for the Study of Asian Problems, Taipei, Oct 14, 1963. Brief introduction to traditional history, scales, notation, and instruments.

2136. _____. "Music Education and Music Activities in the Republic of China" in *Proceedings of the First Asian Pacific Music Conference* (Seoul: Cultural and Social Centre for the Asian and Pacific Region, 1975), p.31-34. NE.

2137. _____. "The Music Education in China" in *ISME International Conference Report, 1963* (Tokyo: 1963), p.292-294.

2138. Terrien de Lacouperie. "On Antique and Sacred Bronze Drums of North-China" *Bab. & Or. Rec.* 7(9):193, May 1894. NE.

2139. Thilman, Johannes Paul. "Etwas über chinesisches Musikleherausbildung" *Musik in der Schule* 7(1):1-8, 1956. Brief report on the author's experiences with teacher training and music education courses in China under the Communists.

2140. Thompson, Jean Graham. *China and Her Music.* M.M. thesis, Northwestern University, 1947. iii+138p. il., bibliog. NE.

2141. Thoresby, Christian. "Chinese Opera Unexpected Success at International Theater Festival" *Musical America* 75(11):15, Sept 1955. il. Review of Paris Festival.

2142. T'ien Han. "Chou Hsin-fang—Fifty Years in Peking Opera" *People's China* 16:32-34, Aug 16, 1955. NE.

2143. _____. "The Composer Nieh Erh" *Chinese Literature* 11:124-131, 1959. il. Eulogy; some revolutionary song texts.

2144. _____. "Mes derniers entretiens avec Mei Lan-fang" *Cahiers Franco-Chinois* 11:26-28, Oct 1961. NE.

2145. _____. "My Last Meetings with Mei Lan-fang" *China Reconstructs* 10(10):35-36, Oct 1961. il. Memorial tribute.

2146. Tiersot, Julien. "Musique chinoise et indochinoise" *Le Ménestral* (Paris), 67(1):--. NE.

2147. _____. "Musique Chinoise et indo-Chinoise" in his *Notes d'Ethnographie Musicale (Première Série)* (Paris: Librairie Fischbacher, 1905), p.39-55. mus. Reprinted from *Ménestral* (1900-1902). Selections from Amiot, followed by comments on music heard at the Exposition, with some thoughts on scale and mode.

2148. Ting Shih-o. "Back to the Working People" in "Between Actor and Audience" *China Reconstructs* 13 (6):8-10, June 1964. il. An actress views modern Shanghai opera.

2149. Tiplady, Eleanor. *The Music of China, History, Scales, Instruments.* M.M. thesis, College-Conservatory of Music of Cincinnati, 1946. mus., bibliog. 96p. NE.

2150. Tökei, F. "Notes prosodiques sur quelques chants de travail chinois" *Acta Orientalia Academiae Scientiarum Hungaricae* 6:53-63, 1956. A scholarly textual study of some work songs from the *Shih Ching* and other Shang and Chou dynasty sources.

2151. Tomkinson, L.   "The Social Teachings of Meh Tse"
      Transactions of the Asiatic Society of Japan 2s
      4:5-179, 1927. See p.156-159, "Against Music and
      Other Luxuries."   A translation of the writings
      of Mo Tzu, generally inferior to that of Y.P.
      Mei.

2152. Torii, R.   "Des instruments en usage chez les Miao-
      tsé dans la Chine de l'Ouest" *Journal of the An-
      thropological Society of Tokyo* 19(214-215):--,
      1904. "A general description of two specimens of
      liu-sheng" (Liu, 1539 above). NE.

2153. Townsend, Edward W. "The Foreign Stage in New York.
      IV: The Chinese Theatre" *The Bookman* 12:39-42,
      Sept 1900. il. Superficial. [RR]

2154. Trautz, F.M.   "Eine erhebende Musikaufführung am
      funffachen Stupa (des Wu-t'a-ssu bei Peking)"
      Asia Major 2:581-596, 1925. il. NE.

2155. Travert, André.   "Caractères originaux et évolution
      actuelle du théâtre Pékinois" in *Les Théâtres
      d'Asie*, edited by Jean Jacquot (Paris: Centre
      National de la Recherche Scientifique, 1961), p.
      99-126. il.

2156. _____. "Récente évolution du théâtre dans la Chine
      moderne" *Comptes rendus mensuels des séances de
      l'Académie des sciences d'outre-mer* (Paris), 20
      (8):320-322, 1960. NE.

2157. Trefzger, Heinz.   "Die Musik in China" *Sinica* 11:
      171-197, 1936. music. NE.

2158. _____.   "Das Musikleben der Tang-Zeit (618-907)"
      Sinica 13:46-82, 1938. il. NE.

2159. _____. "Über das K'in, seine Geschichte, seine Tech-
      nik, seine Notation, und seine Philosophie"
      Schweizerische Musikzeitung 88(3):81-87, 1948.
      il. NE.

2160. _____. "Über das Sheng" *Hug's Musikkurier* 4(1):2f.,
      March 1948. NE.

2161. _____. "Über die chinesischen Notenschriften" *Uni-
      versitas* 6(7):753-761, 1951. il. One plate com-
      pares various scales and respective notations.

2162. _____.   "Über die chinesische Oper 'P'i-P'a-Dji'"
      Neues Musikblatt 16, 1937. NE.

2163. Trippner, P. Joseph. "Das Lied von Ma Wu Ko. Ein Volkslied aus Tsinghai" *Folklore Studies* 17:141-186, 1958. mus. NE.

2164. _____. "Tsing-hai-di Schau Niän Go, die Shao Nien Lieder in Ch'ing Hai" *Folklore Studies*, Supp. I, Peking, 1952. NE.

2165. Tsao Pen-yeh. "*P'ing-t'an* Music—A Preliminary Study" *CHINOPERL Papers* 6:95-119, 1976. A brief introduction, with bibliography, discography and some short transcribed examples. A valuable first step, since little has been written about this narrative ballad genre.

2166. Tscharner, E.H. de. "Un art chinois peu connu: le Théâtre" in *Conferenze Vol. II, Serie Orientale Roma VII* (Rome: Is. M.E.O., 1955), p.185-197. il. plates. NE.

2167. _____. "Chinesische Schauspielkunst" *Sinica* 7:91-106, 1932. NE.

2168. _____. "De l'esthétique du théâtre chinois traditionnel" in *Les Théâtres d'Asie*, edited by Jean Jacquot (Paris: Centre National de la Recherche Scientifique, 1961), p.71-77.

2169. Tscheng Ki Tong. *Le Théâtre des Chinois*. Paris: Calmann-Lévy, 1886. xii+324p. Does not discuss music. Tries to relate Chinese dramatic conventions to Western analogs. Not scholarly.

2170. Tschi Lien-po. "Die chinesische Opernschule" *Theater der Zeit* 12(9):32-37, 1957. NE.

2171. Tsenin, S. "Dva Mes'atsa v Kitae [Two Months in China] *Sovetskaya Muzyka* 4:125f., April 1955. NE.

2172. Tsiang Un-kai. *K'ouen K'iu: Le Théâtre Chinois Ancien*. Paris: Leroux, 1932. 130p. il. A scholarly study of the development, style, texts and literary value of *k'un ch'ü*. Chapter on music gives a non-technical discussion of modes, instruments, singing, and declamation.

2173. Tso Lin. "The Chinese and Western Theatres: A Study in Contrasting Techniques" *Chinese Literature* 8:101-111, Aug 1962. Compares Mei Lan-fang, Stanislavski, and Brecht.

2174. Tsung Chi. "The Seventh 'Shanghai Spring' Music Festival" *Chinese Literature* 9:164-176, 1966. With 4 pages of plates.

2175. Tsung Shu. "New Life for Local Opera" *Chinese Literature* 11:90-96, 1974. il. Report on Peking Festival (Aug-Sept, 1974) at which local opera groups presented adaptations of model revolutionary Peking operas in their regional opera genre.

2176. Tsung Wen. "The Art of the Working People" *Chinese Literature* 3:71-82, 1965. il. On the "Minorities Amateur Art Festival." Good photos.

2177. Tu Chin-fang. "As an Opera Actress Sees It" *Eastern Horizon* 1(2):45-46, Aug 1960. il.

2178. _____. "Die moderne revolutionäre Peking-Oper" *China Report* 7-8:12-13, 1972. NE.

2179. Tu Hsien-jo. "New Music in Shanghai" *China Reconstructs* 10(12):30-31, Dec 1961. il. Report on the second annual Music Festival.

2180. Tuan An-chieh. "Yo-fou-tsa-lou: Notes diverses sur les mélodies" in *T'ang Kien Wen Tse; Florilège de Littérature des T'ang*, edited by Bruno Belpaire (Paris: Editions Universitaires, 1957), II, 287-315.

* Tuan An-chieh. See also under Martin Gimm.

2181. Tuan Jui-hsia. "Not Just One of the Audience" *Chinese Literature* 9:51-64, 1973. Short story on providing a good sound system for performance of revolutionary model operas.

2182. Tung, Constantine. "The Hidden Enemy as Villain in Communist Chinese Drama" *Educational Theatre Journal* 25(3):335-343, Oct 1973. Character and plot studies of contemporary operas, concentrating on "Song of the Dragon River" and "On the Docks."

2183. Tuttle, Lauren T. "Music in the Orient: The Old, The New" *Overland Monthly* 2s 48:79-84, Aug 1906. il. NE.

2184. Twitchett, D.C. and A.H. Christie. "A Medieval Burmese Orchestra" *Asia Major* ns 7(1-2):176-195, 1959. il. Detailed survey of an orchestra presented to the Emperor of China in +802 by the King of Pyu, with annotated translation of a relevant passage from the *Hsin-T'ang-Shu* dynastic history. An important source for the study of T'ang dynasty music.

2185. Tyrrell, Henry.   "The Theatre of New York's China-
      town" *Theatre Magazine* 3:170-172, 1903. il. Vi-
      sitor's impressions.   Splendid photography. [RR]

                 * * * * * * * * * *

2186. Uchiyama, Jun. "Theatre After 1949" *The Drama Re-
      view* 15(3):252-257, Spring 1971.   Translated by
      Tomoko Kusuhara.   Surveys political developments
      in opera and spoken drama.

2187. Umehara, Suiji. "A Study of the Bronze Ch'un" *Mon-
      umenta Serica* 15:142-160, 1956. il. *Ch'un* is an
      upward-facing bell with suspended clapper.

2188. Union Research Institute.   "Cantonese Opera on Mod-
      ern Themes" *Union Research Service* 37(14):206-
      220, Nov 17, 1964. This article and those follow-
      ing consist of selected translations from the
      China Mainland press, with short introductory
      comments by the editors.

2189. _____.   "The Central Huai-hai Road Primary School
      Properly Handles the Activities of Children's
      Ballad Singing" *Union Research Service* 33(25):
      400-402, Dec 24, 1963. NE.

2190. _____.   "Chou Hsin-fang, Peking Opera Actor" *Union
      Research Service* 27(2):19-35, April 6, 1962.

2191. _____.   "East China Stages Operas and Plays with
      Contemporary Themes" *Union Research Service* 40
      (13):185-198, Aug 13, 1965.

2192. _____.   "The Late Dr. Mei Lan-fang" *Union Research
      Service* 25(4):47-62, Oct 13, 1961.

2193. _____.   "Mass Singing Activities in Shanghai" *Union
      Research Service* 42(6):77-82, Jan 21, 1966.

2194. _____.   "Nationalization of Music" *Union Research
      Service* 26(17):280-294, Feb 27, 1962.

2195. _____. "Peking Opera 'Hai Jui Admonishes the Emper-
      or' and Its Author Chou Hsin-fang Subject to At-
      tack" *Union Research Service*.

2196. _____.   "Popularizing the 'Modern Drama'" *Union
      Research Service* 34(24):393-408, March 24, 1964.

                      211

2197. _____ . "Recent Communist Attitudes Toward Traditional Operas" *Union Research Service* 33(21):325-339, Dec 10, 1963.

2198. _____ . "The Reform of Peking Opera" *Union Research Service* 36(6):83-95, July 21, 1974.

2199. _____ . "The Revolutionization of the Chinese Theatre in 1965" *Union Research Service* 42(9):124-139, Feb 1, 1966.

2200. _____ . "The 7th 'Spring in Shanghai' Music Festival" *Union Research Service* 44(12):167-182, 1966.

2201. _____ . "The Socialist Singing Movement" *Union Research Service* 33(25):395-409, Dec 24, 1963.

2202. _____ . "Theatrical Troupes to Tour the Countryside" *Union Research Service* 41(14):195-211, Nov 16, 1965.

2203. _____ . "The 20th Anniversary of Mao Tse-tung's 'Talks at the Yenan Forum on Literature and Art'" *Union Research Service* 29(7):96-108, Oct 23, 1962.

* * * * * * * * * *

2204. V.V.S— OV. "Lady Precious Stream" *Vestnik Kitaia* (Tientsin, China) 1:26, May 1936. NE.

2205. Van Juan'-Fan. "Muzykal'noe Isskusstvo KNR" [The Musical Art of the People's Republic of China] *Muzykal'naja Žizn'* (Moskva) 5:15-16, 1959. NE.

2206. Vanara, Candido. "Il Canto Gregoriano in Cina" *Rassegna Gregoriana* 8:178-183, 1909. NE.

2207. Vega, L.K. "Justinus Kerner und die 'Ombres Chinoises'" *Ciba Zeitschrift* 1(7):235-237, 1934. NE.

2208. Vikár, László. "Adatok a Kínai és Magyar Népzene Kapcsolatahoz" [On the Relations Between Chinese and Hungarian Folk Music] *Új Zenei Szemele* (Budapest) 6(2):7-12, 1955. NE.

2209. _____. "Chinese Folk Songs with Answers at the Interval of a Fifth" *Acta Ethnographica Academiae Scientiarum Hungaricae* 7(3-4):429-432, 1958. On the formal device of transposing thematic material a fourth or a fifth, and repeating sequentially; common in Chinese folk tunes.

2210. Vinogradov, Viktor Sergeevič. "Kompozitory Novogo Kitaja" [Composers in People's China] *Sovetskaya Muzyka* 5:131-140, May 1958. NE.

2211. _____. *Muzyka v Kitaiskoi Narodni Respublike* [Music in the Chinese People's Republic] Modvoe: Sovetskii Kompositor, 1959. 86p. il., mus. NE.

2212. Vissière, A. "Deux chansons politiques chinoises" *T'oung Pao* 10:213-222, 1899. NE.

2213. Voigt, Alban. "Chinesische Musikinstrumente" *Deutsche Instrumentenbau Zeitschrift* 32, 1931. NE.

2214. Volpert, V.V. "Das Chinesische Schauspielwesen in Südschantung" *Anthropos* 5:367-380, 1910. il., mus. See p.372-373. NE.

2215. Voskamp, C.F. "Die tönende Laute. Eine musikalische Geschichte aus dem alten China um 300 vor Christi geburt" *Der Ferne Osten* 1(1):17-23. NE.

2216. Votterle, K. "Altchinesische Kammermusik" *Hausmusik* 5:129-131, Sept-Oct 1959. Short popular article introducing Wang En-shao's *p'i-p'a* concerts.

* * * * * * * * * * *

2217. Wagener, G. "Bemerkungen über die Theorie der chinesischen Musik und ihren Zusammenhang mit der Philosophie" *Mitteilungen der Deutsche Gesellschaft für Volk- und Naturkunde des Orient* 2:42-61, 1877. English abstract in *Nature* 30:565-566, 1884. NE.

2218. Wagner, Eduard. "Verzeichnis Chinesischer Musikinstrumenten" *Jahrbuch des Museums für Völkerkunde zu Leipzig* 11:22-33, 1952. 69 instruments listed by material of construction: stone, metal, wood, bamboo, string, membrane, gourd, clay, shell. There is a short cross-index to selected social functions. Chinese characters given.

2219. Waldrop, Rebecca. *Sacred, Classic, Court and Ritual Dances of the Far East*.   M.A. thesis (physical education), George Peabody, 1935. NE.

2220. Wales, H.G. Quaritsch.   "The Religious Significance of the Early Dongson Bronze Drums" in   *Proceedings of the 23rd International Congress of Orientalists* (Cambridge: 1954), p.270-271. Abstract. Interprets drums as symbolic of a microcosm; part of Shamanistic religion; helps to transport shaman magically to heaven.

2221. Waley, Arthur.   "Chinese Stories About Actors" *The Listener* (London) Feb 7, 1957.   Reprinted in his *The Secret History of the Mongols* (London: Allen and Unwin, 1963; New York: Barnes and Noble, 1964), p.82-88.   Popularly written, anecdotal piece about actors in Peking opera and earlier genres, from Ch'ing sources.

2222. _____ .   "Chinese-Mongol Hybrid Songs" *Bull, School of Oriental and African Studies* 20:581-584, 1957. On Mongol words found in the vocabulary of Chinese drama and song of the Yüan and early Ming dynasties.

2223. _____ .   "The Green Bower Collection" *Oriental Art* ns, 1957. Reprinted in his *The Secret History of the Mongols* (London: Allen and Unwin, 1963;   New York: Barnes and Noble, 1964), p.89-107. Discussion of a Yüan dynasty book *Ch'ing Lou Chi*,   a collection of stories about singing girls of *tsa-chü* and other entertainment genres, together with annotated translations of selected passages. Fascinating material on social history of music and drama.

2224. _____ . "The Lute Girl's Song" *New China Review* 3(5) :376-377, Oct 1921.   Surrejoinder to Giles' rejoinder to Waley's critique of Giles' translation of Po Chu-yi's poem. (See Waley, "Notes on the 'Lute Girl's Song,'" No. 2225 below).

2225. _____ . "Notes on the 'Lute Girl's Song'" *New China Review* 2(6):591-597, Dec 1920.   Annotation of Po Chu-yi's famous poem on a musical subject, with critique of Giles' translation.   See also Giles' reply and Waley's continuation.   Waley defends his translation of Chinese instrument names as "harp" in non-technical work.   "The *kinnor* of the Hebrews was certainly not a harp in the strict sense of the word, yet both A.V. and R.V. translate *kinnor* by 'harp.'   Moreover, the Japanese word *koto* has constantly been translated 'harp' (which sense is given in Brinkley's Dictionary), though no one imagines that it resembles the harp of European concert rooms" (p.569n).

2226. _____. "A Song From Tun-Huang" *Bull, School of Oriental and African Studies* 26:149-151, 1963. NE.

2227. Walker, J.E. "Pentatonic Music: Some Suggestions and Experiences" *Chinese Recorder* 37:497-499, 1906. NE.

2228. _____. "Some Little Foxes" *Chinese Recorder* 33:439-444, 1902. NE.

2229. Walls, Jon W. "Kuaibanshu: Elements of the Fast Clapper Tale" *CHINOPERL Papers* 7:60-91, 1977. il., mus. Excellent introductory survey of this narrative genre with accompaniment of bamboo clappers.

2230. Wan Chi-pao. "China—Drama" in *Encyclopedia Americana*. 1965 ed., VI,551-553. 1971 ed., VI,585-587.

2231. Wan Tung-shu. "The Twelve Mukam of Sinkiang Saved and Revived" *China Reconstructs* 12(2):38-41, Feb 1963. il. Ethnomusicological research and collecting preserves this scarce Uighur vocal genre.

2232. Wang, Betty. "Folk Songs As a Means of Social Control" *Sociology and Social Research* 19(1):64-69, Sept-Oct 1934. Folk songs of American Negroes and China seen acting as a "societal force, cementing the opinions of the people of many generations, influencing people's moral conduct, and making standards of morality" in relation to footbinding, remarriage of widows, etc. Only the song texts are discussed.

2233. _____. "Folk Songs As Regulators of Politics" *Sociology and Social Research* 20:161-166, 1935. Reprinted in *The Study of Folklore*, edited by Alan Dundes (Englewood Cliffs, N.J.: Prentice-Hall, 1965), p.308-313. Folk songs express political thoughts of the masses. Some ancient emperors of China collected folk songs and acted on their complaints and implied injustices. Narrow scope; not covering song in propaganda or education. Only the song texts are discussed.

2234. _____. "Folk Songs in China" *Sociology and Social Research* 19(3):243-246, 1935. Tries to describe nature and function of Chinese folk songs according to 18 characteristics such as: unconscious, spontaneous, somehow group-molded composition; functions to strengthen we-group, ethnocentrism, etc.

2235. Wang Chao-wen. "The Artist and His Audience" *Chinese Literature* 11:89-96, 1963. Some thoughts on traditional Chinese aesthetics.

2236. _____. "The Modern Play and Artistic Taste" *Selections from China Mainland Magazines* 407:32-35, March 9, 1964. From *Hung-ch'i* 2-3, 1964. NE.

2237. _____. "Persist in the Revolutionary Direction; After Watching Numbers Presented During the Festival of Peking Opera on Contemporary Themes" *Selections from China Mainland Magazines* 437:7-22, Oct 5, 1964. From *Hung-ch'i* 16, 1964. NE.

2238. _____. "Some Reflections on Peking Operas with Contemporary Themes" *Chinese Literature* 11:101-109, Nov 1964. Discussion of changes in Peking opera to fit mass society and party line, prediction of future development.

2239. _____. "Szechuan Opera" *Chinese Literature* 7:150-154, June 1959. Describes some individualities of this local tradition, and tells some popular plots.

2240. Wang Ching-hsien. *The Bell and the Drum:* Shih Ching *As Formulaic Poetry in an Oral Tradition.* Berkeley: University of California Press, 1974. xii+ 158p. bibliog., index. An analytic study using computer methods, based on the theories of Parry and Lord on the nature of oral formulaic composition, which are here applied for the first time to an Asian genre.

2241. Wang Ching-ping. "The Development of Chinese Classical Music in the Republic of China" in *Proceedings of the First Asian Pacific Music Conference* (Seoul: Cultural and Social Centre for the Asian and Pacific Region, 1975), p.64-66. NE.

2242. Wang Chi-ning. "A Shining Example in Carrying Our Mao Tse-tung's Thought on Literature and Art" *China Reconstructs* 15(10):26-32, Oct 1966. il. On a military Cultural Work Troupe in Kwangtung. Color photos.

2243. Wang Chi-ssu. "Comedy in the Classical Chinese Theatre" *Chinese Literature* 9:93-99, Sept 1962. Describes comic role-types in Chinese opera.

2244. Wang Chung-yu. "Church Music and Its Condition in the Chinese Church" *Chinese Recorder* 335-340, July 1901. NE.

2245. Wang En-shao. "Chinesische Kammermusik einst und jetzt" *Musica* 4(4):131-133, April 1950. Brief note on chamber traditions for *ch'in* and *p'i-p'a* by noted *p'i-p'a* virtuoso.

2246. Wang Fang-chih. "Laughing Away Old Ideas" *China Reconstructs* 15(6):507, June 1966. il. Contemporary opera in Hunan Province.

2247. Wang, George K.T. "The Singsong Beauties of Nanking" *China Journal* 27(4):178-180, Oct 1937. il. Short note on social status and history of this profession, a life combining entertainment, prostitution, and occasional stardom.

2248. Wang Hsi-cheng. "The Pentatonic and Heptatonic Scales" *Yenching Journal of Chinese Studies* 28: 197-250, 1940. In Chinese with English abstract, p.307-308.

2249. Wang, Johannes Baptista. *De musica sacra in Sinis juxta I concilium sinense et recentiora documenta pontificia.* Rome: Propaganda Fide, 1957. NE.

2250. Wang Kuang-ch'i. "Musikalische Beziehungen zwischen China und dem Westen in Laufe der Jahrtausend" in *Studien zur Geschichte und Kultur des Nahen und Fernen Ostens, Paul Kahle zum 60. Geburtstag* (Lieden: Brill, 1935), p.217-224. Holds that Greek and Chinese music theories stem from Babylon; discusses internationalism of T'ang dynasty; Chu Tsai-yü's invention of equal temperament; the *sheng* and its Western derivation.

2251. _____. *Über die Chinesische Klassische Oper (1530-1860 n. Chr.).* Genf: Bibliothek Sino-International, 1934. 48p. mus. Ph.D. dissertation, Bonn University. Reprinted in *Orient et Occident* 1(1) :9-21, Aug 1934; 1(2):16-33, Sept 1934; 1(3):13-29, Oct 1934. A good survey concentrating on music: tunes, modes, notations. Several musical examples in transcription.

2252. _____. "Über die chinesische Musik" in *Chinesische Musik*, edited by Richard Wilhelm (Frankfurt: A. M.: China Institut, 1927), p.48-56. Also in *Sinica* 2:136-144, 1927.

2253. _____. "Über die chinesischen Notenschriften" *Sinica* 3:110-124, 1928. mus. Beginning with a short historical review, there is technical material on scales, practical considerations of how to read and interpret the various notations. Clear tables and musical examples.

2254. _____. "Über die Metrik der Chinesischen Dichtung" *Sinica*, 1928. NE.

2255. Wang Kuo-wei. "Das chinesische Theater vor der T'ang Zeit" *Asia Major* 10:229-246, 1935. Translation by Eduard Erkes. Part of the first chapter of *Sung Yüan Hsi-ch'ü Shih*. Good survey, based on literary sources, by a respected historical scholar.

2256. Wang Shih-hsiang. "Pigeon Whistles Make Aerial Orchestra" *China Reconstructs* 12(11):42-43, Nov 1963. il. Brief introduction to these unusual instruments, with good photos of eight examples.

2257. Wang Shih-hsiang and Wang Ti. "A 2000-Year-Old Melody" *China Reconstructs* 6(3):18-21, March 1957. il., mus. Story of the old *ch'in* tune "Kuangling-san" and its recent reconstruction by the scholar Kuan P'ing-hu. With photos and transcription of movements 17-20. Also in *Musik und Gesellschaft* 7(8):25, Aug 1957; translated by Heinrich Streicher; and in *Hudebni Rozhledy* 10:506-507, 1957.

2258. Wang Shu-yuan. "Azalea Mountain" *Chinese Literature* 1:3-69, 1974. il. September 1973 script of Peking Opera Troupe of Peking production of this modern revolutionary opera. 12 pages of color plates from the stage production.

2259. _____. "Azaleas Bloom Red Over the Mountains" *Chinese Literature* 1:114-119, 1974. On the background of the creation of the new Peking opera "Azalea Mountain."

2260. Wang Tzu-cheng. "Training People in the Arts" *China Reconstructs* 9(4):34-36, April 1960. il. Integration of education with productive labor.

218

2261. Wang, Dr. Yates. "Une Ancienne mélodie chinoise" *Revue Internationale de Musique* 12:80-82, Spring 1952. mus. Notation and text of a Chinese tune "Pensée des Quatre Saisons" with French translation.

2262. Wang Yü-hsi. "The Cult of Western Bourgeois Music Must Be Extirpated" *Selections from China Mainland Magazines* 462:22-27, March 29, 1965. From *Jen Min Yin-Yüeh*.

2263. Wang Yun-hsi. "The Yüeh-Fu Songs of Ancient China" *Chinese Literature* 4:110-117, 1959. Survey of this important folk song and folk-song-inspired genre, describing the extant poems and sketching the historical development of the form.

2264. Ware, James R. "Query No. 114. Were the Ancient Chinese Weights and Measures Related to Musical Instruments?" *Isis* 37:73, May 1947. Brief query and citation of Pan Ku as authority for affirmative answer.

2265. Waterbury, Florence. *Early Chinese Symbols and Speculations with Particular Reference to the Ritual Bronzes of the Shang Dynasty.* New York: Weyne, 1942. 164p. il. See p.16, 21-23, 28-29, 79-80, 89-91. NE.

2266. Waterman, Richard. "Chinese Music" in *Collier's Encyclopedia.* 1965 ed., XVII,45-46. il.

2267. Weaver, W. "Letter from Venice: The Festival" *Center* 2:17, Nov 1955. Peking Opera troupe at international theatre festival.

2268. Webster, D. "The Philadelphia in China" *High Fidelity and Musical America* 24:MA24-26, Feb 1974.

2269. Wegelin, C.A. "Chineesche Muziek" *China* 4:129-143, 217-231, 1929. il., music. Introductory review from the theoretical side—basic principles, instruments by eight classes, legends, tuning systems, etc.

2270. Wehner, George. "Chinese Music-Drama" *Music Journal* 20:60, 92-93, March 1962. il. Short positive tourist program notes.

2271. Wei Ch'ing. "Another New Flower of Socialist Literature and Art" *Selections from China Mainland Magazines* 725-726:93-98, April 3-10, 1972. On "Ode to the Dragon River." From *Hung-ch'i* 6, March 1, 1972.

2272. Wei, Julie L. "The Singing Role in Yüan Drama" *Dodder* 2:18-23, Jan 1970. Analysis of dramatic function and context of singing role and of the songs.

2273. Wellesz, Egon. "Chinese Music" *Monthly Musical Record* 66:131-132, 1936. NE.

2274. _____. "Vom Geist der chinesischen Musik" *Musikblätter des Anbruch* 1:42-45, 1919. German translations of key sections of the *Yüeh Chi* chapter of the *Li Chi*.

2275. _____. "Vom Wesen der Musik des Orients" *Wiener Beiträge zur Kunst und Kulturgeschichte Asiens* 8 :61-67, 1934. NE.

2276. Wells, Henry W. "Asian Classical Drama Today" *Literature East and West* 10:220-234, Sept 1966. NE.

2277. _____. "Chinese Classical Drama: A View from the West" *Literature East and West* 14(4):535-546, 1970. NE.

2278. _____. "Chinese Drama in English" *Yearbook of Comparative and General Literature* 13:13-27, 1964. NE.

2279. _____. *The Classical Drama of the Orient.* New York: Asia Publishing House, 1965. 348p. index. Nine essays on various facets of Chinese drama, nine on Japanese drama. Music is not discussed; the stress is on form, aesthetics, language.

2280. Wen Chun. "Confucius' Reactionary Views on Literature and Art" *Chinese Literature* 10:111-118, 1974. Another missile in the "Campaign to Criticize Lin Piao and Confucius." Confucius' views on rites, poetry, and music are seen to reinforce the political line of feudal lords.

2281. _____. "An Opera on Proletarian Internationalism" *Chinese Literature* 6, 1972. Reprinted in *Literature and Ideology* (Toronto) 15:59-69, 1973.

2282. Wen I Pao. "Hail the New Achievements of Operettas on Revolutionary Contemporary Themes" *Selections from China Mainland Magazines* 510:14-20, Feb 7, 1966. From No. 10, Oct 10, 1965. NE.

2283. Wen Pin. "Azalea Mountain" *China Reconstructs* 23(2):10-15, Feb 1974. il. Genesis and plot summary of new model revolutionary Peking opera, with color and black-and-white photos.

2284. Wen Shih-ching. "Cheng Yen-chiu; A Great Exponent of Peking Opera" *Chinese Literature* 4:131-134, 1958. il. NE.

2285. _____. "Local Operas on the Peking Stage" *Chinese Literature* 1:152-155, 1958. Reports on performances by companies from seven provinces.

2286. _____. "The School of Traditional Drama" *Chinese Literature* 5:114-121, 1964. il.

2287. Wen Sung. "A Hundred Flowers Blossom in the Field of Dancing" *Chinese Literature* (6):113-120, 1976. il. NE.

2288. Wen Yang. "New Life for Peking Opera" *Chinese Literature* 9:96-102, 1964.

2289. Wen Yu. *Selected Ancient Bronze Drums Found in China and Southeast Asia.* Shanghai: 1955. 64 large quarto photos, rubbings, and drawings of bronze drums and drum-design motifs. Chinese text faces each plate; five-page highly abbreviated English captions are bound in a separate pamphlet. A veritable treasure house of source material for bronze-drum research.

2290. Wendland, Jens. "Filme von Peking-Opern" *Tanzarchiv* (Köln) 20(7):205-206, 211-213, Dec 1972. NE.

2291. Werner, Edward Theodore Chalmers. "Chinese Ditties" *New China Review* 3:259-272, 368-375, 442-450, 1921; 4:23-31, 106-113, 1922. Book form published in Tientsin: Tientsin Press, 1922. 56p. Series of folk songs with Chinese texts and translations. No music.

2292. Werner, Hans. "Chinesische Musik" *Neue Zeitschrift für Musikwissenschaft* 55:359-360, 369-370, 1888. mus. NE.

2293. West, Benjamin. "Chinas Kunst—ein Opfer der Ideologie—Gedanken zur Revision der Peking-oper und anderer Formen der dramatischen Kunst" *Amerika Dienst* 3(4):1-3, 1964.

2294. West, Stephen H. "Some Remarks on the Development of Northern Music Drama" *CHINOPERL Papers* 6:23-44, 1976. Careful examination of the earliest literary sources on the forerunners of the *pei-ch'ü*.

2295. Westharp, Alfred. *The Essense of Chinese Music.* Shanghai: 1913. 9p. NE.

2296. ____. "Music As a Means of Education" *China Review*
1:154-160, July 1914. NE.

2297. ____. "The Musical Soul of East and West" *Music
Mirror* 1(3):2-10, March 1958. NE.

2298. Whaples, Miriam Karpilow. *Exoticism in Dramatic
Music, 1600-1800*. Ph.D. dissertation (music),
Indiana University, 1958. v+415p. mus., index,
bibliog. NE.

2299. Whitaker, K.P.K. "A Cantonese Song Entitled *Kreoy
Keok Lrio Aa Gao*" *Bull, School of Oriental and
African Studies* (London) 36(2):446-459, 1973.
Comparative study of several verions of a *nan-yin*
song, with background historical and contextual
material, texts, and translations. No music.

2300. ____. "Tsaur Jyr and the Introduction of *Fannbay*
Into China" *Bull, School of Oriental and African
Studies* 20:585-597, 1957. *Fannbay* is a type of
Buddhist chanting. This article is essentially
a historical investigation into sources, but
some information on the musical aspect is included.

2301. White, Laura Marsden. "Christian Music in China"
East of Asia Magazine 3:23-28, 1904. A marvelous
mélange of misinformation, missionary zeal, pre-
judice. Do-it-yourself instructions for eliminating Chinese texts, tunes, and voice production,
and substituting Western varieties of the same.

2302. ____. "The Training of Chinese Voices" *Chinese
Recorder* 32:589-592, Dec 1901. NE.

2303. White, Maude. "All the World's a Stage in China"
Theatre Magazine 30:168, Sept 1919. NE.

2304. White-Haired Girl Performing Troupe, Shanghai Ballet
School. "Let Workers, Peasants and Soldiers Stand
Forever Erect on the Ballet Stage" *Selections
from China Mainland Magazines* 629:37-38, Sept 30,
1968.

2305. Whymant, A. Neville J. "Chinese Coolie Songs" *Bull,
School of Oriental and African Studies* 1(3):145-
166, 1920. Some texts first published in *Today*
6(31):25-28, Sept 1919. Ninety short song texts
translated, with brief introduction.

2306. Whymant, N. "Chinese Music and Musical Instruments"
Geographical Magazine 23:189-195, 1950-1951. NE.

2307. Wiant, Bliss Mitchell. *The Character and Function of Music in Chinese Culture*. Ph.D. dissertation, Peabody, 1946. vii+325p. Brief abstract published as: Peabody, Contribution to Education No. 376.

2308. _____. "Chinese Artifacts Inspire Christian Hymns" *The Hymn* 25(4):115-122, Oct 1974. il. NE.

2309. _____. "Chinese Indigenous Hymnody" *Ching Feng* 8(3-4):3-30, Summer-Autumn 1964. NE.

2310 _____. "Chinese Music and Its Use in the Christian Church" *Collectanea Comm. Synodalis* 14:655-674, 1941. NE.

2311. _____. "The Messiah—Oriental Version" *Choral Guide* 6:25-26, Dec 1953. NE.

2312. _____. *The Music of China*. Hong Kong: Chung Chi College, 1966. xii+161p. il., mus., bibliog. Essentially a book version of the author's dissertation. A "social study" with much valuable source material translated from Chinese literature, but not capitalized on. The music *per se* is neglected, the approach anecdotal, but too full of detail and misleading errors for popular consumption.

2313. _____. "New Chinese Regime Favorable to Music. Oratorios Are Sung" *Diapason* (U.S.A.) 45(2):27, Jan 1, 1954. Report of Christian oratorios performed under Communist aegis.

2314. _____. "Oecumenical Hymnology in China" *International Review of Missions* 35:428-434, Oct 1946. NE.

2315. _____. *The Pagoda*. Delaware, Oh.: Cooperative Recreation Service, 1946. 24p. 2nd ed. Hymn-like 4-part piano arrangements of 13 Chinese songs; English text only.

2316. _____. *Possibilities of Polyphonic Treatment of Chinese Tunes*. M.A. thesis, Boston University, 1936. ii+56p. mus. NE.

2317. _____. "What Music Means to the Chinese" *The Hymn* 25(2):37-42, April 1974. mus. NE.

2318. Wieger, L. *Histoire des Croyances Religieuses et des Opinions Philosophiques en Chine*. Hou-kien-fou:Hien-hien, 1917. NE.

2319. Wilhelm, Richard, ed. *Chinesische Musik*. Frankfurt
A.M.: China Institut, 1927. 64p. il. Originally
a special issue of *Sinica* [2:1927]. Includes
Wilhelm's "Die Musik in China," Howard's "Chine-
sische und europäische Musik," Wang Kuang-chi's
"Über die chinesische Musik," and Lo Liang-chu's
"Hauptwerke chinesischer Musik." A rare, sub-
stantial collection.

2320. ____, trans. *Frühling und Herbst des Lü Bu We*.
Jena: Dietrichs, 1928. xiii+541p. See p.54-79.
The only available Western translation of this
important early source of musico-cosmological
theories (Ch'in dynasty).

2321. ____. "Die Musik in China" in his *Chinesische
Musik* (see above). Also in *Frankfurter Zeitung*,
July 17, 1927, and in *Sinica* 2:89-131, 1927.
Translations of relevant passages from Confucius,
Chuang-tzu, Lieh-tzu, Lü Pu-wei, the *Li Chi*, and
Ssu-ma Ch'ien.

2322. ____. "Das Wesen der chinesischen Musik" *Sinica*
2:201-207, 1927. NE.

2323. Wilkinson, J. Norman. "*The White-Haired Girl*: From
Yangko to Revolutionary Modern Ballet" *Educational Theatre Journal* 26(2):164-174, May 1974. Historical survey drawn from English-language sources and reports; done with care.

2324. Wille, O.K. "Deutsche Musik in China" *Deutsche
Militär-Musiker-Zeitung* 28:27-28, 1906. NE.

2325. Williams, Edward Thomas. *China Yesterday and Today*.
5th ed. New York: Crowell, 1932. xvii+613p. See
p.272-273, 281, 377, 380, 381. NE.

2326. Williams, Frank S. "The Chinese Theatre: A Romantic
Institution Fettering the Past and Present in
China" *Asia* 18(4):314-322, April 1918. il. An
interesting, though negative, account of Peking
opera practice, with firsthand comments on theatre life, and photos.

2327. Williams, Samuel Wells. *The Middle Kingdom*. Rev.
ed. New York: Scribner, 1904. 2 vols. See I,424,
672; II,93-104. mus. A standard early general
work on China. Music *passim*.

2328. Wimsatt, Genevieve. *Chinese Shadow Shows*. Cambridge:
Harvard University Press, 1936. xviii+68p. il.
See p.40-43 on music and musical instruments.
NE.

2329. ____. "The Chinese Theatre" *China Review* 5(3):67-70, Sept 1923. il.

2330. ____. "The Curious Puppet Shows of China" *Travel* 46:34-35, Dec 1925. NE.

2331. Wimsatt, Genevieve and Geoffrey Chen. *The Lady of the Long Wall: A Ku Shih or Drum Song of China*. Oxford: Oxford University Press, 1934. 84p. il. NE. Translation of *Mêng Chiang Nü*. Reviewed by: *Times Literary Supplement* 1717:916, Dec 27, 1934; E.D. Edwards in *Journal of the Royal Asiatic Society*, p.124-125, Jan 1937.

2332. ____. "The Mud Men of Tientsin" *Asia* 25(9):768-769, 782-783, Sept 1925. il. On some clay theatrical models.

2333. Winnegerode. *Über Chinesisches Theater*. Oldenberg, Leipzig, [n.d.]. 47p. NE.

2334. Wiora, Walter. *Die Vier Weltalter der Musik*. Stuttgart: Hohlhammer, 1961. il., mus. Both French and English translations have been published. A general history of music, trying to rectify the imbalance typical of Western histories, using ethnomusicological approach to the "Four Ages"—Primitive, Classical Antiquity and the Orient, Development of Western Music, World Industrial Civilization. China is treated briefly in this perspective.

2335. Wisse, Jan. "China" in *Encyclopedie van de Muziek* (Amsterdam: 1956) I,49-52. mus. NE.

2336. Wivell, Charles J. "The Chinese Oral and Pseudo-Oral Narrative Traditions" *CHINOPERL News* 5:115-125, 1975. Essay applying ideas of Parry and Lord to Chinese storytelling genres, trying to clarify the distinction between orally composed narratives and written narratives in oral performance.

2337. Wolpert, Rembrandt. "Einige Bemerkungen zur Geschichte des Streichinstruments in China" *Central Asiatic Journal* 18(4):253-264, 1974. Philological and historical investigations of early distinctions between string instruments 'scraped with a stick' (*ya*) and those 'bowed with a hairstring bow' (*li*).

2338. Wolpert, Rembrandt, Allan Marett, Jonathan Condit, and Laurence Picken. "'The Waves of Kokonor': A Dance-Tune of the T'ang Dynasty" *Asian Music* 5(1): 3-9, 1973. mus. Background study and transcription of a *Tōgaku* composition, trying to reconstruct the effect as performed in T'ang times, rather than following modern Japanese usage.

2339. Wong, Florence Feng Yee [Huang Feng-i]. *Music Education in Modern Chinese Schools.* M.A. thesis, Columbia Teachers College, 1952. Tables, mus. NE.

2340. Wong, Jade Snow. *Fifth Chinese Daughter.* New York: Harper & Bros., 1945. Reprinted, Harper & Row, 1965. Noteworthy remembrance of Chinese opera performance in San Francisco's Chinatown, p.214-216. Note on music at a wedding banquet, p.142. [RR]

2341. Wood, W.W. *Sketches of China.* Philadelphia: Carey and Lea, 1930. See p.155-157. NE.

2342. Wu Ching-Tzu [1701-1754]. *The Scholars* [Ju-lin wai-shih]. Translated by Yang Hsien-yi and Gladys Yang. Peking: Foreign Languages Press, 1957. Reprint, with added Foreword by C.T. Hsia, New York: Grosset & Dunlap, 1972 (Grosset's Universal Library UL263). [x]+692p. A major novel; loosely connected stories of corrupt scholars. Includes many references to music, particularly Chapter 30 depicting an opera contest and Chapter 37 detailing a re-enactment of a Confucian ceremony at a renovated shrine.

2343. Wu Chou-kuang. "The 'Erh-hu' and 'Pi-pa'" *Chinese Literature* 1:100-105, 1975. il. Introduction to these popular string instruments, focusing on post-Cultural Revolution repertoire, and on the performers Min Hui-fen and Liu Teh-hai.

2344. Wu, Hosea K. *Some Theoretical Aspects of Chinese Music.* M.M. thesis, Northwestern University, 1954. NE.

2345. Wu Hsiao-ni. "Plays on Contemporary Themes Being Vigorously Staged in Shanghai" *Union Research Service* 42(9):130-133, Feb 1, 1966. NE.

2346. Wu Hsin. "Proletarian Art Blossoms on Socialist Stage" *China Reconstructs* 16(1):19-25, Jan 1967. il.

2347. Wu Teh-li. "A Challenge to Mao Tse-tung: The Opera 'Three Ascents to Peach Peak'" *Issues and Studies* 10(9):46-56, June 1974. The controversy over this modern opera, taken as a criticism of Chiang Ching, is analyzed as a political event.

2348. ____. "The Maoist Struggle in the Musical Arena" *Issues and Studies* 10(8):30-40, May 1974. Analysis based on published Mainland documents, surveying music during the Cultural Revolution, with particular attention to the campaign against untitled music. The point of view reflects Taiwan's interests, but there is no overt propaganda.

2349. Wu Tsu-kuang. "Liang Shan-po and Chu Ying-tai: An Ancient Folk Tale Comes to the Screen" *People's China* 37-39, Nov 1, 1954. il. Review of film of the Shaohsing opera version.

2350. ____. "Mei Lan-fang—China's Great Classical Actor" *People's China* 18:29-32, Sept 16, 1953. il. Biographical sketch.

2351. ____. "The Stagecraft of Mei Lan-fang" *People's China* (6):28-31, March 16, 1956. il.(cover). Describing a film begun in 1953 "The Stage Art of Mei Lan-fang."

2352. Wu Wei-yun. "The Chinese Puppet Theatre" *Chinese Literature* 2:122-126, 1958. il.

2353. Wulff, K. "'Musik' und 'Freude' im Chinesischen" in *Klg. Danske Videnskabernes Selskab, Historiskfologiske Meddelelser 21, 2* (Copenhagen: Levin and Munksgaard, 1935). 39p. NE.

2354. Wylie, A. *Notes on Chinese Literature*. Shanghai: American Presbyterian Mission Press, 1867. 2nd ed. New York: Paragon, 1964. xl+307p. Valuable annotated book list of Chinese publications on nearly any topic. Short list on music literature.

2355. Whysham, H. Clay. "Chinese Songs and Musical Instruments" *Metronome* 32(9):42-43, 1916. mus. NE.

* * * * * * * * * *

2356. Xia, Ye. "Zur Entwicklung der chinesischen Opern-
stile" *Beiträge zur Musikwissenschaft* 3(3):3-75,
1961. mus. Selected and translated by Gerd Schönfelder. NE.

* * * * * * * * * *

2357. Y.M.P. "Cultural Life: China's First National Music
Festival" *People's China* (20):37-38, Oct 16,
1956. Extensive reviews.

2358. Yang Ai-wen. "Violins and Pianos for China" *China
Reconstructs* 10(7):30-31, July 1961. il. On the
Peking Musical Instrument Factory.

2359. Yang Chen. "Shadow Theatre" *People's China* 13:31-
33, July 1, 1953. il. Descriptive survey.

2360. Yang, Daniel Shih-p'êng. "Censorship: 8 Model Works"
The Drama Review 15(3):258-261, Spring 1971. il.
A brief summary of theatre in Communist China
since the Cultural Revolution. Censorship is in-
terpreted as the outright prohibition of all but
eight approved works.

2361. _____. "Chinese Plays in English Translation, 1741-
1967" *Afro-Asia Theatre Bulletin* 4(1):3-13, 1968.
NE. Also in *Theatre News* 1(2), Nov 1968. NE.

2362. _____. "Peking Drama with Contemporary Themes" *The
Drama Review* 13(4), Summer 1969. NE.

2363. _____. "The Peking Theatre Under Communism" *Theatre
Annual* 24, Dec 1968. NE.

2364. _____. "Staging a Traditional Peking Opera with
American Actors and Musicians" *Educational Theatre Journal* 23(3):307-316, Oct 1971. il. Narrative of problems and solutions in the 1970 production of "Black Dragon Residence" at the University of Colorado.

2365. _____. *The Traditional Theatre of China in its Contemporary Setting: An Examination of the Patterns
of Change Within the Peking Theatre Since 1949.*
D.A., Wisconsin, 1968. 288p. NE.

2366. Yang, Ernest Y.L. and Robert F. Fitch. "Divergent
Opinions on Chinese Hymnody" *Chinese Recorder,* p.
293-300, May 1934. NE.

2367. Yang Pi-wang. "Ancient Bridal Laments" *China Reconstructs* 12(10):42-44, Oct 1963. il. Ceremonial songs sung by brides, collected by folklore research group. Texts only.

2368. Yang, Richard Fu-sen. "Behind the Bamboo Curtain: What the Communists Did to the Peking Opera" *Educational Theatre Journal* 21(1):60-66, March 1969. Documents gradual replacement of traditional operas by revolutionary ones.

2369. _____, trans. *Four Plays of the Yüan Drama*. Taipei: The China Post, 1972. xvi+180p. il. Reliable translations of "Tou O Yüan" [Tou O Was Wronged], "Yüeh-yang Lou" [The Yüeh-yang Tower], "Wu-t'ung Yü" [Rain on the Wu-t'ung Tree], and "Ch'ien-nü Li Hun" [Ch'ien-nü's Soul Left Her Body]. Prof. Yang adds a short introduction and annotations of abstruse passages and references.

2370. _____. "The Function of Poetry in the Yüan Drama" *Monumenta Serica* 19:163-192, 1970-1971.

2371. _____. *Lü Tung-pin in the Yüan Drama*. Ph.D. dissertation, University of Washington, 1955. NE.

2372. _____. "The Reform of Peking Opera Under the Communists" *China Quarterly* 11:124-139, July-Sept 1962. NE.

2373. _____. "Revolutionary Opera in the People's Republic of China" *CHINOPERL News* 5:184-187, 1975. Report from 1972 trip, particularly on "Song of the Dragon River" [Lung-chiang Sung].

2374. _____. "The Social Background of Yüan Drama" *Monumenta Serica* 17:331-352, 1958. NE.

2375. Yang, Richard Fu-sen, David M.Y. Liang, and Myrtle L. Yang. "Poetic Songs of the Yüan" *Chinese Culture* 11(1):82-123, March 1970.

2376. Yang, Schuman Chuo. *Twentieth-Century Chinese Solo Songs: A Historical and Analytical Study of Selected Chinese Solo Songs Composed or Arranged by Chinese Composers from the 1920's to the Present*. Ph.D. (music), George Peabody College for Teachers, 1973. 500p. Abstract in *Dissertation Abstracts International* 34(8): Feb 1974. NE.

2377. Yang Yin-liu. "An Account of the Efforts of Chinese Scholars Towards Solution of the Problem of Equal Tempered Scale in Chinese Music" *Yenching Journal of Chinese Studies* 21:1-60, 341, June 1937. In Chinese; short English abstract.

2378. _____. "Chinese Drums" *Chinese Literature* 4:107-112, 1964. il. A survey of drum types in China, non-technical, too few Chinese words, but nevertheless valuable.

2379. _____. "Erste Untersuchungen zum 'Dreistrophenlied von Yang-guan'" *Beiträge zur Musikwissenschaft* 2 :128-137, 1960. mus. History, text, mode, form of Wang Wei's famous *ch'in* piece are discussed. There is a German translation of the song text, and a reprint of a Western transcription of the music previously published in Peking. English translation by Isabel Wong in *Asian Music* 5(1): 10-23, 1973.

2380. _____. "Recovering Ancient Chinese Music" *People's China* 2:26-30, Jan 16, 1956. il. Report on current research.

2381. _____. "Die Tonskalen des in Xinyang ausgegrabenen Glockenspiels aus der 'Frühlings- und Herbstperiode'" *Beiträge zur Musikwissenschaft* 2:123-127, 1965. Tables. Discussion of pitch measurements of a bell-chime from the late Chou dynasty, which was excavated in 1957. Tables give measurements and comparisons with theoretical Chinese and Western tuning systems.

2382. _____. "Zum Problem der Übertragung von Gong-chi-Notationen" *Beiträge zur Musikwissenschaft* 9(1): 23-40, 1967. il., mus. Translated by Gerd Schönfelder.

2383. _____. "Zur gleichen Existenz pentatonischer und heptatonischer Leitern in der chinesischen Musik" *Beiträge zur Musikwissenschaft* 6(1):42-51, 1964. NE.

2384. Yang Yu. "Hidden Treasures of Folk Art. The All-China Folk Music and Dance Festival" *People's China* 10:33-36, May 16, 1953. il.

2385. _____. "Peking's Children's Theatre" *People's China* 2:20-21, Jan 16, 1953. il.

230

2386. Yao Hsin-nung. "Chinese Drama in Evolution" in *Si-nica: China's Miscellanies*, Tan Liong, editor. Vol. I. [n.p., n.d.], p.275-289, [*ca.* 1939]. il. A good narrative of changes in the traditional opera after the Chinese Revolution.

2387. ____. "Drama Chronicle" *T'ien-Hsia Monthly* 3:45-52, Aug 1936; 5(1):50-58, Aug 1937. il. On the development of modern Chinese drama.

2388. ____. "The Rise and Fall of the K'un Ch'ü" *T'ien-Hsia Monthly* 2(1):63-84, Jan 1936. A good introductory essay on the most refined genre of Chinese classical opera known today.

2389. ____. "The Theme and Structure of Yüan Drama" *T'ien-Hsia Monthly* 1(4):388-403, Nov 1935. General description of *tsa-ch'ü*.

2390. ____. "When Sing-Song Girls Were Muses" *T'ien-Hsia Monthly* 4(5):474-483, 1937. il. Good article on the history of singing entertainers.

2391. Yao Hua. "Songs of New China" *People's China* 9:17-18, 23-24, May 1, 1952. Historical sketch, with texts.

2392. Yasser, Joseph. "Looking Into Chinese Music" *Musical Courier* 88(3):7-8, Jan 17, 1924. il. NE.

2393. ____. "The Rhythmic Structure of Chinese Melody" *Musical News and Herald* 68(1710):6-9, 1925. mus. German translation by Anna El-Tour in *Musik* 17 (3):193-198, Dec 1924. NE.

2394. ____. "Rhythmical Structure of Chinese Tunes" *Musical Courier* 88(14):11-45, April 3, 1924. il., mus. Interesting theory of irregular accent groupings in Chinese melodies. Not followed up or discussed in other works.

2395. ____. *A Theory of Evolving Tonality*. New York: American Library of Musicology, 1932. 381p. il., mus. See p.25-39, "Historic Survey of Chinese Scales" and *passim* references to Chinese scale structures.

2396. Yau Tsih-lam. "Church Music from the Chinese Viewpoint" *Chinese Recorder* 40(6):343-344, June 1909. Letter to the editor: music in churches today is terrible; good translations needed, and new texts; Western music preferable; mixed choirs or students useful as leaders.

2397. Yeh, George. "Cultural Life in Wartime China" *University Review* (Bristol) 15:13-15, Nov 1942. NE.

2398. Yeh Lin. "The People Sing" *People's China* 13:28-31, 1954. NE.

2399. Yeh, Nora. *The Yüeh Chü Style of Cantonese Opera with an Analysis of "The Legend of Lady White Snake."* M.A. thesis (music), U.C.L.A., 1972. 264p. NE.

2400. Yen, Joseph C.Y. "A Study in Detail of the Acting Roles of the Peking Theatre" *Chinese Culture* (Taiwan) 12(2):91-102, June 1971. History, classification, and description of role types; Chinese characters supplied for all terms and names.

2401. Yen Yuan-shu. "Biography of the White Serpent: A Keatsian Interpretation" *Tamkang Review* 1(2):227 -243, 1970. NE.

2402. Yin Cheng-chung. "How the Piano Concerto 'Yellow River' Was Composed" *Chinese Literature* 11:97-102, 1974. A personal, self-critical narrative by the composer-pianist describing his conversion to the goals of art for workers, peasants, and soldiers, and the path to its current implementation.

2403. Yin Fa-lu and Yang Yin-liu. "Chinese Music—Its Past and Its Promise" *People's China* 4:14-18, Feb 16, 1957. il. A good short historical survey, followed by discussion of traditional music's role in the new society.

2404. Yoshikawa, Kojiro. "Martial Songs Accompanied by Tuan-Hsiao" *Tohogaku* 10:1, April 1955. English summary of a longer Japanese text.

2405. Young, Conrad C.S. "Taiwanese Shadow Puppets" Paper presented at Ninth International Congress of Anthropological and Ethnological Sciences, Chicago, 1973. Preprint, 22p. il.

2406. Young, Stark. "Mei Lan-fang" *Orient et Occident* 1(9):35-38, April 1935. NE.

2407. Yu, Alice. *Music and Language—A Case Study of the Melodic Concept in Chinese Music.* Ph.D. dissertation, Columbia University. NE.

2408. Yu Chiang. "The Tung Fang Art Ensemble Returns to the Stage" *Chinese Literature* (1):90-95, 1977. il. Post-"Gang of Four" re-emergence, after 10 years, of a world music and dance troupe doing numbers from Asia, Africa, and Latin America.

2409. Yu Chun-min. "The Story of an Actress" *People's China* 6(6):24-26, 1952. NE.

2410. Yu Feng. "The Shadow Theatre and Shadow Puppets" *Chinese Literature* 6:78-83, 1963. il.

2411. Yu Hsiang. "Folk Music Finds Its Place" *China Reconstructs* 8(9):2-5, 1959. NE.

2412. Yu Hui-Hai. "First Ballet in Chinese Style" *China Reconstructs* 7(5):10-12, May 1958. il. On "The Enchanted Lotus Lantern," a hybrid ballet created by the Central Experimental Opera Theatre.

2413. Yu Kuan-ying. "The Yüeh-fu Folk Songs of the Han Dynasty" *Chinese Literature* 5:67-74, 1963.

2414. Yu Lu-yuan. "The Revolutionary Ballet: 'The White-Haired Girl'" *Chinese Literature* 8:117-132, 1966. With 8 pages of plates.

2415. Yu, P.C. "The Reform of the Classical Chinese Theatre" *People's China* 3(1):12-14, 29, Jan 1, 1951. NE.

2416. Yu Ping. "Social Responses to the Show of Liang Shan-po and Chu Ying-tai Film in Taipei" *West and East* 8(7):7-10, July 1963.

2417. Yu So-ya. "Chinese Puppetry" *People's China* 13:28-30, 1955. NE.

2418. Yu Ta-kang. "The Liang Shan-po and Chu Ying-tai Film and the Tradition of Chinese Opera" *West and East* 8(7):3-6, July 1963.

2419. Yu Tsai-yang. "Cultural Life: Singing Grannies" *People's China* (3):37-38, Feb 1, 1957. The Shenyang Old Ladies' Choir.

2420. Yudin, G. "Kitaiskaia, Cheshkaia, Pol'skaia Muzyka" [Chinese, Czech, and Polish Music] *Sovetskaya Muzyka* 3:135f., March 1959. NE.

2421. Yung, Bell N.   "China, People's Republic of. IV.
Theory" in *Grove's Dictionary of Music and Musicians*. 6th ed. In press.   A general survey, primarily historical, of traditional Chinese theory,
subdivided into: 1) Historical and Philosophical
Background; 2) The 12 *lü*; 3) Scales; 4) Modes;
and 5) Vocal Music.

2422. _____. "Reconstructing a Lost Performance Context:
A Field Work Experiment" *CHINOPERL Papers* 6:120-
143, 1976. il., mus.   On *Nam Jem*, a Cantonese
narrative genre with *cheng* accompaniment.

2423. _____. "The Role of Speech Tones in the Creative
Process of the Cantonese Opera" *CHINOPERL News*
5:157-167, 1975. mus.   A good preliminary study;
this paper was delivered at the 1974 CHINOPERL
conference. Based on field study, the author de-
lineates the basic structural patterns and tonal
rules of Cantonese aria types.

2424. _____. "A Trip to Sok Gu Wan with a Cantonese Opera
Troupe" *CHINOPERL Papers* 7:45-59, 1977.   Field
trip report of a special festival performance.

                    * * * * * * * * * *

2425. Zaluski, Carlo. "La Musica di Chinesi" *l'Orfeo* 31-
33, 1855. NE.

2426. Zbikowski, Tadeusz.   *Early Nan-hsi Plays of the
Southern Sung Period*.   Warsaw: Wydawnictwa Uni-
wersytetu Warszawskiego, 1974. 194p. bibliog.   A
dissertation on the history, repertory, structure and form of the *Nan-hsi*. Includes some discussion of the music, primarily historical descriptions of performance types.

2427. _____. "Kilka uwag o Konwencji w Klasycznym Teatrze
Chinskim" [Some Remarks on Tradition in Classi-
cal Chinese Theatre] *Przeglad Orientalistyczny*
(Warsaw) 1(29):19-30, 1959. NE.

2428. _____. "On Early Chinese Theatrical Performances"
Rocznik Orientalistyczny 26(1):65-77, 1962. Has
plates.   A basic, scholarly study of the Han dynasty pre-dramatic genre *pai-hsi*.

2429. Zeraschi, Hellmut.   "Besuch bei Laurence Picken"
Musik und Gesellschaft 17(1):52-53, Jan 1967.
il. (portrait).

2430. Zoo, T.K. *Songs of Cathay; An Anthology of Songs Current in Various Parts of China Among Her People.* Shanghai: The Association Press, [n.d.]. 25 songs with English translations, piano arrangements.

2431. Zuber, S.M. "Muzikalnuie Instrumentuei I Ikonographi Khara-Khoto" [Musical Instruments in Khara-Khoto Iconography] *Trudi Otdela Vostoka* 3: 325-337, 1940. NE.

2432. Zucker, Adolf Eduard. "The Business Side of the Chinese Theater" *Transpacific* 3(2):61-63, 1920. NE.

2433. ____. "The Changing Theaters of Asia" *Asia* 26(3): 202-209, 260-262, March 1926. il. Surveys current scene in Japan, China, India, Burma, and Indonesia.

2434. ____. "The Changing Theaters of Asia. The Effect of Imitations of European Plays and of Motion Pictures" *Asia* 26:202-208, 260-262, 1926. NE.

2435. ____. "China's 'Leading Lady': The Youthful Female Impersonator Who Is Greatest of the Brethren of the 'Pear Orchard'" *Asia* 24:600-604, 646-647, Aug 1924. il. Firsthand description of Mei Lanfang at the height of his early success, with some fine photos.

2436. ____. *The Chinese Theater.* Boston: Little, Brown & Co., 1925. xvi+234p. il., bibliog. A major survey with much historical material.

2437. ____. "Chinese Wits and the Drama" *Saturday Review of Literature* 1:709, April 25, 1925. NE.

2438. ____. "Oriental Theater" in *Encyclopedia Americana.* 1965 ed. XX,861-865. il., bibliography.

2439. ____. "Peking Playhouses" *Asia* 25(4):306-311, 335-357, April 1925. il. Introduction to the Peking opera; some good photos.

2440. ____. "Théâtre Elizabethain et théâtre chinois" *Revue de Littérature Comparée* 3:497-515, 1923. NE.

2441. Zung, Cecilia S.L. [Ch'eng Hsiu-ling]. *Secrets of the Chinese Drama.* London: Harrup, 1937; and Shanghai: Kelly and Walsh, 1937; reprinted New York: Benjamin Blom, 1964. xxviii+299p. il., index. A detailed exposition of Peking opera techniques, many as demonstrated for the author by Mei Lan-fang. Music treated integrally, but no musicological information. Over 100 pages are devoted to play synopses. Reviewed by: Helen D. Ling in *China Quarterly* 2:561-563, Summer 1937.

[Co-authors, persons written about, and others not accessible through the main alphabetization.]

TOPIC OUTLINE
AND SELECTED READINGS

Offered as a guide for the nonspecialist,
this outline covers the main topics in
Chinese music and suggests some convenient,
representative, and generally reliable
avenues of investigation. Neither the
outline nor the suggestions are complete;
they are just starting points for the
study of Chinese music.

1. General Studies.
   74,622,738,813,829,830,1373,1395,1753,
   1814,1815,1827,1831,1878,1936,2319

2. History.

   A. Early: Prehistory to Northern and Southern
      Dynasties.
      506,507,529,748,826,922,1007,1084,1284,
      1571,1900

   B. Middle: Sui to Sung.
      929,1017,1085,1315,1822,1826,1837,1840,
      1844,1942

   C. Late: Ming, Ch'ing
      14,1190,2127,2342

   D. Modern.

      i. Republic.
         1610,1828,1999

      ii. People's Republic of China.
          19,449,488,489,744,1260,1372,1852,
          1987,2348

      iii. Taiwan.

3. Theory and Analysis.

   A. Pitch, scale, mode, rhythm.
      527,1297,1338,1375,1377,1382,1496,1543,
      1751,1753,1817,1822,1826,1837,1844,2394,
      2421

   B. Acoustics.
      1753

255